GRADUATE ATTRIBUTES, LEARNING AND EMPLOYABILITY

Lifelong Learning Book Series

VOLUME 6

Aims & Scope
"Lifelong Learning" has become a central theme in education and community development. Both international and national agencies, governments and educational institutions have adopted the idea of lifelong learning as their major theme for address and attention over the next ten years. They realize that it is only by getting people committed to the idea of education both life-wide and lifelong that the goals of economic advancement, social emancipation and personal growth will be attained.

The *Lifelong Learning Book Series* aims to keep scholars and professionals informed about and abreast of current developments and to advance research and scholarship in the domain of Lifelong Learning. It further aims to provide learning and teaching materials, serve as a forum for scholarly and professional debate and offer a rich fund of resources for researchers, policy-makers, scholars, professionals and practitioners in the field.

The volumes in this international Series are multi-disciplinary in orientation, polymathic in origin, range and reach, and variegated in range and complexity. They are written by researchers, professionals and practitioners working widely across the international arena in lifelong learning and are orientated towards policy improvement and educational betterment throughout the life cycle.

Graduate Attributes, Learning and Employability

Edited by

PAUL HAGER
University of Technology, Sydney, Australia

and

SUSAN HOLLAND
Edith Cowan University, Perth, Australia

 Springer

A C.I.P. Catalogue record for this book is available from the Library of Congress.

ISBN-10 1-4020-5341-X (HB)
ISBN-13 978-1-4020-5341-2 (HB)
ISBN-10 1-4020-5342-8 (e-book)
ISBN-13 978-1-4020-5342-9 (e-book)

Published by Springer,
P.O. Box 17, 3300 AA Dordrecht, The Netherlands.

www.springer.com

Printed on acid-free paper

Table of Contents

Part III: Graduate Attributes and Employability

LIST OF CONTRIBUTORS

Mark Atlay is Head of Teaching Quality Enhancement and Director of the Centre for Excellence in Teaching and Learning (CETL), University of Luton, United Kingdom. Dr. Atlay spent seven years lecturing in chemistry at the University of Glamorgan before moving on to work on the development of distance learning materials at the Open University in the UK. At Luton he has worked in a number of areas including Quality Assurance, Staff Development, Quality Enhancement and Educational Development. He has coordinated the development and implementation of the University's curriculum model involving a revised approach to skills development linked to progress files and personal development planning (PDP). For its work in this area, the University has received government funding to establish CETL, also known as *Bridges* (see www.luton.ac.uk/bridgescetl), which is supporting the further implementation of PDP processes and employability in the undergraduate curriculum, as well as researching and evaluating their impact.

Ronald Barnett is Professor of Higher Education at the Institute of Education, University of London, United Kingdom, where he is also Pro-Director for Longer Term Strategy. In his research, he has been trying to see whether it is possible to construct an educational idea of the university in the contemporary age and to identify conceptual and practical resources to that end. His books include *The Idea of Higher Education, Improving Higher Education: Total Quality Care, The Limits of Competence, Higher Education: A Critical Business, Realizing the University in an Age of Supercomplexity* and *Beyond All Reason: Living with Ideology in the University*. The University of London has conferred on him a higher doctorate, the Society for Research into Higher Education (SRHE) has made him a Fellow and he is the first recipient of the (new) annual 'Distinguished Researcher' prize awarded by the European Association for Institutional Research. Among his current commitments, Professor Barnett is Chair of the SRHE (an international society). He is also Chair of the Meeting of Professors at the Institute and Chair of the Research Degrees Committee of the University of London: in the latter role, he is particularly interested in trying to improve the quality of the experience of research students.

Simon Barrie is a Senior Lecturer in the Institute for Teaching and Learning at The University of Sydney, Australia. The Institute carries out research and development work in the field of teaching and learning in higher education. Dr. Barrie leads the Institute's Teaching Evaluation and Quality Assurance work and the University's Graduate Attributes project (see www.itl.usyd.edu.au/GraduateAttributes/). Dr. Barrie is exploring teachers' and learners' experiences of university with the aim of using this knowledge to improve the quality of student learning outcomes. His previous research on academics' experiences of the teaching of generic attributes served as the basis for the Conceptions of Generic Attributes (COGA) framework, which underpins The University of Sydney's current policy revision and academic development initiatives related to generic graduate attributes. It is also being used by other universities in Australia and internationally. Dr Barrie's current research focuses on an exploration of the core attributes of graduates of research higher degrees and a project exploring alternative theoretical and conceptual bases for academic development work. He is also part of an ongoing investigation of students' and teachers' experiences of teaching and learning through his involvement in institutional research in the evaluation and quality assurance of teaching.

David Beckett is an Associate Professor and Associate Dean in the Faculty of Education, at The University of Melbourne, Australia. His teaching and research centres on educators' professional development, education and training policy analysis, and in the philosophy of workplace and lifelong learning. His students exemplify training, human resource development, nurse education, community and social work, school principalship and academia. Professor Beckett's recent publications include *Life, Work and Learning: Practice in Postmodernity* (with Paul Hager, Routledge London 2002). In 2004, he was made a Fellow of the Australian Council for Educational Leaders.

David Boud is Professor of Adult Education at the University of Technology Sydney, Australia. Professor Boud has written extensively on teaching, learning and assessment in higher and professional education, and more recently on everyday learning in workplaces. He chaired the working party to develop Graduate Attributes at the University of Technology, Sydney and was chair of that institution's Board of Studies for Work-Based Learning. Currently he is involved in research on informal learning in workplaces and sustainable assessment practices for lifelong learning. His book, *Productive Reflection at Work: Learning for Changing Organisations* (edited with Peter Cressey & Peter Docherty) will be published by Routledge in 2006.

Catherine Down has worked within tertiary education since 1986. During this time she has been involved in curriculum development, professional development and research across a wide range of disciplines. Her experience includes secondments to the Ford Motor Company, Automotive Industry Training Board, Victoria, the Australian Competency Research Centre and the Office of Training and Further Education. For the last seven or so years, her position has been that of Senior Lecturer and Projects Director (Educational Development) within the Royal Melbourne Institute of Technology, Australia. She has now established her own consultancy business in order to work with educational practitioners to enable them, and their learners, to learn more effectively from and through work. Her recently completed doctoral research focused on polycontextual boundary-crossing within situated learning. Her thesis proposed a metaphoric framework in which to better understand how we learn through our work and in particular, how we take what we know and can do and apply it to new contexts and work situations.

Andrew Gonczi is Professor of Education at the University of Technology Sydney, Australia. His scholarly research encompasses vocational and higher education, and learning in the workplace. Professor Gonczi has also published various articles in the area of educational policy. He is particularly interested in the impact of globalisation on educational policy in individual countries.

Paul Hager is Professor of Education, University of Technology, Sydney. His main ongoing scholarly interest is in the emerging field of philosophy of adult and vocational education. This centres on topics such as informal workplace learning, professional practice and the role of generic skills in work. He leads a current Australian Research Council Discovery project investigating context, judgement and learning at work. Paul is also writing another book for Springer on informal learning as it relates to lifelong learning (with John Halliday, University of Strathclyde). He is also researching agency and practical judgement (with David Beckett, University of Melbourne).

Geoffrey Hinchliffe is the Student Skills and Employability Adviser at the University of East Anglia (UEA) in Norwich, United Kingdom. Dr. Hinchliffe also has teaching responsibilities in the Centre for Continuing Education at UEA for the provision of philosophy and politics classes. He is currently exploring the concept of learning as capability drawing on both modern and Aristotelian perspectives.

Susan Holland is an adjunct Professor in Learning and Professional Practice in the Institute for the Service Professions at Edith Cowan University (ECU), Western Australia, where she was previously a Pro Vice-Chancellor and Executive Dean of the Faculty of Community Services, Education and Social Sciences. Professor Holland is currently also an auditor for the Australian Universities Quality Agency and a consultant in higher education. Prior to joining ECU she was CEO of a large vocational institute in Sydney, New South Wales for a number of years and a member of the Council of Macquarie University. She has held several senior executive posts across the educational sectors, in which she was responsible for curriculum development, cross-sectoral policy and equity programs. Each of these roles had a research component. Her current research interests include lifelong learning, leadership development and generic capacities, critical thinking and quality assurance.

Dianne Mulcahy is a Senior Lecturer in the Faculty of Education, at The University of Melbourne, Australia. Her teaching and research centres on curriculum innovation, education leadership and policy analysis, and in the social theory of work and workplace learning. Over the past decade, she has managed several major funded projects on areas such as competency-based training (*Evaluating the contribution of competency-based training,* with Pauline James, National Centre for Vocational Education Research (NCVER), Adelaide 1999), leadership and management (*Leadership and management in vocational education and training: Staying focussed on strategy,* NCVER, Adelaide 2003), and standards of professional practice (*Towards the development of standards of professional practice for the Victorian TAFE teaching workforce,* with Anne Jasman, Department of Education and Training, Melbourne 2003). She has been a team member on other national research projects such as a recent evaluation study of frontline management funded by the NCVER.

Lesley Scanlon is a lecturer in the Faculty of Education and Social Work, at The University of Sydney, Australia. Dr. Scanlon is the First Year Experience coordinator facilitating the faculty mentor programme. Prior to this appointment she spent more than ten years in the Technical and Further Education sector where she taught and pursued her research interests in adult continuing education with specific reference to the segmented world of adult learners and generic competency acquisition. Her current research focus is mentoring student transitions to university and the process of identity construction in transition situations. Dr. Sanlon researches and writes within the interpretive, symbolic interactionist tradition. She is currently engaged in an extensive project investigating the historical, sociological and epistemological aspects of mentoring.

Nicky Solomon is currently Professor and Head of Education and Lifelong Learning in the School of Arts at City University London, United Kingdom. Until recently Professor Solomon has been working in Australia at the University of Technology Sydney. In both places she is involved in teaching, research and consultancy in the broad field of work and learning across various sets of educational and research programmes. Her current research interests focus on the increasing attempts to link work and learning and the way that these links produce different kinds of students, workers and education cultures.

Ina Te Wiata is currently employed in the Training and Development Unit at Massey University, Palmerston North. She has extensive experience working in staff development in Higher Education both in New Zealand and Australia. Ina has contributed to all aspects of staff development including, working as a consultant with groups and individuals, facilitating workshops and seminars, developing resources, and playing an active role in the preparation and implementation of policy. During her teaching career, she has sought to discover what really happens in classrooms and other learning environments (e.g. workplaces) and how teaching practice affects this. Her particular areas of interest (aside from her doctoral studies) remain assessment, course design and curriculum development, and the evaluation of all facets of the teaching-learning enterprise.

Christopher Winch is currently Reader in Education Management and Policy at King's College, London, United Kingdom. A philosopher by training, Dr Winch is interested in various aspects of vocational learning and education, including professional education, the political economy of vocational education and the integration of workplace and academic learning. Previous publications include *The Philosophy of Human Learning* (1998) and *Education, Work and Social Capital* (2000). His *Education, Autonomy and Critical Thinking* was published by Routledge in 2005. He has worked in further, higher and primary education.

EDITORIAL BY SERIES EDITORS

This volume is a further flowering from the *International Handbook of Lifelong Learning*, which was jointly edited by David Aspin, Judith Chapman, Yukiko Sawano and Michael Hatton, published by Springer (formerly known as Kluwer Academic Publishers) in 2001. In the *International Handbook* we laid down a set of agenda for future research and development, analysis and expansion, strategies and guidelines in the field of lifelong learning. It had become clear that the domain of lifelong learning was a rich and fertile ground for setting out and summarising, comparing and criticising the heterogeneous scope and remit of policies, proposals and practices in its different constitutive parts across the international arena. Certainly the scholars, researchers, policy makers, and educators with whom we discussed this matter seemed to agree with us that each of the themes that were taken up in the individual chapters of the original *International Handbook* would merit separate volumes of their own – to say nothing of the other possibilities that a more extended mapping, analysis and exploration of the field might quickly generate.

This volume is an outcome of the important issues that were raised in the *International Handbook*, in particular, by the questions of the development of graduate attributes and their relationship to learning and employability. It is the work of our colleagues Paul Hager and Susan Holland, who have gathered together contributions to this important theme from a range of international scholars and writers in that field. The writers analyse the nature, development and function of generic attributes in an age of uncertainty. They look at the relationship between graduate attributes and changing conceptions of learning, as well as the relationship between graduate attributes and employability, in a world where opportunities for employment and their concomitant requirements are constantly changing. They pay particular attention to the evolution from institutional specifications of skills development to a more student-centred approach, in which the needs, interests and aspirations of the learners themselves play a far greater part in determining the structures and directions of the learning programs that are set up to cater for them. Particular attention is paid to the changing nature, type and function of generic attributes and learning in workplace settings.

Paul Hager and Susan Holland have done us all a signal service in the preparation of this book. Their work has demonstrated a clear commitment to the emancipatory potential of lifelong learning. Their argument is that the contemporary focus on the transition to work and the role of generic attributes, whether for school leavers or graduates, needs to be conceived more realistically and coherently as part of an ongoing and interactive lifelong learning process. The work environment can provide individual and collective opportunities to build on and integrate learnings gained from classrooms, lectures and laboratories. Workplace learning, they argue, is an important part of lifelong learning, as it is a site for personal and general forms of learning, as well as for the further development of technical and professional knowledge. For them, the issue of how to enhance the employability of new entrants to the workforce, by which employers usually mean general capacities like communicating, relating to people, and using technology, is a matter of encouraging better learning, prior to entering and while engaged in the workplace. They believe generic attributes have a valuable role in enhancing learning and hence employability.

We believe that this important work comes forward at an especially significant and fruitful time when the worlds and institutions of learning and work are in a state of considerable, not to say radical change and upheaval. We believe that both employers and institutions will benefit enormously from reading and reflecting on the messages contained in this iconoclastic work. We are pleased that the work helps carry forward the agenda of the Springer Book Series on Lifelong Learning. We thank the anonymous international reviewers and assessors who have considered, reviewed and assessed the proposal for this work and the individual chapters in the final manuscript and who have played such a significant part in the progress of this work to completion. We trust that its readers will find it as stimulating, thought-provoking and controversial as we who have overseen this project and its development have found it. We commend it with great confidence to all those working in this field. We are sure that this further volume in the Springer Series will provide the wide range of constituencies working in the domain of lifelong learning with a rich range of new material for their consideration and further investigation. We believe that it will encourage their continuing critical thinking, research and development, academic and scholarly production and individual, institutional and professional progress.

March 2006   David Aspin and Judith Chapman

CHAPTER 1

PAUL HAGER AND SUSAN HOLLAND

INTRODUCTION

The idea for this book began a few years ago when we, together with another colleague, were invited to write a position paper (Hager, Holland & Beckett 2002) on a similar topic for the Business/Higher Education Roundtable in Australia. Subsequently, in line with our recommendations, this group decided to produce a further position paper showcasing progress and good practice in embedding and assessing generic attributes in universities in Australia (B-HERT 2003).

Since these developments we have had an opportunity to reflect on both the theoretical and practical issues we raised. Not surprisingly these issues have remained topical. Indeed, particularly in these changing and competitive times, there continues to be policy, business and educational interest in the general or generic outcomes of undergraduate programs, and the relationship between graduate attributes and what has come to be termed 'employability'. Our respective research and professional projects are such that we have long had an interest in, and commitment to the emancipatory potential of learning, and the importance of setting undergraduate education in a broader framework of a lifelong learning process rather than as an end in itself. We believe that this kind of approach is important for school leavers as much as for mature adults re-entering formal education with the intent of pursuing degree level or other studies.

Furthermore, we consider that the contemporary focus on the transition to work and the role of generic attributes, whether for school leavers or graduates, needs to be conceived more realistically and coherently as part of an ongoing and interactive learning project. The work environment can provide individual and collective opportunities to build on and integrate the kinds of learning gained from the classroom, lecture or laboratory. Given certain conditions, workers at any level can continue to develop their knowledge and understanding as well as their repertoire of skills and dispositions.

1

P. Hager and S. Holland (eds.), Graduate Attributes, Learning and Employability, 1–15.
© 2006 *Springer.*

We see work-based learning as an important part of lifelong learning as it is a site for personal and general forms of learning as well as for the further development of technical and/or professional knowledge. As such it is a necessary adjunct to the more structured forms of learning usually encountered in academic programs. For us, the issue of how to enhance the employability of new entrants to the workforce, by which employers usually mean general capacities like communicating, relating to people, using technology, and so forth, is a matter of encouraging better learning prior to entering, and while engaged in the workplace. We believe that despite the flaws in the way that generic attributes are often described, seemingly taught and assessed, when their limitations are properly understood and accounted for they have a valuable role in enhancing learning and hence employability.

1. GRADUATE ATTRIBUTES AND RELATED TERMINOLOGY

In an international context there has been increasing educational attention paid to what are variously called 'generic skills', 'core skills' or 'basic skills', or, more recently, 'employability skills'. Sometimes they are referred to as 'competencies' rather than as 'skills'. The term 'generic skills' and its cognates are widely used to refer to a range of qualities and capacities that are increasingly viewed as important in all walks of life, though the main focus is usually on their role in work and in education viewed as a preparation for work. Typical 'generic skills' cluster around key human activities such as communication, working with others, gathering and ordering information, and problem solving.

This contemporary focus on generic skills has spread across education systems, including the university sector, where they are often called 'graduate attributes' or 'graduate qualities'. For the purposes of this book, we will use 'generic attributes' as the meta-level, more encompassing term to refer to these 'skills' or 'competencies'. When we are referring specifically to the higher education sector, as will be the case for much of this book, the preferred term will be 'graduate attributes'.

From the perspective of higher education, a range of 'graduate attributes' has gained attention. These include thinking skills such as logical and analytical reasoning, problem solving and, intellectual curiosity; effective communication skills, teamwork skills, and capacities to identify, access and manage knowledge and information; personal attributes such as imagination, creativity and intellectual rigour; and values such as ethical practice, persistence, integrity and tolerance. This collection of various qualities and capacities is distinguished from the discipline-specific knowledge and associated technical skills that traditionally are associated with higher education.

Generally when people talk about 'generic attributes' they are referring to a very diverse range of supposed 'things' – skill components, attitudes, values and dispositions. Some of these so-called 'skills' may not be the kind of thing that can be improved with practice, in the usual sense of guided repetition. Likewise, even when considering those that most look like they might be genuine skills, some have significant physical components, e.g. body language in interpersonal communication, others are mainly mental, e.g. analytical reasoning. There may be significant differences here that are masked by the blanket term 'skills'. Still others of these so-called 'skills' are, strictly speaking, not so much skills as attitudes and dispositions. As such, they might be more accurately thought of as relational complexes that connect persons and particular contexts, rather than as unitary 'things'. It may be that these attitudinal and dispositional qualities are better seen as products of cultural, ethical and social circumstances that may be refined and modified by knowledge and reflection.

These are the reasons why the more neutral term 'attribute', as preferred in this book, is probably a better descriptor of the collection of diverse qualities that together constitute so-called 'generic skills'. In keeping with our aim to reflect different perspectives there is some variation in the precise terminology adopted by the chapter authors. In a few instances we, and other authors in the book, use the term 'capabilities', particularly in relation to a sense of agency in the workplace, to describe essentially the same constellation of values, dispositions and personal qualities. Some authors have adopted another variation, 'generic graduate attributes'. While we wish to highlight broad rather than narrow understandings, we recognise the wide currency of the term 'generic skills' both in popular usage and in the literature generally. In this regard we trust that the attentive reader will have no difficulty in deploying the thinking behind our usage to a reading of the wider literature on the subject.

2. WHY ARE GRADUATE ATTRIBUTES IMPORTANT

The growing emphasis on graduate attributes in higher education has several sources. One is the increasing evidence of demand from business and employer organisations for graduates to possess generic attributes (or generic skills). This trend reflects recent economic and technological developments. As well, there are a number of educational considerations that have brought graduate attributes to wider attention. The contemporary focus on graduate attributes in higher education is really part of a bigger, as yet unresolved, debate about the purpose of university education and how to develop well educated persons who are both employable and capable of contributing to civil society. So the increasing importance of graduate attributes in higher education policy reflects various cross-sectoral influences.

2.1 Demand for Generic Attributes from Business and Employers

As much recent literature claims, a major feature of current knowledge-based economies is that workers increasingly require a diverse range of generic attributes or skills. These typically include such items as ability to work flexibly as part of a team, the ability to work autonomously, capacity to adapt to change, ability to work creatively, and so on. These diverse generic attributes are increasingly being grouped together with other general job-seeking attributes under the rubric of 'employability skills'. General job-seeking attributes include such things as self-belief and the capacity to obtain and retain employment.

The supposed shift to a knowledge-based economy, that has stimulated this stampede by employers and employer groups to embrace the mantra of generic attributes and employability skills, seems to stem largely from the correct observation that the nature of work has both changed and continues to change, particularly with the continuing spread of micro-electronic technology. As well, there is the ongoing long-term shift to a service economy where information and social skills are increasingly important. But the question is whether these changes are really so fundamental that workers are now required to be new kinds of workers with different sorts of attributes. Even where the term 'knowledge worker' is used, suggesting that the new workplace involves continuous knowledge creation, generic attributes are the core contributors to these work activities. In fact, for most people it is more a matter of locating, managing and disseminating knowledge, rather than creating it.

Nevertheless, a climate has arisen in which workers have seen their tenure in the workforce become more precarious as jobs increasingly require them to exhibit attributes that previously were not so important for most workers. Indeed with rapid and often unexpected changes in the workplace a new kind of attribute has come into demand. The capacity to adapt quickly to changes in the nature of work and take responsibility for self-managing subsequent career shifts is now an important factor influencing success in the workplace. Against this background there is growing interest in lifelong learning. The attributes that are commonly taken to characterise lifelong learning are heavily reliant on a range of generic attributes. This is well illustrated by the following 'profile of the lifelong learner' proposed by Candy, Crebert & O'Leary (1994: 43-4):

An inquiring mind
- a love of learning;
- a sense of curiosity and question asking;
- a critical spirit;
- comprehension, monitoring and self-evaluation;

Helicopter vision
- a sense of the interconnectedness of fields;
- an awareness of how knowledge is created in at least one field of study, and an understanding of the methodological and substantive limitations of that field;
- breadth of vision;

Information literacy
- knowledge of major current sources available in at least one field of study;
- ability to frame researchable questions in at least one field of study;
- ability to locate, evaluate, manage, and use information in a range of contexts;
- ability to retrieve information using a variety of media;
- ability to decode information in a variety of forms: written, statistical, graphs, charts, diagrams and tables;
- critical evaluation of information;

A sense of personal agency
- a positive concept of oneself as capable and autonomous;
- self-organisation skills (time management, goal-setting, etc.);

A repertoire of learning skills
- knowledge of one's own strengths, weaknesses and preferred learning style;
- range of strategies for learning in whatever context one finds oneself; and
- an understanding of the differences between surface and deep level learning.

Linked to these developments is the emerging notion of the 'learning organisation'. The nature and range of generic attributes of staff, including their collective capacity to adapt to change and learn new skills, are coming to be regarded by business leaders and employers as important as the traditional factors of production, labour and capital, in determining the sustainability of enterprises. In these circumstances, there has been a proliferation of attempts to set out discrete lists of generic attributes and employability skills. While much commonality is evident in these various lists, there is also significant diversity. These differences are a reflection of the fact that despite the aura of tangibility provided by codified descriptive lists, much about these supposed generic attributes remains intangible and elusive. However, this has not deterred some employers from the view that they can readily assess the extent of applicants' generic attributes on the basis of job applications and interviews. As various contributions to this book will demonstrate, such confidence is very likely misplaced.

These rapid and accelerating changes have placed pressure on the front-end approach to vocational and professional education. This is reflected, for instance, in growing dissatisfaction with courses for professions (Hager 1996). More and more, a formal two, three or four year course at the start of a career whether in the vocational or higher education sector, is seen merely as the necessary foundation for the early years of practice, rather than as the sufficient basis for a lifetime of practice. Hence the increasing interest in lifelong learning and the growing emphasis on learning in the workplace.

2.2 Adoption of Generic Attributes by Educational Providers

At the same time as business and employers are calling for more emphasis on generic attributes, so too are educational providers. This interest is stimulated, at least in part, by a desire by some to appeal to business and employers in an era of increasing competition and accountability. Some writers (e.g. Bennett, Dunne & Carre 1999; Barnett 1997) have taken issue with the assertion that universities should do what business says it needs merely on the assumption that the outcomes will be beneficial. However, responding to calls from business and employers is not the only reason for the interest in generic attributes by educational providers. There are sound educational arguments for the increased focus on generic attributes. There is growing awareness that well-founded sets of generic attributes have the potential to deliver several educational advantages to course providers whether vocational and/or educational in emphasis. These advantages can be grouped as follows:

- course development
- course delivery and assessment
- quality assurance.

In the area of course development the advantages offered by a sound set of generic attributes are multiple. They add a further dimension to discipline-specific discourse by providing the basis for a consistent terminology for describing course outcomes. The common lack of such consistency, particularly in the higher education sector, means there is no agreed reference point when, for example, academics attempt to develop transdisciplinary courses. So, the terminology of the generic attributes that are required by contemporary work practices not only facilitates links between particular courses and the world of practice, but also creates links between courses of different kinds. These sorts of links are vital, for instance, in incorporating work-based learning in higher education courses. This integration of theory and workplace learning in the vocational sector is less problematic due to different pedagogic traditions.

Generic attributes are, typically, significant components of initiatives to improve teaching and learning. Such initiatives take many forms and have diverse aims. But whether they seek to encourage deeper learning, to make learners more reflective about their learning or to develop more self-directed learners, they characteristically require learners to deploy some combination of generic attributes if they are to be successful. It seems that the strategies needed to develop generic attributes are also the ones that lead to good learning outcomes. Thus, by embedding the development of generic attributes in courses we can improve learning overall. The emphasis here is on how people learn best rather than on how to develop generic attributes. Erik de Corte (1996) has identified a useful set of features of powerful learning environments:

They:
- have 'a good balance between discovery learning and personal exploration, on the one hand, and systematic instruction and guidance, on the other';
- require students to 'progressively increase' their 'share of self-regulation...at the expense of external regulation'; 'provide

opportunities to use a rich array of resources' and for 'social interaction and collaboration';

- 'allow for the flexible adaptation of the instructional support to accommodate individual differences and stages of learning';
- 'facilitate the acquisition of general learning and thinking skills' throughout the curriculum.   (pp. 123–124).

Research on generic attributes teaching and learning methods indicates that they are best developed by active approaches (Moy 1999). Thus, there is a strong and recurrent link between the development of generic attributes by learners and teaching and learning methods that exhibit such features as:

- adult learning principles
- holistic approaches to learning
- problem-based learning
- lifelong learning skills
- learning how, why and exploring what if ... , not just learning received facts
- learner reflection, evaluation and articulation on learning experiences as a critical aspect of the learning process
- active, learner-centred approaches in which integrated thinking and action occurs on tasks that are relevant and meaningful to learners
- the teacher assuming multiple roles, such as mentor, coach, facilitator, evaluator, that include demonstrating/modelling the generic attributes to learners.

But as de Corte's list suggests, these are precisely the features of powerful learning environments.

A good example of a set of generic attributes being deployed to enhance learning is the 'profile of the lifelong learner' (Candy, Crebert & O'Leary 1994) outlined in the previous section. The work of Candy et al. provides a range of ways in which the profile can be incorporated into the pedagogy of various types of courses, thereby fostering the development of lifelong learning capacities by students. A common theme in the literature on teaching and learning of generic attributes is that success depends crucially on the generic attributes being made explicit for students. Leaving them implicit, as happens in many traditional courses, does little to encourage significant learning and development of the attributes.

Generic attributes can also play a significant role in quality assurance measures that are suitable for use in higher education. For example, having a consistent terminology for describing course outcomes can improve course development across an institution. It can also improve communication to those outside of the institution. Likewise, higher education institutions could use well-grounded sets of generic attributes to facilitate recognition and accreditation of prior learning, e.g. of non-graduate students into post-graduate programs. Such a procedure could generate greater public confidence in the assessment decisions that are made by educators.

3. BASIS OF THIS BOOK

In conceiving this book our intention has been two fold. Firstly, we wish to contribute to a fuller and more critical understanding of generic attributes, including their potentialities and limitations in practice. Secondly, we are committed to a progressive agenda for graduate attributes in relation to lifelong learning because of their role in enhancing better learning and employability. Chapter authors were chosen for various reasons. We deliberately left the brief fairly flexible and encouraged diversity of view in an attempt to broaden rather than constrain our present understanding of generic attributes and lifelong learning. Because of our professional commitment to developmental processes we invited some less well known academics, who have undertaken relevant doctoral research, to contribute as well as those with very well established, international profiles. While all the chapters draw on research and practical experience to a greater or lesser extent, inevitably some are more theoretical in orientation than others.

To ensure balance there are different but complementary theoretical perspectives about the nature and purpose of graduate attributes. There is also a chapter concerned with policy issues in an international and cross-sectoral context. A number of case studies highlight direct practical experiences of students or academics in designing and delivering a curriculum that advances a generic learning agenda, in one case on the basis of credit for work-based learning. Others detail, respectively, the experience of mature adults re-entering education, and graduates in the workplace in terms of their perceptions of the value of generic attributes. To reflect something of the developmental potential of generic attributes for lifelong learning, the educational settings for the chapters range across the post-compulsory years of schooling to include re-entry programs, vocational and university study, as well as work-based learning programs.

In some chapters the focus is on generic attributes *per se*, in others the concern is with the generic aspects of higher education, specifically undergraduate programs. In these cases, as already noted, the term 'graduate attributes', is used to distinguish this particular situation from other kinds of educational or work-based settings. The title of the book was chosen as *Graduate Attributes, Learning and Employability* because of the considerable policy and educational debate concerning graduate outcomes in particular. However, we have endeavoured to reflect more than these contemporary concerns by the inclusion of cross-sectoral material. We would have liked to include more discussion of, and case studies pertaining to, the employer perspective. But, despite several attempts, we were unable to elicit this kind of material in any appropriate form.

4. OVERVIEW OF THIS BOOK

Given both the depth and broad spectrum of issues concerning graduate attributes, learning and employability covered by the book, it could have been organised in a number of ways. To assist the reader who may be interested in some aspects more than others, the chapters have been arranged so that the meta-level conceptual discussion comes first followed by the case studies and frameworks. These in turn are divided according to whether the main focus is on learning and educational settings, or on employability and the workplace. Accordingly there are three parts to the book: Meta-concepts, Graduate Attributes and Learning, and Graduate Attributes and Employability. Part One addresses the meta-concepts which are germane to understanding the nature, value, and difficulties in applying generic attributes. Part Two deals with graduate attributes and their relationship to learning. Part Three goes beyond the formal learning context to embrace work-based learning and graduate capabilities in terms of the notion of employability.

In Part One: Meta-concepts, the chapters are primarily theoretical, although their respective arguments are frequently sketched in practical terms. Hager explains why generic attributes remain important in a postmodern world, before examining the typical ways in which they are described and assessed. He argues that learning is primarily a process, and that graduate attributes are inherently holistic and contextual in character. He goes on to argue from this base that there are a number of flaws in the way that graduate attributes are commonly perceived, although he still concludes that they can be valuable in encouraging better forms of learning. All of this has implications for employability.

From another meta-level perspective, Barnett considers what 'graduateness' means in a new, super complex, world order marked by contestability, changeability and uncertainty. He argues that these substantive changes require new knowledges, new adaptations and new skills, including the need for new forms of 'being' in the world. For him the major educational challenge is an ontological one and the graduate attributes of most importance are to do with the development of 'authentic' human beings, including the capacity for engagement with the world, inquisitiveness, and personal qualities like courage, resilience and quietness.

Winch sets out some useful tests for generic attributes that are similar to Hager's characteristics; namely, developmental capacity, coherence, and context independency. And, if, all of these conditions are met, then he posits a final condition to do with transferability. He concludes that a graduate attributes approach in higher education does not easily align with cognitivist and behaviourist models of teaching and learning. On the other hand technical, as opposed to technological, forms of higher education, may provide more opportunities for the development of the generic capacities of graduates, because of the greater time spent in practicum and thus immersion in the social world of the workplace. From his perspective the challenge in developing graduate attributes is not so much ontological as a curriculum or teaching and learning issue.

The last chapter in the first part is by Hinchliffe who explores graduate attributes and the notion of employability. Citing research that examined recruitment policies, plus a number of practical scenarios, he argues that the current expectations of employers concerning graduate attributes are unrealistic for a number of reasons. He suggests that this is so primarily because degree level programs provide insufficient time and opportunity for individuals to develop the kinds of self-narrative apparently expected for success in the workplace. Hinchliffe further develops his argument by indicating the importance of situational understanding for learning. This involves both the recognition of the limits of self-knowledge and an understanding of the inevitable dependency on others in the workplace. His conclusions have pedagogic implications for higher education in general and work-based learning programs in particular.

Part Two of the book, which is concerned with graduate attributes and learning, opens with a policy oriented chapter. Here Gonczi outlines several large

scale cross-national projects, which have been auspiced by the Organisation for
Economic Co-operation and Development (OECD), that have significant
implications for the development and assessment of generic attributes, particularly
beyond the compulsory years of schooling. The Definition and Selection of
Competencies (*DeSeCo*) project, which extended the scope of an earlier project
the Programme for International Student Assessment (PISA), is important for
several reasons. Apart from being international in perspective, *DeSeCo* dealt in
some depth with generic capacities across a broad spectrum of contexts, including
foundations for further learning, transition to work, personal development, and
community engagement. Furthermore, the project was unique in that it involved
discipline experts from different domains in considering how best to define and
construct the kinds of cognitive and personal attributes, which transcend particular
levels or situations of learning.

The rest of the chapters in Part Two are essentially case studies concerning the
development of generic attributes and related curriculum issues in different
educational settings. Scanlon traces the learning experiences of a group of mature-
aged students undertaking a bridging program as a preparation for tertiary study.
Reflecting on their progress as adult learners re-entering formal study the students
highlighted a number of generic attributes as being of particular importance. They
also identified teacher attributes deemed to be essential in providing the kinds of
learning contexts in which they experienced success. The chapter concludes by
emphasising the significance of generic attributes in shaping adult learner
identities. This is an important insight in relation to the factors involved in
facilitating lifelong learning.

Based on the perceptions by academics of the efficacy of various curriculum
strategies used to promote the teaching of generic aspects of undergraduate
education, Barrie has derived a phenomenographical framework for generic
graduate attributes. His chapter outlines the findings from this research, which he
argues provides a conceptual base for lifelong learning. The chapter also describes
the way that his framework has been applied in practice at a strategic and
curriculum level at an established, research intensive university in Australia. He
concludes that any credible attempt to teach generic type capacities must be
transdisciplinary in approach and, also, be based on a cluster of attributes rather
than individual skills.

Atlay also draws on practical experiences but, by contrast, he is engaged in
research in a very different kind of university in the United Kingdom. He
describes a longitudinal study of changing approaches to curriculum planning,
where an important goal of the undergraduate program has been to facilitate the

general learning capacities and personal attributes of a culturally and educationally diverse body of students. Over a ten year period shifts in national policy regarding higher education, as well as feedback from staff and students, have led to significant changes in the way that the undergraduate programs, specifically the Personal Development Program, are designed and delivered. Overall, in an effort to better meet the educational needs of the students, most of whom are the first of their generation to attend university, and to adequately prepare them for the workplace, a more student-centred approach has been adopted with an explicit focus on personal and career development.

The chapters in Part Three of the book each describe aspects of workplace learning and in that sense have something to say about graduate attributes and employability. Down, draws on action theory to argue that workplace performance depends on the ability to learn from workplace experiences and the capacity to adapt practice to meet the challenges encountered at work. From her qualitative analysis of interviews with supervisors, trainers and workers in different vocational settings, she considers that workplace agency and what she terms 'affordances' determine access to opportunities for learning at work. She concludes, given her view of the duality of work as learning and learning as work, that tertiary students, including those engaged in vocational forms of study, would benefit from a capability-driven approach to curriculum design.

Exploring the theme of work-based learning from another perspective, Boud and Solomon recognise it is the nature of the work itself that provides the basis for the curriculum. Furthermore, to legitimate this kind of learning in higher education it is often necessary to adapt programs and courses to reflect the unique work experience of the learner. In their chapter they outline the processes and problematics involved in credentialling work-based learning at another university in Australia, one which has made a strong and explicit commitment to promoting practical forms of learning. In engaging with colleagues to validate work-based learning as the curriculum, they have encountered several logistical and conceptual issues. Against this background they agree with Barrie that a transdisciplinary framework affords the best opportunity for academics to build shared understandings of, and create consensus for, the teaching and learning of graduate attributes.

Reflections on critical incidents was the approach adopted by Te Wiata to capture the realities of the first few years of work experience for recent graduates employed in different professions. This set of novice professionals identified a number of clusters of generic capacities in relation to workplace success. These generic capacities which included, critical thinking, problem solving, communication and interpersonal understandings, were seen by the novices as being important for several reasons: in underpinning and helping to make sense of their daily work routines; in conducting technical or technological aspects of their work; and in enabling them to meet unexpected or challenging situations with a sense of purpose and confidence.

In the context of an increasing emphasis on 'knowledge' work, as well as the contingent nature of work, Beckett and Mulcahy consider how best to describe the kinds of attributes that are regarded by employers as being valuable in contemporary workplaces. They argue that rather than merely citing lists of functional type skills, a better way to capture the kinds of attributes that employers value is to regard these kinds of generic attributes as 'employ-abilities'. Using cases of professionals in practice they illustrate that enacting personal agency in the workplace, deciding what to do and how to proceed, is powerfully shaped by communal self-correcting processes, particularly those judgements which are articulated by and amongst peers. They suggest that their approach provides a more sophisticated account of the role of graduate attributes in professional formation.

The final chapter in the book, by Holland, outlines a lifelong learning framework for graduate attributes. This chapter is a synthesis in that it attempts to reflect both the theoretical discussion in the first part of the book and the case studies described in the second and third parts of the book. Holland argues that the development and acquisition of generic type capacities is an ongoing process requiring engagement in learning in both educational and work-based settings. She suggests that the characteristics of graduate attributes of most relevance to their application in practice are their tendency to cluster, to be contextual and to have contingent aspects, including their limitations with respect to transferability. While her focus is on personal agency and development, she also recognises the importance of collective forms of learning. Holland posits three distinct phases: tertiary study, professional practice and ultimately, leadership development, in a lifelong learning agenda, which is concerned with developing and refining generic capacities through exposure to a mix of learning and working settings, reflection and self-development, peer judgement and feedback. She identifies the learning outcomes from each phase as respectively, graduate capacities, professional capabilities and leadership capabilities.

While the content of the chapters in each part is broadly similar, there is nonetheless some overlap as few of the authors are entirely theoretical or practical in approach, nor are they necessarily only concerned with the issues flagged by the title of the respective parts. This means that the book can be fruitfully read in any order depending on the purpose of the reader. Overall, the chapter order is broadly consistent with the logic of the framework developed in the final chapter, but this is not intended to direct the reader to only these conclusions. The book attempts to answer many questions about generic attributes, learning and employability, but it is also the case that much remains problematic in this increasingly debated area of educational policy and practice.

5. REFERENCES

Barnett, R. (1997) *Higher Education: A Critical Business*. Buckingham: SRHE/Open University Press.

Bennett, N., Dunne, E. & Carre, C. (1999) 'Patterns of core and generic skill provision in higher education', *Higher Education*, Vol. 37, pp. 71–93.

B-HERT (Business/Higher Education Round Table) (2003) 'Developing Generic Skills: Examples of Best Practice', *B-HERT News*, Issue 16.

Candy, P.C., Crebert, G. & O'Leary, J. (1994) *Developing Lifelong Learners Through Undergraduate Education*. Commissioned Report No. 28. Canberra: National Board of Employment, Education and Training.

de Corte, E. (1996) 'New Perspectives of Learning and Teaching in Higher Education', in A Burgen (ed.) *Goals and Purposes of Higher Education in the 21st Century*. London: Jessica Kingsley. pp. 112-132.

Hager, P. (1996) 'Professional Practice in Education: Research and Issues', *Australian Journal of Education*, Vol. 40, No. 3, pp. 235-47.

Hager, P., Holland, S. & Beckett, D. (2002) *Enhancing The Learning And Employability Of Graduates: The Role Of Generic Skills*. Business/Higher Education Round Table Position Paper No. 9. Melbourne: B-HERT.

Moy, J. (1999) *The Impact of Generic Competencies on Workplace Performance*. Review of Research Monograph Series. Adelaide: National Centre for Vocational Education Research.

CHAPTER 2

PAUL HAGER

NATURE AND DEVELOPMENT OF GENERIC ATTRIBUTES

1. INTRODUCTION

It is surely a scandal that much contemporary educational policy makes assumptions about learning that are directly contradicted by the best research and theorising of learning that has occurred over the last decade and more. This worrying mismatch is largely attributable to adherence by policy makers (and other key stakeholders such as employers), to common sense notions of learning transfer, notions that have long been abandoned by researchers and educational theorists. Employability skills, generic attributes, key skills, and learning to learn skills all provide clear examples of policies based on simplistic notions of transfer. As nations have sought to respond to globalisation by enriching, expanding and better recognising the skills profiles of their labour force, policies to promote and reward employability skills, generic attributes, key skills, and learning to learn skills have become common concepts at all levels of education systems. However, almost invariably, these purported skills are envisaged as being a series of discrete, decontextualised atomic elements or competencies, which learners are thought of as needing to acquire one by one. Once acquired, it is assumed that these skills can be transferred unproblematically by learners to diverse situations. Certainly, in policy literature emanating from employer groups, this assumption is very common (Hager, Holland & Beckett 2002). Yet as contemporary theoretical and research-based accounts of learning at work suggest, the contextuality of actual work processes severely curtails naïve expectations of unproblematic generic transfer. From the perspective of this chapter, what is especially revealing in this type of policy literature is the way the two metaphors of transfer and acquisition are employed ubiquitously to reinforce and support one another.

17

P. Hager and S. Holland (eds.), Graduate Attributes, Learning and Employability, 17–47.
© 2006 *Springer*.

As was noted in Chapter 1, though people commonly talk about 'generic attributes' as if they are all of a kind, in fact they include a range of diverse and fundamentally different kinds of entities such as skill components, attitudes, values and dispositions. This lumping together of significantly distinct kinds of entities is enough in itself to muddy the waters. It results from the common but dubious assumption that if a term such as 'generic attributes' can be applied meaningfully to a diverse range of entities, then they must have something significant in common. Whereas what actually might be occurring here is the lazy use of language. This possibility becomes more than likely when the putative entities that are supposed to be pretty much alike turn out, on closer inspection, to be significantly diverse, abstract and elusive, encompassing such varied 'things' as skill components, attitudes, values and dispositions. However, and importantly, this is not the only misconception about generic attributes that arises from taking them at the face value suggested by common sense. This chapter will begin by outlining five common conceptual mistakes that, it is argued, bedevil thought and talk about generic attributes in general. In the process, it will become abundantly clear that much of this thought and talk about generic attributes does indeed involve uncritical use of language and easy reliance on common sense metaphors, the applicability of which is very debatable. The five common conceptual mistakes about generic attributes are:

I That they are viewed as *discrete or atomic entities*, thus they can be acquired and transferred singly.

II That the learning of each of them is thought to be a relatively quick, once-off event. They are *acquired complete and finished* (this follows on from I).

III That they are thought of as being acquired by *individual* learners. So the learning is located within individuals. (This view is often linked with I, but is actually not at all entailed by it).

IV It is thought that we can *readily recognise them* when we see them. (It is easy to conclude from I and II that if typical generic attributes are discrete entities and can be acquired readily, then it must be straightforward to identify when someone exhibits them).

V It is thought that they are *readily and unequivocally describable in language*. Hence it is straightforward to develop descriptive understandings of typical generic attributes and to convey these understandings to others in written form. (V may seem to follow from IV, but this is not the case, as will be shown below).

The case for viewing each of these as a conceptual mistake will now be presented in some detail. The main problems that will be identified are uncritical reliance on dubious assumptions and adherence to unhelpful metaphors for thinking about learning. Following this discussion the chapter will go on to develop some key ideas that are claimed to be crucial for a more accurate understanding of the nature of graduate attributes. These key ideas include viewing learning as a process, paying due regard to the holism of graduate attributes, taking proper account of the influence of social/group factors and contextuality on graduate attributes, and the relevance of these graduate attributes for lifelong learning.

2. COMMON MISUNDERSTANDINGS OF THE NATURE OF GENERIC ATTRIBUTES

2.1 The First Common Misunderstanding of the Nature of Generic Attributes is that they are Thought of as Discrete or Atomic Entities to be Acquired and Transferred Singly

Generic attributes are widely, but mistakenly, viewed as being discrete or atomic entities, which can be acquired and transferred singly. (By 'discrete or atomic' I mean that they are thought to stand alone from other generic attributes). There are two key points here. First that generic attributes are viewed as discrete, self-contained items or things; second, that like all such tangible things, they are thought of as being acquired by persons or groups and transferred from place to place. There is nothing in the notions of acquisition and transfer that restrict them to individuals alone. For instance, a sporting team can be thought of as acquiring teamwork, and their coach might hope that they can transfer it from one season to the next. Both of these key points about generic attributes employ metaphors. But because these metaphors accord with common sense notions, it is often overlooked that such talk and thought is metaphorical. This concordance with common sense makes it seem 'natural' to view generic attributes as discrete or atomic entities that can be acquired and transferred as needed. In this respect generic attributes accord with the dominant understanding of learning. As Lakoff & Johnson (1980) stress, the natural or common sense understanding of learning views the mind as a 'container' and 'knowledge as a type of substance'. Thus, learning becomes 'adding more substance to the mind'. Bereiter (2002) dubs this picture of the accumulation of atomistic products as the 'folk theory' of learning.

> Under the influence of the mind-as-container metaphor, knowledge is treated as
> consisting of objects contained in individual minds, something like the contents of
> mental filing cabinets. *(Bereiter 2002: 179)*

These are very seductive metaphors because their very pervasiveness and homeliness means that they are easily accepted as the plain truth about learning, thereby masking that, being metaphors, they are not factual descriptions, and may, in some respects at least, even be misleading. Certainly, when it comes to thought and talk about generic attributes the widespread uncritical employment of these metaphors overlooks some inherent problems.

Firstly, transfer has come to seem to be a far from straight-forward notion. Even within its own specialist research field it is found to be a surprisingly rare happening (Bransford & Schwartz 1999). It seems that something more complex is involved than the simple transfer metaphor would suggest. Secondly, typical generic attributes are not at all plausible candidates for the status of discrete 'things', rather they have the character of relations of various kinds. Thirdly, although it appears that the use of metaphor is inevitable for thought and talk about learning, recent research favours different metaphors that would suggest other ways of thinking about generic attributes.

2.1.1 According to the best available research literature, learning transfer is anything but ubiquitous
Despite increasing power of experimental techniques, transfer "seems to vanish when experimenters try to pin it down" (Schoenfeld 1999: 7). Accepting that transfer is indeed rare if it is restricted to 'replicative' transfer, Bransford & Schwartz (1999) point to the need to reconceptualise transfer and, by implication, learning. They propose that we broaden the notion of 'transfer' by including an emphasis on 'preparation for future learning', the ability to learn in new environments. According to them, the point of transfer is not replication, but a contribution to facilitating ongoing learning. It seems that rather than any common-sense conception of direct transfer being applicable to typical life situations, it is more realistic to view 'transfer' as renovation and expansion of previous knowledge via the experience of dealing with new situations in new settings. Here, learning is more accurately viewed as an ongoing process than as a series of discrete acquisition events. If this is the norm for learning, then both the transfer and acquisition metaphors threaten to muddy and mislead our thinking about learning. They simply omit the crucial importance to learning of changing

contexts. As will be argued later in this chapter, learning is more fruitfully viewed as an ongoing process rather than as a series of acquisition events.

However, the power of the common sense understanding of learning is such that it also holds sway in the arena of the practical. Having learnt to do X, is equated with acquisition of a something followed by the transfer of it as needed. Hence the atomistic approach to skill which has plagued both the competence agenda around the world and generic attributes policies in particular. Not surprisingly, then, in the popular mind, learning to perform in human practices is seen as a series of discrete acquisition events followed by transfer as circumstances warrant it. Surely a better view of learning to perform in human practices is that it is a developing capacity (i.e. a process, something that evolves over time).

2.1.2 Typical generic attributes are not at all plausible candidates for the status of discrete 'things', rather they have the character of relations of various kinds
As was noted in chapter one, generic attributes encompass a diverse range of very different kinds of 'things'. Some may be 'skills' of various types. Others are, strictly speaking, not so much skills as attitudes and dispositions. These might be more accurately thought of as relational complexes that connect persons and particular contexts, rather than as unitary 'things'. Hence, these attitudinal and dispositional qualities may be more accurately viewed as products of cultural, ethical and social circumstances that can be refined and modified by knowledge and reflection. In these circumstances, notions of acquisition and transfer of discrete entities by individual learners are simply misleading ways to think about what is happening here.

2.1.3 Though the use of metaphors for thinking about learning seems to be inevitable, more useful alternative metaphors are available for thinking about generic attributes
As an examination of the history of educational thought shows (Hager 2004a), it seems that we are unable to talk about learning without resorting to metaphors. Exactly why there is this strong link between learning and metaphor is a very interesting question, but not one that can be pursued here (see Hager 2004a for more discussion of this). Sfard (1998) argued that two basic metaphors – learning as *acquisition* and as *participation* – have underpinned much educational thought. As we have seen, the acquisition metaphor has long been very influential. It subordinates the process of learning to its products – the something acquired (knowledge, skills, attitudes, values, behaviour, understanding, etc). Sfard

contrasts this metaphor with the participation one which recently has become increasingly influential in educational writings. Sfard claims that neither metaphor by itself is adequate to understanding of the full complexities of learning.

My view is that *acquisition* emphasises learning as a product and the common sense view of learning, i.e. a mind accumulating stable, discrete substances or atoms. In contrast, the *participation* metaphor presents learning as either a product or a process. This is because while participation itself is a process, the learner belongs more and more to the community of practice by acquiring the right characteristics (products of learning). A metaphor not mentioned by Sfard that I suggest better accords with learning as a process is *construction* (*or re-construction* – to emphasise its ongoing character). This includes the construction of the learning, of the self, and of the environment (world) which includes the self.

I suggest that participation accounts less well than does construction for change. So the latter has an extra dimension. Rogoff (1995) seemingly recognises the limitations of mere participation as a metaphor. Her sociocultural approach proposes viewing learning and development within a community in terms of three ".... inseparable, mutually constituting planes comprising activities that can become the focus of analysis at different times, but with the others necessarily remaining in the background of the analysis." (p. 139) The three planes of analysis are:

> Apprenticeship (community/institutional)
> Guided participation (interpersonal)
> Participatory appropriation (personal)

It is the third of these that particularly involves constructive processes, since appropriation of a personal kind clearly implies something stronger than mere replication.

Overall, various metaphors are available for thinking about learning. It is far from clear that the transfer and acquisition metaphors are very illuminating for understanding generic attributes. Both the participation and construction metaphors seem to offer more scope for illuminating the process aspects of learners developing proficiency in deploying generic attributes. Certainly, participation and construction connect better with the suggestion of viewing generic attributes as relational complexes that connect persons and particular contexts.

The various metaphors about learning link differently to lifelong learning and related concepts. The acquisition metaphor has unattractive implications for lifelong learning, suggesting endless accumulation of discrete pieces of learning. One imagines over-crammed filing cabinets. If learning is centrally about minds acquiring propositions, lifelong learning is potentially about perpetual enrolment in formal accredited courses. The individual learner is in danger of being condemned to learn all subjects/disciplines. In this respect, part of the 'folk theory' of learning is an acceptance of a 'quiz show' view of what it is for someone to be learned. (This contrasts with the Socratic view that the more you 'know', the more you know that you don't know). As well, the focus here is firmly on the individual learner. Illich (1973) was right that we have been schooled to accept a 'consumer of formal courses' view of knowledge acquisition. By contrast, the participation metaphor is undoubtedly more congenial for lifelong learning. People participate in many activities at many levels, signalling much scope for learning. This learning is at whole person level rather than just being centred on the mind. As well, rather than focussing solely on individual learners, the participation metaphor accepts the importance of learning by groups, communities and organisations. However, participation in itself does not ensure learning. Quite the opposite, as is demonstrated by participation in closed societies or organisations that are dedicated to resisting change (e.g. certain religious societies). The construction metaphor, however, with its tripartite focus on the construction of learning, of learners, and of the environments in which they operate, has a wider scope. One in which change, learning and human flourishing are inextricably enmeshed.

2.2 The Second General Misunderstanding of the Nature of Generic Attributes is that the Learning of each of them is Thought to be a Relatively Quick Event. Thus, they are Believed to be Acquired Complete and Finished (This Follows on from 1)

The common sense view of learning regards it as the accumulation of distinct items. It thereby focuses on the products of learning as discrete atoms. It says little about how processes of learning might occur, other than that the learning product is somehow transferred to the learner. The metaphors of acquisition and transfer serve to direct attention away from actual processes. Their focus is on the accumulation of learning *products*. Hence, the influential idea that learning is a kind of *product* has become pervasive. Hence, the common sense view of generic attributes as simple products to be acquired. Just as persons can easily and completely acquire the latest compact disc and play it wherever they like, so it is thought, they can acquire generic attributes quickly and completely and apply them wherever they happen to be. This seductive common sense understanding of generic attributes has promoted their popularity with employers and politicians as a 'quick-fix' for perceived shortcomings in existing vocational education and training arrangements. More surprisingly, policy makers have accepted this superficially attractive position. Thus policy implementation around generic attributes has been clouded by systematic mis-understanding of their nature and what is involved in learning them. As this chapter will demonstrate, generic attributes are not acquired in one-off learning events. Rather their development is an ongoing process. Nor are they discrete items or products that can be readily transferred to any situation. Instead they are significantly contextual, thereby requiring further learning for their successful application in novel contexts. Of course, the flawed common sense view suggests that the acquisition of generic attributes is obviously the responsibility of formal education at all levels. Clearly this is a very attractive option for employers as it relieves them of any responsibility. The alternative view, located in research, is much less congenial. If development of generic attributes is an ongoing and highly contextual process, then significant learning in the workplace is needed. This is a message that many employers and politicians do not wish to hear.

The pervasive common sense view of learning involves two particularly important basic assumptions. Firstly, the stability assumption, which requires the products of learning to be relatively stable over time. This stability enables learning products to be incorporated into curricula and textbooks, to be passed on from teachers to students, their attainment to be measured in examinations, and the examination results for different teachers and different institutions to be readily amenable to comparison. Thus formal education systems depend for assessment purposes on learning that is stable, familiar and widely understood. Secondly, there is the replicability assumption – that the learning of different learners can be literally the same or identical. That is, they have acquired identical products. The sorting and grading functions of education systems requires the possibility of this kind of foundational certainty of marks and grades. Hence it is seen as important that generic attributes fit this mould, so that individual students can be graded accordingly. Unfortunately our best understandings of generic attributes make a mockery of these pretensions.

The dominant influence of the common sense understanding of learning is also apparent in the workplace. Educators use the terms 'learner' and 'learning' in unproblematic, relatively neutral ways. Likewise those interested in such topics as workplace learning, lifelong learning, and organisational learning, readily associate the terms 'work' and 'learner' and 'working' and 'learning'. However, such terminology becomes more problematic for typical workers. Here the common sense understanding of learning exerts its sway. On the product view of learning a learner is someone who has yet to acquire all of the requisite products or mental items for carrying out the work. Thus to be a learner in the workplace on this view is to have a deficit (not having acquired yet) and therefore have less power or position.

Research reported by Boud & Solomon (2003) suggests, in workplaces not too far removed from the academy, being associated with terms such as 'learner' and 'learning' can be very problematic. It can conflict with workers' overall perception of their identity and status within the organisation. It is precisely because of the dominant learning as product view that in the community at large, being a learner can be seriously problematic. On the product view of learning a learner is someone who has yet to acquire all of the requisite products or mental items for carrying out the work. The Boud and Solomon research found that to be a learner in the workplaces they studied is:

- to have a deficit, e.g. to be inexperienced or not yet competent.
- to therefore have less power, position, recognition, or legitimation.
- to need to leave behind the role of 'learner' as quickly as possible (the 'L plate' syndrome).

As will be argued in this chapter, a different account of learning does not have these consequences. However, the efficacy of lifelong learning discourse is clearly reduced by workers having perceptions such as these, which is not to deny that this discourse has had some success in changing peoples' understandings of 'learning'. However, the dominance of the common sense understanding of learning means that there can be tensions in being both a worker (or professional) and a learner at the one time. Terms such as 'learner' and 'learning' do different work in different contexts. So the act of naming someone (including oneself) as a learner can be controversial. Though, as Boud and Solomon's research suggested, the act of naming something as learning is usually somewhat less controversial.

The pervasive influence of the 'learning as product' view can perhaps be thought of in terms of Bourdieu's concept of habitus. For Bourdieu (1990), habitus is a kind of socialised subjectivity, that is socially acquired, embodied systems of dispositions. As such, they represent a fine balance between structure and agency:

> Agents to some extent *fall into* the practice that is theirs rather than freely choosing it
> or being impelled into it by mechanical constraints. *(Bourdieu, 1990: 90)*

The suggestion is that 'learning as product', as socially acquired habitus, is not immutably entrenched. However, change is possible only to the extent that the wider social forces that transmit it are themselves altered.

Overall then, there has been a naïve tendency to view generic attributes as discrete or atomic entities that once acquired can be transferred to any situation. Here 'learning as product' muddies the waters. However, consistent with development of generic attributes being an ongoing process rather than a once-only acquisition event, research indicates that their transfer is severely limited as contexts change. It seems that rather than any common sense conception of direct transfer, it is more realistic to view transfer as application of previous knowledge to new settings that result in learning of significant new knowledge. On the 'learning as a process' view, to be discussed later in this chapter, generic attributes need to change and evolve with circumstances.

2.3 The Third General Misunderstanding of the Nature of Generic Attributes is that they are Thought of as Being Acquired by Individual Learners. So the Learning is Viewed as Being Located Within Individuals

Learning is essentially an individual activity. This is a virtually universal assumption in the literature on learning. Not surprisingly, it is central to the common sense understanding of learning. This assumption that the individual is the correct unit of analysis is so entrenched that almost all learning theories focus on individual persons or minds. The power of the individuality assumption is such that the first conceptual mistake about generic attributes (that they are discrete or atomic entities that can be acquired and transferred singly) is usually read as applying to individuals only. However, as argued above, it can equally apply to teams or groups. So, restricting generic attribute learning to individuals is a further assumption, one that this section argues is mistaken.

This assumption about the individual has been variously challenged. It is claimed that it is founded on a faulty view of the individual self (Usher, Bryant & Johnston 1997: 97-100). Crucially, however, this assumption discounts the possibility, indeed the likelihood, of communal learning, i.e. learning by teams and organisations that may not be reducible to learning by individuals. Understandings of learning centred on the individuality assumption offer no "convincing account of the relationship between 'knowledge' as the possession of individuals and 'knowledge' as the collective property of communities of 'knowers'..." (Toulmin 1999: 54). Likewise the assumption that meaning is established via individual minds creates the problem of accounting for collective knowledge (Toulmin 1999: 55). Adopting the individuality assumption has wide-ranging implications for vocational education, e.g. human capital theory incorporates this assumption. This is evident from a typical definition of human capital: '[T]he knowledge, skills and competences and other attributes embodied in individuals that are relevant to economic activity' (OECD 1998: 9).

However, as Winch stresses, the implications of the social nature of learning go far deeper than remedying a failure to account for collective knowledge. In crucial senses we need to recognise "the necessarily *social* nature of learning" (Winch 1998: 183). Normative learning of all kinds, including the important case of learning rule-following, presupposes the prior existence of social institutions. "No normative activity could exist *ab initio* in the life of a solitary" (Winch 1998: 7). Clearly, when considering learning, the isolated *individual* is often not the appropriate unit of analysis.

Not unexpectedly, the individual is the focus of generic attribute policies and programmes. Yet many of the putative generic attributes are inherently social. For instance, one generic attribute often mentioned by employers is 'customer satisfaction skills'. It should be clear that in a large firm that enjoys good relations with its customers, it is both unlikely and implausible that all staff have the same generic 'customer satisfaction skills'. Rather the customer relations of the firm is a complex whole that many staff contribute to and develop in their different ways. In an important sense, the firm's customer relations is an evolving social construction. One problem with the focus on individual acquisition of generic attributes is that it cuts out contextual features of such attributes. Yet the customer relations of the firm will be something that is highly contextual. As staff come into the firm they bring their own take on customer relations and proceed to develop and adapt it to their new circumstances. In the process they help to shape the evolving social construction that is the firm's customer relations. But to simply focus on customer relations as internalised by a given individual is to miss the rich fabric of this social construction.

Customer relations as internalised by given individuals will vary significantly. Quite simply, the learning histories of staff, for example, will rarely if ever be the same because of the contextuality and particularities of their different work experiences. Hence it makes little sense to look for exact *replicability* of learning histories across individual workers. Of course, there will be some commonalities. For instance, all proficient workers in the firm will need to be able to recognise certain basic customer relations strategies. But even here differences in learning histories and/or pattern recognition capabilities might well lead to subtle differences in how a given situation is read by different workers.

In a discussion of different ways of understanding skills, Stasz & Brewer compare and contrast what they call two "conflicting theoretical perspectives about skills" (1999: 14). The first perspective is a "positivist" view which "conceives of skills as unitary, measurable traits that individuals possess". In other words skills are learned by, and attach to, the individual and can be transferred to different contexts. This is, of course, the perspective that is implicit in most generic attributes literature.

The second perspective outlined by Stasz & Brewer is a "situated" view, which

> assumes that skills are larger than the behaviour and cognitive processes of a single person. Rather, individuals act in social systems that help determine skill requirements, distribution of skills in the work setting, and other important factors. Direct transfer of skills from one setting to another is rare *(Stasz & Brewer 1999: 71)*.

This perspective obviously denies that achievement of a set of generic attributes, in (say) customer service, would equate with workplace proficiency in the firm discussed above. This is clearly so since the skills are attached to the job rather than to the person. The neophyte accredited with generic attributes in customer service would need to go through a learning process to acquire proficiency in the customer service practices of the firm. Stasz & Brewer suggest that neither of the two perspectives provides a complete picture of the place of skills in work. It seems very clear that the individualist perspective is wholly inadequate for understanding generic attributes such as customer relations.

A further important dimension to the viewpoint that generic attributes are socially situated comes from writings that emphasise the roles of power and gender in the construction of skills (see, for example, Bradley 1989, Butler 1999). The main claim is that certain occupational groups succeed in having their work viewed as skilled irrespective of the nature or complexity of the tasks involved (e.g. Shields 1995). Strong contexuality of generic attributes is a seemingly inevitable implication of theories that view skill formation as inherently social (see, for example, Lave & Wenger 1991, Guile & Young 1998, Waterhouse, Wilson & Ewer 1999, Engestrom 2001, Hodkinson & Hodkinson 2003). If the social characteristics of a workplace shape the range and deployment of skills in that workplace, then there will be an inescapable mismatch with standardised or generic competence descriptors. As Waterhouse, Wilson & Ewer (1999: 37) put it:

> Competencies, when carefully considered in context, are both subtle and complex in ways that may not be reflected in simple or generic descriptions. The social and collective nature of competence is also often not reflected in the individualistic approaches that underpin many training needs analysis and curriculum design processes. ....Yet without the mediating influence of wider industry, social and individual learner concerns even this finely contextualised and well-grounded focus could be short sighted. Learners also need to extend their horizons and stretch their capacities beyond the immediate context.

2.4 The Fourth General Misunderstanding of the Nature of Generic Attributes is that it is Thought that we can Readily Recognise them when we see them. (It is easy to Conclude from I and II that if Typical Generic Attributes are Discrete Entities and can be Acquired Readily, then we must be Straightforward to Identify Their Presence or Absence)

For the common sense understanding of learning, to have successfully learnt is to know what it is that you have learnt. Learning that is non-transparent, that the learner cannot tell you about, is inferior learning. Winch puts this point as follows:

> It is natural for us to talk about learning as if we recognise that we have both a capacity to learn and a capacity to bring to mind what has been learned. *(1998: 19)*

This second capacity trades on the image of the mind as the home of clear and distinct ideas. If we have really learnt well, we will be able to bring the learning to mind. An inability to do so is a clear indicator that learning has been imperfect or unsuccessful. Here propositions are the model. If we really understand (have learnt) a proposition then we will be able to 'bring it before the mind'. Inability to do so indicates ineffectual or inferior learning. So, for the common sense understanding of learning, non-transparent learning, such as tacit knowledge, informal learning, and the like, is either an aberration or a second rate kind of learning. However, as was pointed out in chapter one, There is significant diversity evident in the various proposed lists of generic and graduate attributes. It was argued that these differences are a reflection of the fact that despite the aura of tangibility provided by codified descriptive lists, much about supposed generic attributes remains intangible and elusive. So generic attributes clash with the transparency assumption.

However, the transparency assumption is challenged by the increasing recognition of the importance of non-transparent types of learning, one of which, dispositional learning, is presupposed by other forms of learning (Passmore 1980). These dispositions include a range of abilities or capacities that underpin other forms of learning. Winch (1998: 19) argues that knowledge is largely dispositional, thereby taking the central focus firmly away from transparent propositions in minds. These capacities, abilities, and skills are non-transparent are closely related to generic attributes. Recent recognition of the importance of non-transparent or tacit types of learning (Hager 2005) means it should not be seen as a limitation of graduate attributes if they turn out to be significantly tacit. One of the lessons from the implementation of the competence approach has been the realisation that the underpinning constituents of competence cannot be precisely specified (Hager 2004b). Early proponents of competence thought otherwise. But it is performance rather than human capabilities that can be accurately and meaningfully represented in statement form.

It is precisely because performance is describable, observable, measurable, and assessable, while the capabilities, abilities, and skills that constitute competence are inaccessible, that judging competence always involves inference (Hager & Beckett 1995). We infer on the basis of performance various propositions about a person's capabilities, abilities, and skills. But this remains territory where contestation and diverse views are inevitable. Much human know-how is inexplicit. This is the case for generic attributes. Their precise specification remains elusive. Unfortunately, this is not something that is at all understood by the many policy makers and industrialists who, seemingly all around the world, make confident, but hollow, assertions about the exact range of generic attributes supposedly needed universally by workers in a given nation, whatever the exact nature of the work in which they happen to be engaged (see, for example, Hager, Holland & Beckett 2002).

2.5 The Fifth General Misunderstanding of the Nature of Generic Attributes is that they are Thought to be Readily and Unequivocally Describable in Language. Hence it is Regarded as Straightforward to Develop Descriptive Understandings of Typical Generic Attributes and to Convey These Understandings to Others in Written form

This point largely follows from the previous one. However, it is worth making on its own because many seem to believe that if only the descriptions of generic attributes or graduate attributes can be polished and perfected then everything else will fall into place. However, it is because, as argued in the previous section, that much knowledge of generic attributes or graduate attributes is tacit, that verbal descriptions of such attributes will necessarily be incomplete. Consider, for instance, the case of face recognition. Humans can easily pick out a familiar face from thousands of unfamiliar ones. But to state in words exactly how this is done is something that remains elusive. As Lum (1999: 410) succinctly puts it, the assumption that "human capabilities can be unequivocally described and accurately communicated by means of language" is unfounded. So, at best, lists and descriptions of generic attributes can be rough and ready guides. This is not to deny that they might sometimes be useful. But it is a warning that all such lists and descriptions will have inherent limitations and disadvantages. In particular, there is an ever present tendency to assume that reality is exhausted by attempted descriptions of it. This is rarely the case.

Thus when we make inferences about a person's attributes (capabilities, abilities, and skills) on the basis of performance, such attributions always involve assumptions about the nature of these capacities. The nature of the capabilities, abilities, and skills involved in performances of various kinds are typically contested, as also is the best way to develop such capabilities, abilities, and skills.

We have seen in this section that there are various seductive conceptual confusions about generic attributes that need to be guarded against. What aids are available to help us to achieve this? This is the focus of the next section.

3. PRINCIPLES FOR A MORE ACCURATE UNDERSTANDING OF THE NATURE OF GENERIC ATTRIBUTES

In this section key ideas that are claimed to be crucial for gaining a more accurate understanding of the nature of graduate attributes are outlined. These key ideas include:

I Viewing learning as a process.

II Paying due regard to the holism of generic attributes.

III Taking proper account of the influence of social/group factors.

IV Recognising the contextuality of generic attributes.

V Recognising the relevance of generic attributes for lifelong learning.

As will become apparent in the following discussion, these five key ideas interconnect with and reinforce one another. Some of these five key ideas relate to more than one of the five conceptual errors discussed in the previous section. The order of presentation has been chosen for ease of exposition. Hence, these five key ideas definitely should not be regarded as matching their same-numbered counterparts in the previous section on conceptual errors.

3.1 Viewing Learning as a Process

The idea that learning is most fruitfully viewed as a process has become increasingly prominent in educational thought of the last hundred or so years. Dewey, for instance, views learning as an ongoing process (or, more accurately, as a dialectical interplay of process and product). Viewing learning primarily as a process rather than as a product provides an alternative and more fruitful conception of generic attributes, one that enables different features to be emphasised. Learning becomes a process that changes both the learner and the environment (with the learner being part of the environment rather than a detached spectator – see Beckett & Hager 2002, section 7.9). As the learner and their relationship to their surroundings is reshaped by learning, so is their generic attribute repertoire reshaped. This view of learning resonates with other key ideas that will be considered in this section. It underlines its contextuality, as well as the influence of cultural and social factors. It is also holistic in that it points to the organic, whole person nature of learning, including the importance of dispositions and abilities. On this view, graduate attributes are central to learning and lifelong learning becomes normal rather than abnormal. Following the discussion of metaphors in the previous section, the favoured metaphors for learning as process are participation and construction. This view of learning underlines its contextuality, as well as the influence of cultural and social factors. It is holistic in that it points to the organic, whole person nature of learning, including the importance of dispositions and abilities.

The following definitions highlight the contrasts between the two views of learning – product vs. process. According to the *Oxford English Dictionary*, learning means: "To acquire knowledge of (a subject) or skill (an art, etc.) as a result of study, experience or teaching." Besides portraying learning as a product, this definition is in danger of limiting learning to propositions and skills. The more holistic emerging view of learning is captured in Schoenfeld's (1999: 6) definition: "… coming to understand things and developing increased capacities to do what one wants or needs to do …".

While there is a strong convergence between traditional notions of apprenticeship and recent influential theories of learning, in that both emphasise learning as a process, much recent vocational education and training policy development is completely out of step with this. Far from viewing vocational learning as a process, learning is too often thought of as unit-by-unit acquisition of independent atoms of knowledge and skill. Work performance is broken down into a series of such decontextualised atomic elements, which novice workers are thought of as needing to gain one by one. Once a discrete element is acquired, transfer or application to appropriate future circumstances by the learner is assumed to be unproblematic. Further, it is assumed, apparently, that learners have an innate capacity to combine appropriate learned elements to produce the required holistic response to real work situations that may be more or less novel. In other words, it is assumed that the main learning task is to acquire the atoms that underpin performance. But what if real work performance is something much richer than anything that a mere list of discrete atoms can capture? The notion of discrete unit-by-unit mastery of skills and understanding omits the crucial need for an overall grasp of the whole. Rather than unit-by-unit acquisition of independent skills, a better image to represent the gaining of high level proficiency in an occupation might be something like the 'gradual clearing of a fog in a landscape'. This image captures the idea of the increasingly proficient performer gaining a growing appreciation of the relationships between various skills and of their significance for the whole.

Some might claim that the description in the previous paragraph is a caricature. But certainly something close to this constitutes the underlying principles implicit in official Australian documents relating to Competency-Based Training. Likewise Training Packages are consistent with this reading (see Hager 2004b). What other understanding is available to poorly qualified trainers working from the thin guidance contained in a Training Package? Likewise, Australian documents on generic attributes (key competencies, core or basic skills) assume similar principles. In particular, generic attributes, such as communication and problem solving, are clearly presented as discrete, decontextualised atoms that once acquired can be transferred simply to diverse situations. Certainly, literature emanating from employer groups reflects this common assumption (see, for example, Hager, Holland & Beckett 2002).

3.2 Paying due Regard to the Holism of Generic Attributes

While it is useful in developing our understanding of generic attributes to consider them individually, in practice they overlap and interweave like the threads in a carpet. So, for example, you don't need to go far into a consideration of teamwork before communication becomes an issue. Likewise, to use a workplace example, answering the telephone effectively in a business situation may be good customer relations, but it can also involve simultaneously communication, gathering of information, analytical reasoning, and problem solving, all of a high order. Research shows very clearly that in workplace situations of all kinds generic attributes cluster (Moy 1999, Hager 1997).

So, universities that identify graduate attributes need to avoid the danger of treating them as a simple mechanistic list of separate traits. A familiar analogy will help to illustrate the problem. Think of the capability of driving a motor car. A simple analysis might break this activity into (say) 80 discrete components, e.g. start engine, release hand brake, turn steering wheel through ninety degrees, know meanings of road markings, exercise care when reversing, etc. The discrete components represent a mix of knowledge, skills and dispositions (attitudes and values), ie. a mix of attributes. However, not much thought is required to see that someone might be capable of demonstrating each of these discrete attributes yet still be an incompetent driver. Driving is a holistic activity which depends mainly on a capacity to bring together the various 'discrete' attributes in an appropriate way determined by changes in conditions and contexts. The real skill in driving is in putting together the attributes in changing combinations. This principle is general. In particular, professional practice is holistic in this way. So, for example, a professional identifying a problem and developing a solution might be simultaneously communicating with a client, reasoning analytically, and acting as a mentor.

While it is useful for many purposes to distinguish the various generic attributes, their integration in real life practice should never be overlooked. This has important implications in, e.g. assessment of generic skills. The Australian Council for Educational Research (ACER) has developed *Graduate Skills*

Assessment Tests that measure isolated skills or traits (see Hager, Holland & Beckett 2002). It may be that scores on a series of traits say little about a graduate's higher level capacity to integrate generic attributes together with other knowledge and skills to frame an appropriate response to a given contextual situation.

This holism of generic attributes and the requisite capacity to deploy them seamlessly in appropriate ways in changing conditions and contexts, means that in a significant sense one's generic attributes capacity is a reflection of the kind of person that one is. Thus, having well-developed generic attributes may have the effect of improving self esteem and self-confidence. In other words, graduates may be more likely to see themselves as competent people and be perceived as competent by others (including prospective employers). For example, Brennan et al. (1993: 144) cited evidence 'of a demand amongst graduates themselves for a greater emphasis on a broader general education in those skills areas which can be seen to make for a "competent person".' Barnett (1994) has written about moving from academic competence to operational competence. Development of generic attributes (or practice knowledge) while a student may thus be important for job selection and initial work.

The last two sections have stressed the importance for understanding generic attributes of viewing learning as a process and taking account of the significance of their holism. These should encourage a different outlook on vocational learning. If vocational learning is not centrally about unit-by-unit acquisition of atoms, but, rather, is an integrated, ongoing process of coming to understand a whole complex of knowledge and skills, including generic attributes, then much current policy overlooks, and even discourages, this vital dimension of learning. It is only by developing understanding of a whole complex of knowledge and skills, and how the various parts relate to one another, that workers can develop skilled responses to relatively novel or even unique circumstances. This gradually acquired capacity to tailor skilled responses to changing contexts is not something that can be captured in a short term check list. It is because this rich, synthetic dimension of learning is absent that research finds that trainees have a

> .... low opinion [of] the concept of 'ticking off' outcomes or competencies from workbooks or training records. Quite simply, these lists of outcomes were seen by the trainees as a 'thin' account of their work experience and learning. *(Hager & Smith 2004: 42)*

Another research project found that 70% of work sites studied used the training workbooks that encapsulated the check list of competencies approach, while 30% admitted to neglecting the workbooks. What was interesting here was that

> ..... the 30% who admitted neglecting them often included firms that were clearly providing good training. The reasoning here seems to be that the holism of real work situations is such that long lists of outcomes are seen as but pale representations of the real thing. So, thoughtful training arrangements lead people to go beyond this approach. *(Hager & Smith 2004: 42)*

Thus, it seems that people who are good trainers may know that what has been served up to them by policy makers is a sham, but they get on with good training regardless. The worry is the majority who apparently accept the thin conception of training that underpins much current vocational education policy.

3.3 Taking Proper Account of the Influence of Social/Group Factors

Social and group factors are important influences on the development and deployment of generic attributes. Earlier in this chapter, it was argued that it is a common misunderstanding of the nature of generic attributes to view them as being acquired by individual learners, with the learning regarded as being located within these individuals. The isolated *individual* is often not the appropriate unit of analysis. Yet, shaped no doubt by the power of the learning as product view, educational policies, including those that impact on workplace learning, tend to focus almost exclusively on individual learners. This near universal adoption of the individuality assumption is no doubt reinforced by the popularity of human capital theory, which, as noted earlier, focuses on the knowledge, skills and competences embodied in individuals. The competencies agenda as implemented in many countries provides an illustration of the powerful attraction of the individuality assumption and human capital thinking. However, recent work suggests a growing interest in social capital (see, for example, Winch 2000, Beckett & Hager 2002: 80ff.).

Not surprisingly then, there have been various theories of workplace learning that focus on individual learners acquiring learning as products. Such theories align closely with human capital theory (Hager 2005). Given this, there is a temptation to oppose these individualistic theories with social learning theories that centre on group learning as a participatory process based on social capital theory. However, such a move is certainly too simplistic. This is so because some significant learning theories challenge the idea that learning has to be exclusively either individual or social. These theories accept that, while all learning is in some sense social, this is compatible with some instances of learning being learning by individuals, and other instances of learning occurring at the communal level (Hager 2005: 838-839). Thus at least some social learning theories include a place for learning by individuals that is different from pure communal learning. In the context of the development of generic attributes this is highly relevant, since it is a plausible claim, given the diverse nature of generic attributes (discussed earlier), that both individual and social learning are different but important dimensions of the learning of these attributes.

Thus, while the main point of this section is to urge that proper account needs to be taken of the influence of social/group factors on the development of generic attributes, it is not suggesting that these factors explain everything nor that learning by individuals is of no significance. Rather, the claim is that both individual and communal learning are important categories for understanding learning of graduate attributes. As noted earlier in this chapter, Toulmin is one writer who takes this possibility seriously. In arguing that understandings of learning centred on the individuality assumption offer no "convincing account of the relationship between 'knowledge' as the possession of individuals and 'knowledge' as the collective property of communities of 'knowers'..." (Toulmin 1999: 54), he draws attention to these two dimensions of graduate attribute learning. All of the social accounts of learning recognise "the necessarily *social* nature of learning" (Winch 1998: 183). This means that normative learning of all kinds, including the important case of learning rule-following, presupposes the prior existence of social institutions. "No normative activity could exist *ab initio* in the life of a solitary" (Winch 1998: 7). However, none of this rules out the possibility that, in coming to understand learning of graduate attributes, the focus might be sometimes on the learning by individuals and sometimes on the communal learning that transcends the learning of any individual.

The social learning theories mentioned in this section (e.g. Lave and Wenger 1991, Wertsch 1998, Engestrom 2001) recognise that workplace learning and performance are embodied phenomena; that they are significantly shaped by social, organisational and cultural factors, thereby extending beyond the individual; and that they seamlessly integrate a range of human attributes that is much wider than just rationality. In doing so, they tend to problematise or seek to re-theorise learning. In doing so they offer a fresh take on the development of generic attributes.

Overall then, for a nuanced understanding of generic attributes to be developed, we need to take account of both social and individual factors. Neither approach on its own, is likely to be able to provide a sufficiently rich understanding of generic attributes.

3.4 Recognising the Contextuality of Generic Attributes

Generic attributes and the ways that they cluster are strongly shaped by the particular features of the context in which work is carried out (Hager 1997: 13-15). The influence of the context is such that it is unhelpful to identify the generic attributes of an occupation or profession. The relative importance of these generic attributes and the ways that they cluster will very much change with the workplace context. The notion of 'context' is itself complex and includes a multiplicity of workplace-related factors such as:

- The specific history of a workplace or company
- Its particular culture and norms
- Its institutions and practices, e.g. work organisation, career structure
- Its economic and social environment
- Its strategic needs
- Its deployment of technology
- The extent and intensity of change to which it is subject.

Research on the workplace role of generic attributes shows that there is significant variation in competence requirements across work sites within the one occupation. Such variation means that pre-specified skill development outcomes, including standardised generic attributes, cannot meet all of the requirements of particular work sites. For example, in the USA Stasz et al. (1996) found differences in generic attributes needed across occupations, but also in the same occupation practiced in different organisations and work sites. They concluded (Stasz et al. 1996: 102) that

> .... whereas generic skills and dispositions are identifiable in all jobs, their specific characteristics and importance vary among jobs. The characteristics of problem solving, teamwork, communication .... are related to job demands, which in turn

depend on the purpose of the work, the tasks that constitute the job, the organization
of the work, and other aspects of the work context.

Thus, even within the same occupation, job demands can vary so much between different companies or work sites that it makes little sense to try to specify the exact generic attributes mix for a particular occupation. The high contextual sensitivity of generic attributes requirements of work is further illustrated by the later research findings of Stasz & Brewer (1999).

Similar findings emerged from Australian research on the role of generic attributes ("key competencies") in the workplace (Gonczi et al. 1995, Hager et al. 1996, Stevenson (ed.) 1996, Hager, Garrick et al. 2002). Gonczi et al. (1995) found that hairdressing, for example, is practised somewhat differently in different types of businesses, thereby creating diverse contexts within the industry. For instance, a hairdressing salon that was part of a flourishing small chain of salons saw itself as maintaining an edge on its competitors due to its significant investment in generic attributes training. Hairdressing is an occupation that is typically entered via an apprenticeship, which, of course, includes a substantial component of on-the-job training. This chain of salons featured continuous training activities for all of its staff. Besides keeping up-to-date with the more technical skills of hairdressing, there was an ongoing emphasis of the importance of the softer skills (generic attributes) that were seen as underpinning the business focus of the chain. This centred on the provision of a kind of service to customers that would bring them back regularly. The achievement of this end depended as much on the softer skills of the staff as it did on basic and advanced technical skills. This becomes evident from a consideration of how the staff went about their work.

Staff typically spent significant time in consultation with customers to establish their needs and offer a range of alternatives to help meet the identified needs. The emphasis was on formulating the various alternatives in a clear way so that customers could make informed choices. Customers often are not sure of what they want. The staff role was to formulate ways to make the customer look better and to present the options to the customer clearly so that they could make an informed decision. It was emphasised that staff must present options to the customer, not as a hard sell, but in a helpful, constructive way. As well as the initial presentation of options to the customer, staff also had to provide sound advice on post-treatment care. Advice on post-treatment care included recommending to the customer, and selling to them, products for after care.

As part of the normal service, staff were required to design a program for customers to manage their hair after the treatment. A copy of the care program that had been supplied to the customer was retained on the records, thereby enabling management to monitor ongoing staff performance in this area. Staff likened this part of their work to the responsibility of a doctor for sending a patient away with the correct prescription. Other aspects of planning/organising were to ensure that customers were not kept waiting longer than necessary and that they were looked after with coffee, newspaper, and so forth.

The General Manager of this hairdressing salon reported that though graduates of the vocational education college certificate possessed the requisite technical skills, they usually lacked the level of soft skills required by the business philosophy of this chain (Gonczi et al. 1995: 106). Thus for staff of this business, workplace competence included the capacity to make some very context specific judgements shaped by the company approach to customer service. It appeared that a significant level of in-house training was needed to achieve this. Further evidence of variation in soft skills requirements between workplaces carrying out the same occupation was found by Hager et al. (1996). This study examined five occupational areas across twenty-two work sites.

Further support for the inherent contextuality of competence in general, and of generic attributes in particular, comes from the increasing prominence of the "new workplace". Here the focus shifts from the competencies of individuals to organisational capacity, that is, the combined assets of the organisation's staff and resources. So the new workplace is marked by generic attributes that go beyond the technical, such as 'teamwork', 'innovation', 'taking responsibility', 'planning', 'solving problems', 'communicating effectively' and 'creating new knowledge'. These generic attributes are required to be deployed in combinations that meet the demands of unique and continually changing work contexts. As such they demand on-going learning by workers that are adaptable, multi-skilled and flexible in the face of evolving circumstances. While traditional training to specified outcomes is well-suited to the imparting of technical skills, these generic attributes appear to require continuing learning in novel work contexts.

Although there is a strong temptation to think about an individual's generic attributes in isolation, employers are really interested in the capacity to deploy them holistically for successful performance in a particular workplace. Organisations that are seeking to foster a strong learning environment for employees implement their own internal learning and cultural programs for this purpose. In the information technology industry, Hewlett-Packard Australia, for example (see Hager, Holland & Beckett 2002), hires graduates from a range of disciplines, apart from computer science, and try to select those that are 'flexible', 'adaptive' and capable of 'learning on the job' because of the need to develop such contextual attributes as 'business savvy' and 'customer focus'. This firm views itself as committed to lifelong learning and has identified its values which are used to determine the 'cultural fit' of employees.

People are such that we should not be surprised to find that they fit into some workplaces better than others. This is borne out by the familiar example of undergraduates who undertake a series of work placements. Typically, students do very well in some workplaces (even being offered a job), but not so well in others. The suggestion is that this is because, in part at least, their generic attributes and their capacity to tailor them to particular contexts suits some workplaces more than others. In short, they are more adept at responding to some workplaces than to others. Once again, these kinds of considerations cast strong doubts on the worth of context-free generic attributes profiles that treat the generic attributes singly.

This marked contextuality of generic attributes provides another argument for the educational value of developing them. They provide the means for learners to gain types of knowledge and learning not otherwise readily available to them, i.e. types of professional knowledge often overlooked in professional education courses. Eraut (1994), for example, argues that professional education typically can be mapped as providing specified disciplinary knowledge and related technical skills, but that there is another realm of knowledge and skills required for practice as a professional that lies outside the standard syllabus. This practice knowledge (communication, dealing with people, etc.) typically is seen as implicit knowledge — something you have naturally or not, or something you pick up along the way — and not normally spelled out. The argument can be made that such practice knowledge can be equated to some extent with the graduate attributes that people talk about. To the extent that higher education is a preparation for professional work for many graduates, the development of 'practice' knowledge should be as much an explicit part of the curriculum as disciplinary knowledge. This is not to overlook the broader purposes of higher education such as preparation for active citizenship.

While we might want to say that university graduates develop a range of generic attributes of more significance is their capacity to deploy suitable combinations of these attributes to deal with the particular professional situations in which they find themselves. In these circumstances, a series of scores on individual generic attributes may mean very little in relation to performance in real workplaces and only serve to confuse thinking in this important area of educational debate. The term 'capability' may be useful as an overarching concept to reflect the clustering of attributes and skills. The various combinations of attributes and skills that a graduate deploys in a series of different situations can be called capabilities.

The contextuality of generic attributes means that it is important that only a relatively small number of general generic attributes is proposed as standard graduate outcomes. It seems that different professions and occupations have somewhat different generic attributes profiles, particularly when they are practiced in many different sorts of contexts. Thus, the greater the number of generic attributes that are detailed and distinguished, the less likely it is that a proposed general profile will be suited to every university program. Hence an appropriate level of generality is needed. This also means that if a general profile is to be widely used by faculties and/or programs, e.g. in developing a work-based learning degree (see Boud & Solomon chapter 11), there is a need to contextualise the generic attributes to the particular profession or discipline area.

3.5 Recognising the Relevance of Generic Attributes for Lifelong Learning

The preceding considerations suggest one way of thinking about lifelong learning. From the early years of schooling and before, learners can be expected to be in situations in which they would be acquiring some basic proficiency in deploying at least some common generic attributes, for example, using household microelectronic technology. One outcome of a sound education would be a growing capacity to deploy successfully generic attributes in an increasingly diverse range of situations and contexts. This suggests that the development of generic attributes should become gradually more integrated and holistic as young people move through schooling. The idea is that sound performance in very many of life's situations centres on successful deployment of suitable combinations of generic attributes. Such a staged development of generic attributes would facilitate students' transition to vocational training, higher education, work and other post-school activities.

In the Australian vocational sector the recent agenda to embed generic attributes in the training courses is an attempt to achieve a balance between the capacity for lifelong learning in the longer term and employability in the short term. The greater articulation between vocational education courses and university courses, as well as more clearly delineated curriculum pathways are, of course, an identifiable form of lifelong learning.

The development of graduate attributes by universities is closely linked to their role in fostering graduates with a capacity for lifelong learning. Various graduate attributes have been recognised as important for lifelong learning (see, for example, Candy, Crebert & O'Leary 1994). Developments at the University of Otago provide an example of the close links between these two notions. Viewing lifelong learning as an element of 'graduateness', a concept elaborated by the English Higher Education Quality Council (HEQC 1996), the university has instituted an iterative process in which links are strengthened in its courses between the fostering of desirable attributes and the deployment of innovative teaching and instructional design strategies. Part of this iterative process is the obtaining of ongoing feedback from both employers and recent graduates on the generic attributes required of graduates.

It is also crucial that generic attributes should be thought of more broadly than in terms of just university and work. These attributes represent a basis for lifelong learning in all kinds of life situations. Rather than being viewed as discrete attributes that people learn to transfer, generic attributes should be seen as learnt capacities to handle an increasing variety of diverse situations. Thus transfer becomes more a growth in confidence and adaptability as learners experience ever more success in their deployment of generic skills in a range of situations. To put it another way, perhaps it is not so much generic attributes that transfer, as growing understanding of how to deal with different contexts. In this way, non-work experiences can benefit workplace performance and vice versa.

4. CONCLUSION

This chapter has argued that the value of generic attributes initiatives will hinge crucially on how well they are conceptualised. Popular common sense understandings of these matters have been shown to be seriously flawed. Five conceptual errors that abound in generic attributes literature and practice have been outlined and discussed in some detail. The chapter then presented and expounded five principles that need to inform a sounder understanding of generic attributes.

5. REFERENCES

Barnett, R. (1994) *The Limits of Competence: Knowledge, Higher Education, and Society.* Buckingham: The Society for Research into Higher Education/Open University Press.

Beckett, D. & Hager, P. (2002) *Life, Work and Learning: Practice in Postmodernity.* Routledge International Studies in the Philosophy of Education 14. London and New York: Routledge.

Bereiter, C. (2002) *Education and Mind in the Knowledge Age.* Mahwah, N.J./London: Lawrence Erlbaum Associates.

Boud, D. & Solomon, N. (2003) ' "I Don't Think I Am a Learner": Acts of Naming Learners at Work', *Journal of Workplace Learning*, Vol. 15, Nos. 7-8, pp. 326-331.

Bourdieu, P. (1990) *In Other Words: Essays Towards a Reflexive Practice.* Cambridge: Polity Press.

Bradley, H. (1989) *Men's Work, Women's Work: A Sociological History of the Social Division of Labour in Employment.* Cambridge: Polity Press.

Bransford, J.D. & Schwartz, D.L. (1999) 'Rethinking Transfer: A Simple Proposal With Multiple Implications', *Review of Research in Education*, Vol. 24, pp. 61-100.

Brennan, J.L., Lyon, E.S., McGeevor, P.A. & Murray, K. (1993) *Students, Courses and Jobs: The Relationship Between Higher Education and the Labour Market.* London: Jessica Kingsley.

Butler, E. (1999) 'Technologising Equity: The Politics and Practices of Work-Related Learning' in D. Boud & J.Garrick (eds.) *Understanding Learning at Work.* London & New York: Routledge.

Candy, P.C., Crebert, G. & O'Leary, J. (1994) *Developing Lifelong Learners Through Undergraduate Education.* Commissioned Report No. 28. Canberra: National Board of Employment, Education and Training.

Engestrom, Y. (2001) 'Expansive Learning at Work: Towards an Activity-Theoretical Re-conceptualisation', *Journal of Education and Work*, Vol. 14, No. 1, pp. 133-156.

Eraut, M. (1994) *Developing Professional Knowledge and Competence.* London: Falmer Press.

Gonczi, A., Curtain, R., Hager P., Hallard A. & Harrison J. (1995) *Key Competencies in On-the-Job Training.* Sydney: University of Technology, Sydney.

Guile, D. & Young, M. (1998) 'Apprenticeship As a Conceptual Basis for a Social Theory of Learning', *Journal of Vocational Education & Training*, Vol. 50, No. 2, pp. 173-92.

Hager, P. (1997) *Learning in the Workplace*. Review of Research Monograph Series. Adelaide: National Centre for Vocational Education Research.

Hager, P. (2004a)'The Inescapability of Metaphors for Thinking about Learning', in G. Jover & P. Villamor (eds.) *Voices of Philosophy of Education, Proceedings of the 9th Biennial Conference of the International Network of Philosophers of Education*, Madrid, Spain: Complutense University, pp. 143-51.

Hager, P. (2004b) 'The Competence Affair, or Why VET Urgently Needs a New Understanding of Learning', *Journal of Vocational Education & Training*, Vol. 56, No. 3, pp. 409-433.

Hager, P. (2005) 'Current Theories of Workplace Learning: A Critical Assessment' in N. Bascia, A. Cumming, A. Datnow, K. Leithwood & D. Livingstone (eds.) *International Handbook of Educational Policy*. Part Two. Dordrecht: Springer, pp. 829-846.

Hager, P. & Beckett, D. (1995) 'Philosophical Underpinnings of the Integrated Conception of Competence', *Educational Philosophy and Theory*, Vol. 27, No. 1,pp. 1-24.

Hager, P., McIntyre, J., Moy, J., Comyn, P., Stone, J., Schwenke, C. & Gonczi, A. (1996) *Workplace Keys: Piloting the Key Competencies in Workplace Training*, Sydney: University of Technology, Sydney.

Hager, P., Garrick, J., Crowley, S. & Risgalla, R. (2002) *Generic Competencies and Workplace Reform in the Australian Construction Industry*. Sydney: University of Technology, Sydney.

Hager, P., Holland, S. & Beckett, D. (2002) *Enhancing The Learning And Employability Of Graduates: The Role Of Generic Skills*. Business/Higher Education Round Table Position Paper No. 9. Melbourne: B-HERT.

Hager, P. & Smith, E. (2004) 'The Inescapability of Significant Contextual Learning in Work Performance', *London Review of Education*, Vol. 2, No. 1, pp. 33-46.

Higher Education Quality Council (1996) *Academic Standards in the Approval, Review and Classification of Degrees*. London: Chameleon Press.

Hodkinson, P. & Hodkinson ,H. (2003) 'Individuals, Communities of Practice and the Policy Context: School-Teachers Learning in Their Workplace', *Studies in Continuing Education*, Vol. 25, No. 1, pp. 3-21.

Illich, I. (1973) *Deschooling Society*, Harmondsworth: Penguin.

Lakoff, G. & Johnson, M. (1980) *Metaphors We Live By*. Chicago: University of Chicago Press.

Lave, J. & Wenger, E. (1991) *Situated Learning: Legitimate peripheral participation.* Cambridge: Cambridge University Press.

Lum, G. (1999) Where's the Competence in Competence-based Education and Training?, *Journal of Philosophy of Education*, Vol. 33, No. 3, pp. 403-18.

Moy, J. (1999) *The Impact of Generic Competencies on Workplace Performance*. Review of Research Monograph Series. Adelaide: National Centre for Vocational Education Research.

Organisation for Economic Cooperation and Development (OECD) (1998) *Human Capital Investment: An International Comparison*. Paris: OECD.

Passmore, J. (1980) *The Philosophy of Teaching*. London: Duckworth.

Rogoff, B. (1995) 'Observing Sociocultural Activity on Three Planes: Participatory Appropriation, Guided Participation, and Apprenticeship' in J.J. Wertsch, P. del Rio & A. Alvarez *Sociocultural Studies of Mind*. Cambridge: Cambridge University Press.

Schoenfeld, A. H. (1999) 'Looking Toward the 21st Century: Challenges of Educational Theory and Practice', *Educational Researcher*, Vol. 28, No. 7, pp. 4-14.

Sfard, A. (1998) 'On Two Metaphors for Learning and the Dangers of Choosing Just One', *Educational Researcher*, Vol. 27, No. 2, pp. 4-13.

Shields, J. (1995) 'A matter of skill: the revival of apprenticeship in early twentieth-century New South Wales', *Journal of Industrial Relations,* June, pp. 236-262.

Stasz, C., Ramsey, K., Eden, R., Melamid, E. & Kaganoff, T. (1996) *Workplace Skills in Practice*. Santa Monica, CA: Rand/National Center for Research in Vocational Education.

Stasz, C. & Brewer, D. J. (1999) *Academic Skills at Work: Two Perspectives*. Santa Monica: Rand Education (reprinted from the National Center for Research in Vocational Education).

Stevenson, J. (ed.) (1996) *Learning in the Workplace: Tourism and Hospitality*, Brisbane: Centre for Skill Formation Research and Development, Griffith University.

Toulmin, S. (1999) 'Knowledge as Shared Procedures', in Y. Engestrom, R. Miettinen & R. Punamaki (eds.) *Perspectives on Action Theory*. Cambridge: Cambridge University Press.

Usher, R., Bryant, I. & Johnston, R. (1997) *Adult Education and the Postmodern Challenge: Learning Beyond the Limits*. London and New York: Routledge.

Waterhouse, P., Wilson, B. & Ewer, P. (1999) *The Changing Nature and Patterns of Work and Implications for VET*. Review of Research Monograph Series. Adelaide: National Centre for Vocational Education Research.

Wertsch, J. W. (1998). *Mind as action*. Oxford and New York: Oxford University Press.

Winch, C. (1998) *The Philosophy of Human Learning*. Routledge International Studies in the Philosophy of Education. London and New York: Routledge.

Winch, C. (2000) *Education, work and social capital*. London and New York: Routledge.

CHAPTER 3

RONALD BARNETT

GRADUATE ATTRIBUTES IN AN AGE
OF UNCERTAINTY

1. INTRODUCTION

We live in a changing world; that much is a commonplace. But, in the present
context, there are two further points that can be made immediately. Firstly, the
range of the changes confronting the world and those who live in it are surely not
always appreciated. Secondly, the working out of the implications of change for
higher education is still a task that is largely before us. By addressing both of these
challenges, we shall necessarily come to a more informed appreciation as to what
'graduateness' might mean in the twenty-first century and also gain some further
insights into lifelong learning as a personal and social project.

2. A WORLD OF CHANGE

The world has been destabilized in numerous ways. Technologies, systems,
institutions, languages and social practices change not just daily but with ever-
increasing rapidity. One manifestation of these changes lies in dictionaries:
compilers agonize over what is to be included, as new idioms arise, and know that
any such publication is out of date as it is published. For many, this is a 'runaway
world', in which traditions are being 'disembedded' and in which our ethical
frameworks are failing to keep pace with the challenges that our technologies – in
medicine, in surveillance techniques – are presenting to us (Giddens 1992, 2002).
We hardly know how to live in such a world, it seems, except through retreating
into ourselves, into our own projects. We go 'bowling alone' (Putnam 2000) in an
increasingly individualized society.

P. Hager and S. Holland (eds.), Graduate Attributes, Learning and Employability, 49–65.
© 2006 *Springer.*

Some of these readings can be and surely are overdone. While there are signs of the weakening of cultural ties, there are also signs of strengthening of such ties: communities seem often determined to reassert their sense of themselves in themselves, whether on a very local or a regional or a national level. Some regional languages revivify even as others threaten to disappear. Considerable efforts are invested in order to try to place some new technologies, at least, under some kind of rational and even ethical control. At the same time, the ideas of 'MacDonaldization' and 'globalization' are testimony to a potential emergence of world-wide cultural identities (Ritzer 1997). So the theme of 'runawayness' should not beguile us; it should not runaway with us. Nevertheless, I believe that we are into a new world order in which a vocabulary of change has a particular resonance.

We may term this world order a world of complexity. In itself, however, to invoke 'complexity' is a crude move and on two accounts. Firstly, complexity itself comes in all manner of forms, for example, as between systems complexity and ethical complexity, between statistical complexity and emotional complexity. Such complexities can be extended in range very considerably indeed. Secondly, complexity can all too easily simply convey a sense, however justified, of an external environment and, in the process, fail to indicate the internal challenges, as it were, to human beings of living amid complexity. Daily, single situations of the kinds that graduates face in professional life, present a range of complexities in themselves – in systems, in interpersonal relationships, in ethical matters, in roles and responsibilities. If the first consideration points us towards a *horizontal* sense of an unfolding range of complexities *in extenso*, the second consideration points us towards a *vertical* sense of complexity. Here, in this latter manifestation of complexity, its challenges reach deeply into human beings, often in a submerged form, hidden from view and yet reeking its havoc, to appear as stress and even suicide.

An environment of radical uncertainty and complexity both brings about changes in human beings and calls for changes. The changes are at once substantive – new knowledges, new adaptations, new skills – and superstructural. By superstructural, I mean change in human being as such: new dispositions, new qualities, new forms of being in the world. The superstructural changes are much more important than the substantive changes. Indeed, it is only by there being changes in human being as such that new knowledges and new skills are going to be acquired and, then, put to use.

Human beings won't, for example, take the time and trouble to learn a second language on top of a busy professional and home life unless they have already come to a view that this is important to them (for whatever reason): a certain kind of state of being is necessary before any sought-for change in knowledge and skills. We can say, therefore, that the fundamental educational problem of a changing world is neither one of knowledge nor of skills but is one of *being*. To put it formally, the educational challenge of a world of uncertainty is ontological in its nature.

Our first point, then, as to graduate attributes in the context of lifelong learning, is that *'attributes' have to be understood generously to embrace human being as such*. The first task of higher education is to prepare the ground for forms of human being that are going to be able to withstand profound and incessant change.

It may be that 'attributes' is a misleading term here. One alternative that we might be tempted to summon in aid is that old-fashioned term 'character'. A problem with that term, however, is that it can all too easily divert us into a concern with the overt way in which a person presents herself to the world - her 'characteristics' – when much more before us are the inner structure of the person's being. Is it of the kind that is going to be adequate to a world in which all bets are off, when nothing can be taken for granted and in which every act, and every utterance and every outcome of one's acts and utterances are liable to be questioned from opposing quarters? Can we, in turn, construe of and develop a higher education that is going to be concerned with a mode of being for a world of uncertainty?

Our second point, then, has to be that *higher education needs to undergo a fundamental shift, not exactly to cast off concerns either with knowledge or with skills but to place at its centre a new concern with being as such*.

3. SUPERCOMPLEXITY

The matters that we are exploring here are clearly matters of general concern; they do not just come into view in the context of 'graduate' abilities or the situations in which graduates are likely to face. Nevertheless, we may plausibly contend that, characteristically, the situations in which graduates are likely to find themselves through the rest of their lives are likely to be positions of openendedness, of value conflict, of insufficient information and so forth; in short, situations of complexity.

We may even observe that such situations are *supercomplex* in their nature for these situations are, if not formally undescribable, are susceptible to multiple and proliferating descriptions. If only one had more time, more resources and more information, many of the challenges of complex situations would dissolve. (That one doesn't have the time, resources or information bring in their wake real and often stressful challenges.) Amid supercomplexity, in contrast, the matter is even more problematic for one finds oneself in the presence of situations that are inherently unresolvable in the sense that they cannot even be described with unanimity in the first place.

To put it even more sharply, we may distinguish complexity and supercomplexity in this way. Situations of complexity are situations in which the entities are so numerous and interwoven that the outcomes of interventions are difficult if not impossible to predict. Complexity may be understood, therefore, as *systems* complexity. Situations of supercomplexity, on the other hand, are situations where there is no unanimity even in describing the situations themselves.   Such a situation of multiple and conflicting interpretations is recursive: if we cannot be sure even of our descriptions of a situation – and therefore of the character of the situation itself – we cannot, in turn, be sure of ourselves, of our own identity and our relationships with the world.

The Israel-Palestinian crisis; the American 'war on terror'; and the termination of unborn foetuses are examples of supercomplex situations for there is no apparent possibility of the parties to the conflict even agreeing on the nature of the situation in which they are placed. This world of supercomplexity bears in generally on all in society but it is a feature especially of professional life. How, for example, are we to understand the professional-client relationship? Is it one of purchaser/supplier, or of expert/novice, or of practitioner/recipient or of sage/supplicant or (in an Internet age) one of dialogue between equal knowledges or …? Unless we are clear about the character of the relationship, we cannot specify the roles and responsibilities of the parties. The point is that, nowadays, that relationship is open to multiple interpretations and has continually to be renegotiated; but underlying those negotiations are going to be many sentiments, values and hopes that won't be voiced.

It is hardly surprising if doctors find it difficult to administer to themselves, for their roles – as we have just observed – are inherently unstable. But this is but a cameo of professional life in general and of its daily character, if not its hourly character. Professional situations are inherently lacking in clear descriptions. Indeed, we may say that part of 'professionalism' in an age of supercomplexity lies in the capability of living effectively amid such openendedness.

Our third point, then, is that *a higher education, if it is to be adequate to the challenges of professional life, has to incorporate moments of supercomplexity into the curriculum – such as situations bearing multiple descriptions and the handling of multiple identities and value conflict.*

For example, should doctors see themselves as the healers of disease, or the preventers of disease or enablers of individuals in handling their own health care? Should those studying chemistry come to see themselves as manipulators of existing compounds, or as the creators of new compounds or as adding to the chemical interventions and risks in our environment? These different interpretations of a role ultimately call for different kinds of curriculum and learning experience; and even of course aims and objectives. To say that the roles – of doctor or chemist – are all of those readings solves nothing; it merely indicates that the supercomplexity of the world has to be brought into the curriculum so that the curriculum becomes a vehicle for comprehending and living with multiple identities *which may not be coherently be brought together.*

Our fourth point, therefore, is that, *in an age of supercomplexity, the curriculum becomes a vehicle not for knowledge or skill acquisition but for living effectively in the world.* In such an age, the curriculum becomes an ontological project.

4. TIME

While the changes in human being that we are exploring can be begun in higher education, they cannot be fully achieved. They constitute, indeed, a lifelong challenge. At one level, this is manifestly the case. If the world is inherently unstable, if it is liable to present with new experiences, new ideas, or new dilemmas at any time, human beings have to be ready to respond anew on a continuing basis. Human being is, accordingly, a continuing project; it has no end. But there are two other senses in which the dimension of time comes into play here.

Firstly, the world is such that we are continually trying to anticipate the future, even though we know such an effort is fraught with difficulty. Precisely because the world is unstable, we try to buy a little security by anticipating the world as it might be at a future point (Nowotny 1996). Institutions, accordingly, conduct their forecasts, produce projections of their future size or budgetary situation, or compute the pattern of trends in the environment in which they are situated. The future comes into the present. We come increasingly to live in the future even though we are condemned to live in the present. The result, of course, is that our current situation becomes all the more complex and challenging, living both in the present and in the future simultaneously. Time itself is destabilized in this milieu. We live amid different time horizons all at once. *Our fifth point, then, is that higher education that is going to be adequate to the challenges of the twenty-first century has, therefore, to build into its curricula a sense of and a responsiveness to multiple time horizons.*

The second way in which the dimension of time comes into play is that the laying down of these forms of human wherewithal that we are drawing out has to unfold over time. They cannot be accomplished in a short span of time. Even, say, a four year honours course of study cannot fully meet this bill, although properly organized and carried through, it can do much. The three or four levels of intellectual and professional functioning that typically attach to an honours degree programme is indicative of the point here: degree courses seek to take students onto successively higher levels of achievement. But, in principle, there can be no end to such ladders of achievement. What is in question here, after all, is the changing of human being as such.

We should recognize that we do not even know if the kinds of change that we are sketching out here *can* be accomplished in any determinate way. For this is, arguably, a new educational project, at least on a mass scale. It could be said that the Oxford Greats experience, exposing students to the languages and ideas of ancient cultures, was a course of study of this kind, that laid down the human qualities appropriate to facing situations of uncertainty and strangeness (of the kind that might be encountered in administering an Empire across the globe in distant lands). But to tackle such an education on a mass scale is surely a new educational challenge.

The point remains that the formation of human being that is going to be adequate to a world of incessant unpredictability and to acting with effective purpose within such a world is not going to be accomplished in a short frame of time. What is before us is a process that will go on over time.

The comparison with Oxford Greats may be further instructive. Such an education could be predicated on the basis of considerable social and personal capital already in the possession of the students concerned, coming as they did from a particular social stratum and having already acquired a broad education at English 'public' schools. A key issue, therefore, is how a social and personal capital appropriate to a world of uncertainty, conceptual messiness, and value conflict is to be developed under conditions of mass higher education. An answer suggests itself in the form of a sixth point: *that graduate attributes for an age of uncertainty are to be developed not only over time, but through a continuing dialogue – as it were – between situations for reflection and situations of challenge.*

Increasingly, curricula in higher education are coming to be designed that set out to do just this. Clinical experience, backed up by a reflective journal, is interspersed with reflection and analysis; cognitive problem-solving is set off against 'real-life' problem-solving; action in the community is complemented by theoretical enquiry in the library; action research is underpinned by data analysis. The signs of a potential curriculum movement in the desired directions are already evident. There surely remains, though, scope for more insight into the personal challenges in handling situations that can never yield stable and secure outcomes.

5. GRADUATENESS AS ENGAGEMENT

In the UK alone, there are some 2 million+ students in higher education taking some 50,000+ courses. Under those circumstances, where a very wide range of course aims and objectives are being pursued, what counts as an appropriate frame of mind can obviously vary considerably. But it remains an open question as to whether we can envisage that there might be some features of the development of mind that might be commonly sought for in higher education. Such, at least, was surely implicit in the major exercise pursued by the former Higher Education Quality Council in its 'graduateness' programme (HEQC 1997); that there might be qualities or attributes of mind that all courses in higher education should embrace.

In the Western conception of higher education, the beginnings of such a pursuit, to specify generic features of graduateness, would doubtless be founded on fundamental values of respect for persons and of a concern for the open society. Values such as these, in turn, would generate a vocabulary of 'graduateness' that included such terms as 'criticality', 'care', 'understanding', 'truthfulness', 'dialogue' and 'opennness'. But such a pursuit would quickly run into difficulty. On the one hand, there is the problem of context specificity: do terms such as 'criticality' or 'truthfulness' have anything in common in the ways in which they are exemplified in practices across the disciplines? On the other hand, there is the problem of value conflict.

For example, some and perhaps many might say that 'engagement' not only should be a core value but that it is already (Bjarnason and Coldstream 2003): graduates, it might be said, should be able effectively to engage with their immediate environment. When pressed, such an advocate might even want to substantiate the plea by arguing that students already are expected to engage in a first-hand way with the experiences to which they are exposed in their course of study. In other words, graduateness implies capacities for interchange with the wider environment; the graduate isn't simply someone living in his or her own world. But that having been said, all kinds of difficulty arise. Is 'engagement' with a field of knowledge the same kind of process as 'engagement' with a social or physical environment? In the social world, is an 'engagement' that amounts to endorsing traditional practices to count for equal value as compared with an 'engagement' that seeks to overturn existing practices?

The point here is that ideas of 'engagement' can quickly turn out either to be empty or to overlay complex issues over which there may be profound value conflict. Spelling out 'engagment' is a nice example of supercomplexity: the differences of view to which its definition gives rise yield no easy resolution and, indeed, probably no straightforward resolution at all.

6. AUTHENTICITY

The kinds of change in human being that we are exploring here take time to unfold because, implicitly, what is at stake is authenticity. If we were only to be in the presence of inauthenticity, then it is likely that change – even of an apparently effective variety – could be accomplished quite quickly. But change that seeks to usher in a new form of authentic human being has to take time.

Forming of the requisite kind can only take place on the basis of *unforming*. University lecturers would not uncommonly say to new undergraduate students that they had to forget all that they had learnt. Tutors of adult learners sometimes consider that such participants come to the pedagogical situation with undue 'baggage' that may impede their learning. Prior learning can hinder effective learning, particularly when the new learning takes a different form from that previously encountered. Or, rather, students may not always come at their learning experiences with a frame of mind appropriate to the kinds of development their educators hope of them.

What is an 'appropriate' frame of mind? This, clearly, is a matter of dispute; at least, at one level. Again, different courses may look to sponsor a very wide range of forms of knowing, and understanding, and intellectual capability in relation to those forms of knowing and understanding. These days, too, we have come to have a sense that the ends that courses might serve are not just intellectual but should speak to students' capability in the world and their personal hold on the world, including their self-understandings. And, in all these ways, courses will vary. This is one justification for the modern injunction that course 'aims and objectives' be spelt out. A course can only seek to hope to accomplish a small range of its potential possibilities so there had better be some clarity about the enterprise.

And, yet, despite the profoundly different kinds of human development that curricula are intended to bring about, can we not also continue to believe that courses – in Western universities in general – might have certain kinds of educational validity in common? Can we not also say that, in order to count as a valid programme of study in a university (or a university-like institution) that, in relation to the aims and objectives in question, students are to be encouraged to come to a position of authenticity. We want the students not just to believe in what they say, do and feel but also to be able to back up those utterances, interventions and intuitions through their own reasoning.

Assessment criteria will, indeed, often include terms such as 'independence of thought', 'creativity', 'critical thought' and, even, 'originality'. We want to feel that we are in the presence of firsthandedness, that students' judgements are theirs. Of course, those judgements will be set in the milieu of the collective standards of the relevant intellectual fields and often, in professionally oriented programmes, standards set down by professional bodies. Students don't work in a vacuum but act and speak amid intellectual and professional communities. Even if, in a sense, their utterances and their actions have had their precursors, still we want to feel that student are personally involved in their texts, whether spoken or written or in other media. That there is so much concern over plagiarism is itself surely an indication of this value embedded in Western higher education, namely that the kind of offerings sought from students should be the student's own.

But – and here arises our seventh point – all this is to remind ourselves that *what is in question in higher education is authentic being*. Higher education, we may say, is precisely a form of education that is intended to bring about a state of *authentic being*. Authentic being is neither, it will be clear, an isolated individualism nor self-indulgence nor a form of anarchic being. It is that state of being in which one's sentiments, utterances, offerings, actions and understandings are oneself's *and* possess a legitimacy. The tests of legitimacy will vary but, typically, there are relevant standards to hand, whether in the form of disciplinary standards or in the form of the standards embodied in a profession.

Of course, legitimacy is also to be found in acts and utterances that set out to contest established standards or bend the local rules; but those acts and utterances still get their bearings from those standards or rules, even if they are going in the opposite direction. The point is that while authenticity demands that the self be the generator of acts and utterances, there is also an external point of judgement. Authenticity is not a recipe for 'anything goes'.

It may be objected that all this talk about authenticity is pure casuistry, calling up philosophical considerations that have little or no purchase in the modern age. Such an objection must be repudiated directly. Graduateness in the modern age, if it is to mean anything at all, has surely to include the capacity for genuine thought and action. That this is particularly difficult in an age of supercomplexity, beset as it is by rival interpretations of the world, is precisely why (point eight) *higher education – as part of lifelong learning – has to take on this task, of furnishing a human wherewithal that is adequate to such incessant contestability and challengeability.*

7. INDIVIDUALITY

It may be objected, especially by those who have been particularly persuaded by poststructuralist or postmodern perspectives, that the argument being advanced here is self-contradictory. On the one hand, it recognizes a world that is fragmented, non-unitary and lacking in firm anchors, a world that assaults the self and threatens its dissolution (and, thereby, falls in with several poststructuralist and postmodern doctrines). On the other hand, it seems to imply that, with a bit of effort, a unitary authentic self can be uncovered and maintained. It also seems to imply that a durable self can be developed through the lifespan, even as it is assaulted from different directions. All that is needed, perhaps, is a bit of support from higher education in coming intermittently into play, to offer space and time out from the hurly-burly of the world.

Actually, I believe this caricature to be true so far as it goes; but it *is* a caricature. Authenticity in an age of supercomplexity cannot demand that there be a unitary being that provides the bedrock of the self's thoughts and actions. It cannot demand, either, that the self's thoughts and actions form a coherent whole or that the self should not change through the lifespan. But these reflections as to the difficulties or even the impossibility of identifying an enduring or unitary self, or secure standards of judgement, in no way render the concept of authenticity passé.

In an age of uncertainty and change, in which one's thoughts and actions are constantly challenged, authenticity has to be continually revisited and remade. Our ninth point, then, is that *higher education has the challenge of establishing a personal infrastructure that will make possible this continuing remaking of the self but lifelong learning has the challenge of furnishing the conditions under which that remaking is accomplished.* This may seem far-fetched or hopelessly abstract but, in fact, we see this latter task being achieved day-in and day-out where individuals have 'come back into' higher education to participate in programmes of study that provide a space for personal and professional reflection.

But, still, we have so far evaded trying to offer a definition of authenticity, a definition, too, that has to make sense in an age of supercomplexity. I would say that authenticity is an achievement, namely the achievement of individuality. If the world is continually changing, is continually presenting conceptual and value challenges, and continually calls us into new relationships with others, with technologies and social structures, then individuality has to be remade anew each day. This, then, points to our tenth point, that *the first task of higher education in an unstable world is to call students and course participants into a state of being in which they can contemplate identifying and expressing their individuality on a continually changing basis.* (Other tasks include the acquisition of perspectives for knowing and skills for engagement but those tasks – of theory and practice – remain subsidiary to those of meeting the ontological challenges that we have been sketching out.)

Students often become understandably apprehensive in realizing that this is what is expected of them, especially international students from cultures where the making of oneself and the projection of oneself is not played up. Part of the apprehensiveness here, I take it, lies precisely in the apperception that the call from their tutors and lecturers that their own ideas are important requires continuing attention on the student's part. Individuality is not a once-and-for-all achievement; it is an always unfinished task. But it is a task that comes prominently into play in lifelong learning where, even on instrumentally oriented courses, the unspoken question lurks for many participants: 'who am I?'

The idea of authenticity is not, of course, exhausted by mere talk of individuality. We saw earlier how authenticity has to be anchored in traditions and standards, even as it furnishes creativity. We have, then, at this stage in our inquiry, three moments of authenticity: social and epistemological change; traditions and standards; and individuality.

Those who have been influenced by Pierre Bourdieu may wish to invoke the idea of *habitus*: it may be felt that what is at issue here is the making clear both to oneself and others the continually shifting nature of one's *habitus*. Higher education helps form the *habitus* while lifelong learning helps both the unforming and the redefining of the *habitus*. This perspective and the distinction that it offers us between initial higher education and lifelong learning is, I think, helpful but it is a limited help. The difficulty for us here, I think, in the concept of habitus is that it does not fully allow for an individual's struggles nor does it fully allow for the normative aspect of authenticity, to which the dimension of standards begins to point us.

If authenticity, then, is to be distinguished from individuality (it includes individuality but goes beyond it), it is also to be distinguished, for example, from integrity. Integrity takes on a particular difficulty in an age of supercomplexity for the unitary self, from which integrity gains its purchase, is problematic. Authenticity, on the other hand, is not dependent in the same way, on the idea of a unitary self. We can still find space for authenticity amid the multiple identities that constitute the self at any one time. Authenticity now becomes that state of being in which thought or action is anchored in the self: the self gives the utterance or the action a purposiveness, an energy. The self wills the utterance or the action into life which, in turn, have their validity enhanced by being tested against traditions and standards. That the individual can bring multiple selves to bear is no repudiation of the idea of authenticity: the point is that the utterance or the action should come significantly from within and have personal meaning invested in it.

There is, lastly, a further element that is part of authenticity. If we put together the elements that we have so far identified – social change, traditions and standards, individuality and personal will – we are surely pointed towards a self-monitoring capability. Authenticity is not a form of personal licence but involves the capacity for self-control. Authenticity speaks outwards and inwards at the same time. It points to the internalisation of critical standards, even as ideas and actions are imbued with personal energy. In an age of supercomplexity, of course, what is to count as the relevant critical standards is itself a matter for debate, not to say personal anxiety. Precisely that difficulty again points to an eleventh point, namely that *a value of lifelong learning lies in its offering a space where new critical standards can be taken on board, so that authenticity can be continually won anew.*

8. A NEVER-ENDING VOYAGE

Against considerations of the kind sketched out here, what we might understand by the term 'graduate attributes' widens and, in turn, the role of higher education itself widens. Higher education would be falling short of its challenges if it did not seek to lay down the human wherewithal for individuals to face up to a world of incessant change and contestation. We are well used to a vocabulary of 'flexibility', 'adaptability' and even 'self-reliance' coming to the higher education sector from the world of work. Such a vocabulary is a sign, surely, of a wish to see higher education reframed along the lines of our discussion. What is in question is the capacity *and the will* for self-monitoring and self-renewal.

A twelfth point emerges here. It is surely now evident that *'graduate attributes' should not primarily be construed as sets of skills or even knowledges. What is required are certain kinds of human dispositions and qualities. Qualities* that a world of incessant unpredictability and challengeability calls for would include qualities of courage, resilience, fortitude and quietness (for otherwise, one is hardly going to understand the strangeness that the world presents). *Dispositions* that such a world calls for include an orientation towards self-change, engagement with the world, inquisitiveness, and a will to communicate (for otherwise, one will be lost in a solipsistic space, unable to test one's responses on and in the world).

It cannot be part of our purpose here to try to go deeply into the structure and character of the necessary qualities and dispositions. The key point is a negative one; that what matters here, in the carving out of 'graduate attributes' in a world of uncertainty, is that we should take on an ontological perspective. The main educational challenge in a world of uncertainty is that neither of knowledge nor of skills but of *being*. How are we to *be* in such a world? What kind of human being is appropriate to a world of irredeemable contestability? And how are we to prosper in a such a world?

Higher education, then, conceived in this way, takes on the character of the beginnings of a personal voyage of human becoming. This is not new. Indeed, it is happening every day in our institutions of higher education as the not-infrequent comment – 'you have changed/ transformed my life' – from a successful and grateful student indicates. But the changes in human being that such utterances imply are primarily – we may intuit – neither the acquisition of some new skills nor of some new forms of knowledge but of new relationships to the world and to oneself. The skills and the knowledge newly acquired are doubtless contributory to the changes in question but, fundamentally, what is being brought out here are changes in human being as such.

The changes, indeed, are those that enable the individual to become an individual, to become authentic. She has been brought to a new situation in which she has command over herself in ways that she could not earlier have imagined. She stands in a steady and resolute stance to the world. She has – to use Heideggarian terminology – come to 'sever' herself from the world and to come into a space independently of the 'they': she has, in short, fulfilled the assessment criterion that speaks of 'independent thought'. She has found a way of coming into herself, at least in that area of the world that has formed the heart of her studies. She stands for and by herself 'on her own two feet' (as Richard Peters used to put it).

This is an extraordinary achievement; and yet it happens, day-in and day-out, in institutions of higher education. But this bringing of students to a point where they can stand independently of the world, and form authentic thoughts and actions, has to be – in an age of supercomplexity – but a start of a journey, a continual lifelong journey of personal becoming and *re*-becoming. If the world is incessantly changing, then a position of independence and authenticity has to be continually struggled for and won anew. In professional life, for example, every day is different; one never knows what the world is going to throw at one. One is being asked and often required continually to take on new challenges – whether, for example, of external quality audits or of new practices within the profession or of challenges to one's professional identity and self-perception. The potentials for independence and for authenticity with which one entered professional life, therefore, have all the time to be revisited and re-embedded.

This is an uncertain voyage of personal re-making and personal discovery. One may be inclined to think of 'personal discovery' as a kind of digging into the self, to find its 'true' substance; going through layers of veneer to a kind of personal bedrock. Such geological metaphors are misleading, for they imply an enduring core to the self and a withdrawing into that inner core. Even if there is such a 'core to one's being', the key point – in an age of supercomplexity – is that authenticity is (as Heidegger made clear) relational. It arises out of relationships between human being and the world. Authenticity arises not out of a retreat into the self but through engaging with the world and in the world. And, for human being that is sensitive to the world (to use another term of Heidegger's, has a 'care' towards the world), there is bound to be uncertainty not only about what the world throws at one but about the character of one's responses and, in turn, the world's responses. We are, therefore, into an infinite etceteration of mutual responses between the self and the world: the self, in other words, is embarked on an uncertain voyage of discovery of the self-in-the-world.

Our thirteenth point, therefore, comes into view. *Lifelong learning, seen from the perspective that we have sketched out, becomes thereby a matter of continually engaging in forming a sense of oneself in the world.* In a changing world, this process of forming-a-sense-of-oneself-in-the-world is necessarily never ending. While higher education is not discrete (typically, it builds on a substructure developed elsewhere), it harbours the potential for laying down the personal infrastructure – of qualities and dispositions – that enable authenticity to go on being continually remade through the subsequent lifespan, through lifelong learning. Higher education can, in turn, also provide a site for personal renewal and development of qualities and dispositions, sometimes even in a new setting, as an individual looks for a mid-career change of a fundamental kind.

9. SUMMARY AND CONCLUSION

A world of incessant change in which one's beliefs, values and hold on the world are continually contested is a world of ontological challenge. Human being as such is continually challenged. Individual psychologies differ: some thrive on such a world; others respond by falling into a state of anxiety and self-doubt. Either way, it is surely clear that the fundamental educational challenge in such a world is neither one of knowledge or skills but of being itself. Is the self strong enough to cope with incessant assaults on it? How is it to live with multiple identities? How is it to withstand the never-ending uncertainties that complex – especially supercomplex – situations bring? If education is to be adequate to such a world, it has explicitly to add a dimension of self and of human being to its work.

Higher education is implicated in these challenges in two ways. Firstly, as a stage of initial higher education, it has the challenge of setting in place infrastructures in human being that are going to offer personal resources of independence of mind and action. Such independence is a necessary condition of those thoughts and actions being authentic. Authenticity won't necessarily, by itself, bring a calmness to human being amid complex situations but it remains central to the educational task in this milieu.

It is particularly apposite that such an education should be associated with higher education for the processes of human development that are implied are higher order processes. They are processes of a higher learning where what is acquired is none other than the human wherewithal to carve out a personal space amid the incessant and unpredictable challenges that daily assault human being. 'Graduate attributes', understood in this way, have to be seen as a shorthand for the capabilities, qualities and dispositions that constitute a personal infrastructure that makes possible an individual and authentic space in such a world.

But such a process has no end, if only because the world moves on and continues to demand new positionings of self. In particular, professional life – in which most graduates will find employment – is itself chock-full of ambiguities, value conflict and continuing demands to take on new forms of professional identity. Lifelong learning, under such conditions, becomes a social and personal space in which new resources, new understandings, new senses of the self can be laid down. Such learning can be accomplished by the individual but it is likely to be aided by an environment for collective reflection.

It is hardly surprising that many mid-career professionals say, on being asked what they most gain from their part-time programmes of study – often added to the continuing responsibilities of professional life – that they find their programme 'therapeutic'. It may be that talk of a 'reinvention of the self' goes too far but, at least, a continuing reshaping of the self is called for. In the process, individuals may come to a state of calmness in the throes of their own *complexity-in-being*.

At stake here is a never-ending voyage of personal re-discovery and re-adjustment. The voyage will go on anyway, with or without higher education. But higher education has the potential to take on board this agenda of human becoming and re-becoming. It is utopian only in the sense that the scale of the enterprise – in which institutions and the academic community seriously come to understand themselves in this way – is enormous. But, in its essence, it is entirely practicable and feasible for it is already happening, in many institutions, and on many programmes of study. The problem is, however, that such processes of human becoming are taking place subliminally, as unforeseen consequences of the kinds of programmes of study often to be found in Western universities. It remains to be seen whether this tacit project of human becoming can become an explicit project and so go much further in realizing its potential in an age of supercomplexity.

10. BIBLIOGRAPHY

Bjarnason, S. and Coldstream, P. (2003) *The Idea of Engagement: Universities in Society.* London: Association of Commonwealth Universities.

Giddens, A. (1992) *The Consequences of Modernity.* Cambridge: Polity Press.

Giddens, A. (2002) *Runaway World: How Globalisation is Reshaping Our Lives.* London: Profile.

HEQC (1997) *Assessment in Higher Education and the Role of 'Graduateness'.* London: HEQC.

Nowotny, H. (1996) *Time: The Modern and Postmodern Experience.* Cambridge: Polity Press.

Putnam, R. (2000) *Bowling Alone: The Collapse and Revival of American Community.* New York: Touchstone.

Ritzer, G. (1997) *The McDonaldization Thesis: Explorations and Extensions.* London: Sage.

CHAPTER 4

CHRISTOPHER WINCH

GRADUATE ATTRIBUTES AND CHANGING
CONCEPTIONS OF LEARNING

This chapter discusses the question as to whether there are generic learning
outcomes of degree programmes, that can be identified across the range of such
programmes, or at least *a* range of them. Related to this is the question of whether
new conceptions of learning are being introduced into degree programmes in order
to develop these generic outcomes. It is argued that degree programmes are
designed to develop a mainly 'technological' rather than a 'technical' employment
capacity in graduates and that such a technological capacity only allows for the
limited development of generic learning outcomes.

1. THE CONCEPT OF HIGHER EDUCATION

The focus of my discussion will be on generic graduate education as a preparation
for professional formation and professional education. Generic graduate education
involves studying a subject to degree level prior to occupation specific
preparation. Professional education at the graduate level involves occupation
specific preparation at the graduate level, resulting in a full or intermediate
professional qualification.

The question of the nature of higher education is controversial and I will not
attempt to settle it here. I will, however, adopt as a working conception, the view
that education that issues in a first degree qualification (graduate level education)
involves the acquisition of theoretical knowledge at a certain degree of
abstraction, complexity and difficulty, making it distinctive in terms of degree
from education offered at a lower level. However, graduate level knowledge is
often thought to be *applied*, or at least *applicable* and it is the nature of this
applicable knowledge that I will be principally concerned with. I wish to

67

P. Hager and S. Holland (eds.), Graduate Attributes, Learning and Employability, 67–89.
© 2006 *Springer.*

characterise the nature of applicable graduate level knowledge as, at least in part, *technological* as well as *technical*. Technical knowledge involves putting into effect a body of theoretical knowledge in a particular context for a particular purpose.[i] *Technological* knowledge, on the other hand, involves the capacity to contribute to the theoretical component of that applicable knowledge, at least in that area of the theoretical knowledge which is closest to application. Thus, although a technician may be an innovator in respect of the ways in which applied theoretical knowledge is actually applied, the technologist is expected to be an innovator in respect of the knowledge which *underlies* the development of new technique. A graduate, then, may be expected on this conception, to be capable, *qa* graduate at any rate, of contributing to the theory of applicable knowledge rather than to the application of that theory. It is a moot point whether or not technological knowledge always presupposes technical knowledge, and there is probably no simple answer to this question. Some degree programmes do include the acquisition of technical as well as technological knowledge, but in those occupations that do not presuppose such technical knowledge, the assumption must be that at least a certain level of technological knowledge may be acquired without acquiring technical knowledge. The expansion of graduate study has led to a whole new range of graduate subjects some of which are technological like some of the more traditional ones. The discussion applies to both the older and the newer groups of subjects.[ii]

There is an important distinction between the knowledge and skill that graduates develop as part of their study, and that which they develop through work. These latter skills may or may not require graduate education in order to be developed. There are also issues concerning whether or not employers want these broader skills beforehand or whether they prefer to develop them themselves. The technical skills and some aspects of applied theoretical knowledge may prove difficult to develop 'in house' and it may be more valuable for employers to receive these from their employees' university education. The 'broader skills' may, on the other hand, be too context-specific to be developed other than in the workplace. But before we can sensibly pose this question, however, we need to ask whether such skills exist and whether it is plausible to suppose that they can be developed as part of university education.

2. GENERIC GRADUATE ATTRIBUTES

There has been increasing emphasis on the generic attributes which consist of alleged *generic* knowledge and skill, as well as subject specific *transferable* knowledge and skills that have been developed as part of degree programmes. Graduate learning has also come to be seen more as a social and independent process than was previously the case. (for example, through the development of seminars, the dissertation, team working and the assessment of oral and aural skills). The sources for these developments can be found in much of the work that has gone on in management education during the last half century. Management education, particularly as it has developed in the US and the UK, is seen as a preparation for a generic skill of management which is applicable across a range of industries. A liberal education, together with communication and presentation skills, as well as the more nebulous generic skills (see below), are increasingly seen by employers as desirable entry attributes to a career in management. At the same time, views about the 'graduateness' of higher education qualifications have developed to include attributes including knowledge, skills and attitudes, which, it is supposed, the modern workplace requires.

It is thought by some academics that a range of skills are developed in graduate education, which cross disciplinary boundaries.[iii] Furthermore, it is thought that these skills are *transferable* so that they become a valuable component of the skills developed in the workplace. Current wisdom has it that these should be taught *both* in the context of liberal and of professional higher education. These skills include: written and spoken communication skills; information searching and organisation; specific rhetorico-logical skills concerned with presenting arguments and criticising them; critical thinking and problem solving skills; more nebulous attributes such as emotional intelligence and creativity; social skills such as the ability to work in teams. Also significant are: research skills, use of information technology, using written language for specific purposes. While some of these pass muster without much difficulty as generic skills, for example, writing and arithmetical abilities, others are more dubious.[iv]

A generic item of knowledge or skill is one specific to more than one activity or subject matter. Being generic is, then, a matter of degree. In order to be *transferable*, it is necessary for an item to be generic; if it is not applicable outside the subject matter in which it is learned then it cannot be transferred outside that subject matter. Thus, an ability that is specific to a particular subject matter will not be transferable, while one that is generic *may* be transferable. Particularly problematic ones are: critical thinking, problem solving, and creativity. There are four areas of difficulty in characterising them as generic skills: 1] Conceptual – What are they and can they coherently be defined? 2] Contextual – If they can be said to exist at all, how context dependent are they? 3] Practicality – Can they be developed as part of graduate education? 4] Transferability – Given positive answers to the first three questions, are they transferable? These questions will be explored later in the chapter and some tentative answers will be suggested.

3. TRADITIONAL PROFESSIONAL EDUCATION
AT THE GRADUATE LEVEL

Western universities were developed in the Middle Ages, partly to provide a professional formation in law, theology and medicine. The idea that they were essentially the site of liberal education and nothing else is a misreading of their history. At the same time, the schools of Greek antiquity could not but exercise a profound influence on their development. These schools had provided an education in rhetoric and logic as well as philosophy, and what they provided was at least partly liberal in nature, being concerned with the development of knowledge as an intrinsic good and the cultivation of an appropriate attitude to life. The mediaeval institutions, although incorporating many of the traditions of antiquity, together with subjects like grammar, rhetoric and logic, had complex aims. They were concerned with professional formation as well as with liberal education and some of the subjects on the curriculum appeared to have generic qualities and to be at least potentially transferable.

As such they provided graduates with the basic technical knowledge necessary to practice in these professions, together with sufficient knowledge of the theoretical background to make a technological contribution as well. Later, various non-vocational subjects came to be incorporated into a liberal conception of graduate education. Often these were disciplines that, at least in part, constituted segments of the older professional formation. Mathematics, Philosophy and Classics were examples. Later still, such subjects as History, English and Modern Languages came to be part of this liberal curriculum. Subsequent graduate professional formation then came to build on the knowledge and skills that these subjects developed.

Both the vocational and the liberal features of the mediaeval university survived into the traditional graduate education of the post-war period. At the same time, the natural sciences and a certain number of technological subjects, based on the natural sciences had become incorporated into the curriculum during the nineteenth and twentieth centuries. Professional graduate education incorporated the traditional theology, medicine and law of the mediaeval universities, but now also encompassed subjects such as engineering and physics. The idea was that the theory necessary to a profession such as engineering would be developed both broadly and in some depth at the degree level. This would allow the graduate to move to probationary practice, but would also mean that he or she could use the theory in a way not really possible for someone acquainted with the occupation at a technical level only. The graduate thus has the capacity to manipulate the theory by reconfiguring it, adapting it for particular purposes and for altering it in the light of technical problems. The graduate has also, arguably, the ability to make new contributions to theory, although this is more debateable (this is connected with alleged features of the 'honours' degree, which is sometimes said to involve a research element in contrast to the subhonours degree, which does not). This is the main terrain in which the claim to a specific 'graduate' level of knowledge is staked out.

4. THE QUEST OF THE SEMI-PROFESSIONS FOR GRADUATE STATUS

Then there are issues here to do with the transition of semi-professional education from diploma to degree level, for example in professions allied to medicine in the UK. This transition includes a shift to the social sciences and to sociology in particular away from technical knowledge (including applied theoretical knowledge), together with an emphasis on the research element to ensure 'honours' status. The implication of this shift is that the technical skills used in practice may not be characteristic of graduate knowledge within the occupation. Although the social sciences clearly are an established part of graduate education the question is whether this shift away from the practicum towards social sciences and research skills really does make for a more competent practitioner, which in turn raises issues about the validity of alleged criteria of graduateness as indicative of occupational competence. One might, for example, query whether the reduction in the clinical practice element of a radiology degree actually reduces the level of technical skill available to the newly-qualified practising radiologist. It may be replied that transition from diploma to degree is necessary to develop technological as well as technical knowledge, but then one has to inquire whether knowledge relevant to technological capability is being developed in a graduate programme. It is not obvious, for example, that instruction in the social sciences is capable of developing the anatomical and physiological knowledge necessary to make a podiatry graduate a technologist of podiatry. Technical skill and knowledge are both developed in undergraduate programmes and used within graduate occupations for example, in such subjects as computing. There is also evidence that the employers of graduates in occupations where technical skill is required expect that undergraduate degree programmes develop these skills in students; teaching is a good example.

In this respect the quest of the semi-professions for graduate status has been confused. On the one hand it has been associated with the transition from technical to technological knowledge, on the other with the transition from subject specific to generic knowledge. But there is no reason to suppose that technological knowledge is generic in nature, although it may rely on some transferable elements. In this respect, the various campaigns that the semi-professions have undertaken to secure graduate status have tended to concentrate more on the achieving of the graduate entry qualification rather than the specific gains in terms of type of knowledge that would come from doing so. As a result the exact nature of the graduate attributes that have been developed through the transition have remained unclear.

5. THE DEMAND FOR NEW KINDS OF GENERIC ATTRIBUTES IN THE WORKPLACE

The theory involved in professional practice is, arguably, part of what one means by a liberal education, which does not have an immediate vocational objective (although this is harder to maintain for such occupations as medicine, nevertheless the natural sciences are now accepted as a possible means of developing a liberal education). It is arguable, for example, that managers need a broadly based liberal education in order to function effectively in the complex situations in which graduates, as potential mangers, are likely to find themselves given the dynamic nature of the business environment in which most enterprises now have to function. The requirements of this environment include knowledge of geography, politics and history of the societies within which businesseses are operating and, more generally, an awareness of and sensitivity to the fact that there are significant cultural, social and historical differences between societies even in a largely globalised marketplace.

5l Workplace Communication Skills

Increasingly, transferable communication skills have come to be seen as important, particularly in relation to the management of social relationships, effective co-ordination and decision-making within the workplace. These aspects of graduate education, once largely confined to the development of written communication skills, are now increasingly emphasised in relation to speaking and listening and working in teams. They are valued as part of a growing concern with the ability to communicate in a broad sense, through spoken and electronic means, as well as through writing. As such these skills are seen as a key aspect of what is needed to be effective in the workplace at a managerial and technological level.

This is particularly apparent in the shift towards service sector employment generally, where far more contact is required with the public than in manufacturing, for example. But it is also important in relation to the 'quality revolution' more generally, one of whose main characteristics has been the development of a notion of quality in terms of specification as the 'fitness for purpose' for the client of a product or service.[v] This 'quality revolution' has also penetrated the public services where effective communication with the client, whether they be patient, parent or passenger has become crucial to the continuing legitimacy of the service being provided.

The form of the 'knowledge economy' being pursued in sectors of the Australian, UK and US economies also relies heavily on the capacity of graduate to manage unskilled or semiskilled employees. Managing in such contexts also importantly involves the ability to communicate, but here the emphasis might be a different one. Whereas the 'client interface' requires a relationship between equals or even between the superior client and the subordinate employee, the management of inferior workers requires persuasive skills of a different order. In the former case, much of the work involves learning about the client's needs and the transmission of appropriate information or counsel to the client. In this latter case, the emphasis is on getting the subordinate to carry out tasks for which they may, in certain cases, have limited enthusiasm. While in both cases, persuasion is important, in the latter case the kind of persuasion required may rely more heavily on covert and manipulative techniques than the former.[vi] This is not to say that such techniques are not used in the *client* relationship (e.g. the doctor's 'bedside manner') but they exist within a somewhat different mix of rhetorical techniques within a different status hierarchy.

There is also evidence that work hierarchies have changed to a certain extent and that within firms autonomous and semi-autonomous teams, whose effective knowledge is collectively based, may be crucial to the success of the enterprise. Such groupings also require workers to have the ability to effectively communicate with each other and to come to decisions based on something like a consensus.[vii] Such decision making will be based on the specialist knowledge of the team, but its effectiveness will depend on an ability to solve strategic, operational and tactical problems and to be innovative in dialogue with peers who are one's status and cognitive equals.

2 Research Skills

One other attribute that deserves mention is the ability to conduct research. This is sometimes seen as the basic ability to conduct research within one's own discipline, to become potentially a technologist or even an innovator rather than a technician. Less ambitiously it relates to having the developed ability to *evaluate* research, having acquired *some* of the skills needed to conduct it. Thirdly, it may be thought necessary to carry out research in the course of one's occupational duties. Graduate attributes now tend to include research skills, meaning the acquisition, selection and use of information through the use of new technologies, the capacity to distinguish between information and knowledge and the organisation of knowledge for particular purposes. This is becoming true, not only of professional higher education, but also within those higher education subjects which have tended to think of themselves as liberal rather than vocational in orientation.

6. LEARNING WITHIN GRADUATE PROGRAMMES

With the allegedly increasing emphasis on the social nature of the skills that graduates bring to their work, is a growing emphasis, particularly within assessment regimes, on the social nature of the skills developed. This is partly the reason why there is an increasing focus within degree level education, on both individual and group project work and presentations. To some extent this can be attributed to the view that the 'soft skills' of sociability, empathy and co-cooperativeness are, to an increasing degree to be required in some forms of the modern workplace (Hodgson 1999). But this is not the only possible scenario. Not only is there no single unambiguous trend towards collective forms of working, but in certain ways, some of the modern technologies used in the workplace have a solitary and in some cases, individualistic rather than collective aspect. This tendency is also to be found within pedagogical theory. Thus, modern learning theory has, with relatively few exceptions, a strongly individualistic bias (but see Winch 1998; Beckett and Hager 2002). Even communicative technologies like email, which are used both in the workplace and in educational contexts, tend to promote physical isolation and facilitate communication at a distance, rather than face to face. So there are no unambiguous trends, either towards individualism or collectivism, to be discerned in the modern workplace.

It is true, however, that the tendency in higher education is in the collectivist direction to a certain extent. The new emphasis on 'graduateness' is partly a reflection of the assumption that the future of the workplace is collective rather than isolated. At the same time, however, there are good reasons to suppose that the use of these technologies is most successful when they are embedded in a social context, including a structured educational environment (Langhammer 2002). The use of collective approaches to the deconstruction of text, presentation of arguments and collective discussion are all emphasised in the context of working in teams within the modern workplace. Rightly or wrongly, the emphasis on collective forms of learning is thought to develop generic skills which can be applied to the operational context of the workplace. At the same time, the individualistic bias of such technologies as the internet and information-handling software are transferable in an obvious way to the modern office workplace.

7. THE NATURE OF APPLIED THEORETICAL KNOWLEDGE: IMPLICATIONS FOR THE DEVELOPMENT OF GENERIC ATTRIBUTES

Professional and technical education involves the acquisition of applied theoretical knowledge. Given that the main contribution of a university will be to the teaching of applicable theory and, to a lesser extent, the development of skill in putting that theory into practice, the question arises as to whether or not the university has any contribution to make to generic skills. While it is unlikely that the application of theoretical knowledge at graduate level depends only on generic abilities, it may be that a significant amount does. If so, then the development of useable generic skills may have a vital part to play in the development of applied theoretical knowledge.

This raises the very interesting question of the nature and possibility of applied theoretical knowledge. In addressing it, we shall also find ourselves concerned with the distinction between the technical and the technological, not to mention the issue of generic skills and their transferability. Although the concept of applied theoretical knowledge is most readily intelligible in those industries and occupations that are based on the natural sciences, it is applicable to those based on the social sciences and also to normative disciplines, such as the law. It may be thought that the very concept of applied theoretical knowledge is a problematic one. How does one apply theory? After all, a theory is an intellectual construction while technical operations involve manipulation of the physical environment. So how do they connect with each other? This is not the place to examine this issue in detail, however, the possibility of applied theoretical knowledge does not depend on a dualist account of mental operations in which a mental operation of judgment based on theory is put into physical effect through a volition. What it *does* require is an intelligible account of the relationship of the propositional knowledge encapsulated in theory with the practical knowledge expressed in activity and this can be given without recourse to a dualist ontology.[viii]

Applied theoretical knowledge at the technical level often requires collective action before it can be made effective. Such a situation arises when the different knowledge and skill of different members of a team have got to be brought to bear and organised to carry out a particular task. We can thus see that technical knowledge is very often collective, but does this apply to technological knowledge of the kind that a graduate might acquire? It does to the extent that technology requires the formulation of problems, their solution and the testing of those solutions in a social environment. But we cannot assume that this will be the case with every graduate occupation.

The use of applied theoretical knowledge is, however, an essential component of the work of many graduates at both technical and technological levels, and the question arises as to the extent to which gaining a degree contributes to the acquisition of such knowledge and the extent to which what is learned during a degree programme is transferable to the occupation in which the graduate is working. It may be helpful to approach this by considering the following questions in relation to graduate education: 1] To what extent is the theoretical knowledge that they require *generic*? 2] To what extent is that knowledge *transferable*?

3] What skills do graduates need to acquire if they are to apply their theoretical knowledge? 4] Are some of those skills transferable? If we succeed in answering these questions, we will have come closer to answering our original question as to the existence and nature of graduate attributes.

An initial point of reference would be to remind ourselves that the graduates are primarily technologists in their disciplines, rather than merely technicians. This implies first that they have a thorough grounding in the theoretical knowledge underlying the technique and second, that they are able to reconfigure that knowledge to make it available for particular purposes and also, to an extent, contribute to that body of knowledge, particularly to that part of it that is concerned with the way in which the theory is put into practice, through the use of instruments, devices etc. whose construction itself depends on a degree of depth of theoretical knowledge. Of course, some of this will come from their knowledge of the subject, which is in part practical anyway, for example knowledge of the methods of verification and inference within the parent discipline. However, we should not assume that this knowledge is either generic or transferable, although some of it may be, for example mathematical knowledge. However, given that much applied theoretical knowledge is collectively held and developed, it is plausible to suggest that social and communicative abilities are crucial to its successful deployment. If this is right, then communicative abilities of the appropriate kind are a necessary attribute of successful technological workers. In order to make a contribution to the applicable side of theory, they will need to be able to work with others and to explain and justify their work within teams. The question now arises as to whether such abilities are generic and, if they are, whether they are transferable from one subject matter to another. If they are then they are part of the applied theoretical knowledge of a particular subject matter and thus a proper part of graduate education.

8. CANDIDATES FOR GENERIC GRADUATE ATTRIBUTES – AN EVALUATION

8l Mathematical Knowledge/Skills

Mathematical knowledge is a persuasive example of a graduate attribute. A social researcher, for example, will need statistical skills acquired during a quantitative research methods part of a social science course. These skills may be applied to a range of research subjects and much of the technical skill involved in using them may consist in knowing which test to use in which circumstances. However, it may be the case that a social researcher sees the need to modify a particular test to answer a certain purpose. If the researcher is to do this successfully, it is necessary for him or her to understand the mathematical principles underlying the test. Such principles are generic in the sense that they apply to more than one subject matter and transferable in the sense that they can be applied within the work situation. Such an ability is also technological to the extent that grasp of the underlying mathematical basis allows for new techniques to be developed. In many cases, however, the learning of such knowledge within a degree programme is only at the technical level. If generic knowledge of this kind at graduate level were largely technical, this would raise serious doubts as to whether it could really be described as an aspect of degree level knowledge. These reservations aside, here we do have an apparent example of a graduate attribute that contributes to applied theoretical knowledge and is both generic and transferable.

& Communication and Information Gathering Skills

While these begin to be acquired in the primary school, it is arguable that the level of complexity and sophistication that is required to use them at graduate level necessitates their further formal development. In one important respect there is a difference between mathematics and communication, in that one does not normally learn the theory of communication and then learn how to communicate. First, it is not clear that there is a requisite theory in this sense and second, because it seems that these are practical abilities *par excellence*, to be acquired in a practical way. But it does not follow from this that they may not be a *component* of applied theoretical knowledge. If we accept that mastery of a subject matter involves knowing how to find things out through investigation and inference in that subject, then the ability to read and research within the subject for example, is properly part of someone's knowledge of that subject matter. Grasp of a subject does not just consist in knowledge of the truth of propositions but of how they are connected and validated (Hirst 1974). Likewise, if knowledge needs to be demonstrated discursively if it is to be useful, the user is going to make use of generic communicative techniques. It may follow, then, that some emphasis on reading and writing skills, perhaps centred around particular genres such as the report, the position paper and the dialectical consideration of a particular case may be of some benefit to graduates in the wider context beyond the university or the particular subject matter being studied.

It might be replied in objection to this that such techniques are genre specific and hence non-generic and thus not susceptible of transfer. But this is to suppose, wrongly, that genres, although they may adopt different conventions, are hermetically sealed from each other. In any case, even were it partially true, one would expect there to be some fit between the degree subject and the occupation in which it is applied.

However, it can be argued that there is a theory of written and spoken communication which assists its practice. Thus the theory of rhetoric provides maxims for effective communication in written and spoken modes. It is doubtful, however, whether graduates studying learning to communicate within degree programmes devoted to other subjects can or should acquire communicative skills at anything more than the technical level. In fact, it is questionable whether they need to even acquire elements of rhetorical theory to put rhetorical maxims into effect.

8 Argument Analysis Skills

The above point also applies to argument analysis. Even if we admit, following the general thrust of Toulmin's claim that argumentation is context-specific, that it is not possible to apply techniques derived from the formal theory of deduction in any straightforward manner to subject-specific argument, it does not follow that we should not analyse arguments, nor that there are not some general principles for doing so. Toulmin himself outlines these general principles and other authors such as Fisher and Levi have developed his approach (Toulmin 1958; Fisher 1988; Levi 2000). What such an approach does preclude, however, is that such techniques can simply be applied to a subject matter without any consideration of its nature and structure. There is little or no evidence that such programmes form a significant part of any undergraduate programme, let alone a significant generic component of a wide range of degree programmes. Deductive logic programmes do exist, on Philosophy and Mathematics courses, but deductive logic courses, if Toulmin's arguments are taken seriously, cannot be deployed in particular subjects and situations without the need for close acquaintance with those subjects and situations, except to a limited extent.[ix] To the extent that critical thinking skills are based on the assumption that deductive logic is relevant and deployable across a wide range of contexts, it is doubtful whether they can be developed as generic and transferable graduate attributes without compromising the amount of curriculum space available for subject-specific knowledge.

What about inductive reasoning? Some aspects, such as statistics and probability theory, are undoubtedly applicable across a range of subject matters. These areas are usually considered to be a branch of mathematics, and as such applicable in just those areas which will benefit from specialised mathematical techniques. On the other hand, principles concerning whether or not an argument is inductive or deductive, whether some particular evidence constitutes adequate support for this conclusion in this context, and whether or not one should adopt this or that test of significance are going to be questions the correct answer to which depends to a degree on the subject matter or context that is involved. Since this is the case, general principles of inductive reasoning, like general principles of deductive reasoning, are going to be of limited assistance in subject areas with which the graduate is unfamiliar.

It would be wrong to deny that there are some general elements in applied theoretical knowledge within particular subject matters (e.g. general principles of inductive and deductive logic, statistics, which might apply in areas of both natural and social science). The critical issue is to do with the points of salience within disciplines – inferential warrants; key backing statements, central concepts, methods of truth determination and verification. Handling these presupposes a sound knowledge of the discipline concerned. This aspect of applied theoretical knowledge must therefore be context dependent. It is obvious that these points place severe limitations on what can be achieved with general principles of inference.

8/ Problem Solving Skills

Much the same points can be made concerning problem solving skills. There are, no doubt, certain maxims for the solution of problems which apply across a range of different areas, such as 'first establish what the problem is before you devise a strategy to solve it.' However, if the solution of practical problems depends on contextual knowledge and skills, then it is at the least a moot point as to whether one can advance beyond such rather banal maxims to contentful as opposed to banal, but at the same time, context-free maxims for action to solve problems. Indeed, to the extent that problem solving involves, as a necessary component, the construction and evaluation of trains of reasoning, much the same considerations as apply to critical thinking skills apply as well to alleged generic problem-solving skills. First because problem solving involves the ability to reason, at least to a considerable extent, and second because the grasp of problems and their possible solutions relies on detailed knowledge of particular subject areas.

&Creativity

What of creativity – another attribute that it is sometimes claimed is developed by graduate programmes? This concept has proved to be highly problematic, and analysis of the concept provides scant comfort for those tempted to consider creativity a graduate attribute. Indeed it is hard to see how it can be a generic, let alone a transferable attribute at all. Commonly, three distinct concepts are bundled together under the heading of 'creativity'. The first is that of *self-expression*. To the extent that self-expression signifies anything at all, it seems to denote the process of expressing one's point of view, emotions, feelings or whatever. We may take it that, in this context, we would be primarily concerned with the expression of an individual point of view. But to dignify this kind of activity with the adjective 'creative' seems to devalue it. Someone's expressing themselves may not even be particularly *original*, but even if it were, the production of something that had not been made before, this would not warrant its being called 'creative'. For this to be the case, we would expect a contribution to an established genre, whether it be in music, art, literature, dance or whatever that not only conforms to the conventions of the genre, but also exploits its possibilities to the fullest extent and perhaps even extends or subverts our conception of what that genre is (Barrow and Woods 1975: Ch. 8; Gingell 2001). We can take the notion of creativity in this sense to include occupations, so one can be genuinely creative in relation to an occupation by, for example, extending its theoretical underpinning or by inventing a new process, procedure or artefact that enhances its operation.[x]

It follows from this, that we should be reluctant to apply the term 'creative' to any authentic product, even an original one, unless it was in some way exceptional, either in the way in which it exploited and extended the possibilities inherent in a genre, or in the way in which it had a similar effect on an occupation, by making a ground-breaking technological advance, for example. One difficulty here is that the term 'creative' is apt to be used as a surrogate for 'innovatory'. It is quite possible, indeed normal, to innovate without being creative. One can make improvements to a mode of operation or to the theory underlying a mode of operation without pushing at the boundaries of a genre or an activity. We would expect skilled technicians and technologists to be capable of being innovatory in this sense. A technician might make an effective modification to a technique, while a technologist might devise a new piece of equipment. With respect to graduates, whom we have primarily characterised as technologists rather than technicians, we would expect their capacity for innovation to extend beyond operational matters (the province of the technician), to critical engagement with the applicable theory connected with the occupation such that the theoretical aspect of applied theoretical knowledge is employed to alter practice for the better. This might, perhaps, seem obvious in relation to traditionally technological activities such as engineering, but can also be seen in those professions which are said to rely on a research base, such as medicine or teaching. Thus one might expect a doctor or surgeon to use physiological or pharmaceutical knowledge to help to develop a new treatment, or for a teacher to use her knowledge of applied linguistics to develop a new literacy programme. But, to the extent that we do expect graduates to be capable of innovation in this technological sense, we can only do so to the extent that they have sufficiently mastered the theoretical basis of their occupation. While this theoretical basis may contain generic elements, one cannot assume that the innovatory capacity *per se* can be understood as a generic graduate attribute, rather than something that is originally developed during theoretical formation within the discipline in the first instance and is then brought to fruition through engagement with the occupation to which the theoretical discipline is applied.

9. IS THERE EVIDENCE THAT GRADUATE ATTRIBUTES ARE GENERIC?

What can we conclude from this survey of alleged graduate attributes? There is no clear answer to the question of whether there are distinct qualities that graduates possess as a result of their studies, in contrast to non-graduates. One point to make about surveys of graduates designed to discover what they think the skills that they have gained from their degrees are, is that one cannot infer from what graduates *think* they have developed from their degree studies either the existence of such attributes or their origin within the student's graduate programme, even if it *is* acknowledged that they exist. The only sure way to discover whether generic knowledge exists on degree programmes is to examine the curricula of those programmes to see if such items occur. As far as skills are concerned, one would need to look at the pedagogic and assessment procedures as well as the curriculum in order to determine whether or not such items occurred. To see whether items of knowledge, either propositional or practical, were transferable, one would then have to trace the item from its acquisition on a degree programme to its use as a part of a graduate's work. For example, one might identify a course on social statistics on a social science degree as a generic item, because statistical knowledge and skills can be used across a variety of disciplines. One could then examine whether or not the graduate used their knowledge of statistics in the workplace. If so, it would be transferable in a narrow sense if it were used within a social science context in the workplace, for example, if the graduate were working for a market research organisation. It would be transferable in the broad sense if it could be shown that the statistical knowledge originally acquired in a social science context were then extended and applied in another work context (e.g. in product quality assurance in manufacturing).

Similar investigations could be conducted in relation to communication skills, particularly written communication, which makes use of distinct genres which are very often practiced as part of the assessment process in many undergraduate programmes. Broad transferability could be demonstrated by the development of writing skills in cognate genres (from argumentative essay to position paper, for example) or the use of those genres and their cognates under operational constraints such as time pressure or the need to preserve confidentiality. However, the position becomes less clear when we come to attributes about which we can feel much less confident that they have a generic character (thinking, reasoning and problem-solving skills) or which we cannot reasonably expect to be developed on undergraduate programmes (creativity).

The most that one can plausibly say about these attributes is, first, that there are some very general maxims that might be extracted from them. Thus one might say that reasoning requires that one identifies the premises and conclusions of arguments, seeks to identify the kind of argument that one is dealing with, establishes inference warrants and suppressed premises, and tries to establish whether or not the argument is a sound one. However, the very generality of such maxims masks the fact that putting them into effect is likely to involve a detailed engagement with the subject matter in question. Second, it is plausible to suggest (and this may be a more general point) that certain intellectual virtues are developed on demanding graduate programmes. These may include patience, being systematic, perseverance and so on, which although contoured by the activity in which they are learned are, nevertheless, applicable in other contexts. However, to characterise them as knowledge or skill is misleading. There is a danger that in looking 'in the round' for what is developed by advanced study, we may omit to look in areas where we unaccustomed to look. That is, we focus on skills rather than virtues or character traits.

10. INCREASING DEMAND FOR THE "MANAGEMENT SKILLS' OF GRADUATES IN THE "KNOWLEDGE ECONOMY"

One of the reasons for the massive expansion in funding for higher education in the last two decades is the perception that graduates are required in the emerging 'knowledge economy.' However the term itself obscures two possible, but somewhat distinct, lines of development. There seem to be emerging two kinds of high skill economy. One, which emphasises the role of technical workers (the level 3 model, where entry qualifications are based on the use of theoretical knowledge at sub-degree level) is based on the idea that high specification and high performance systems require workers with a high degree of discretion, polyvalent skilling and the capacity to work in teams (Hodgson op.cit.; Prais 1995).[xi] This model presupposes a large corps of graduate technologists and managers, but sees a particular co-ordinative role for them in a relatively non-hierarchical structure in which level 3 technical workers occupy a critical role. Typically, the manager has technological and often technical knowledge of a branch of the industry, as well as some of the specific knowledge concerned with managing an enterprise, such as production management, quality assurance, accountancy or human resources development. It is common for such managers to be recruited from within the industry and to have received further training in management skills subsequent to their graduate education as technologists within the industry.

The Level 4 model (where operatives are educated to degree level), exemplified by the US and the UK emphasises the role of the graduate as manager supervising workers at craft and sub-technician level. In this model there is a steady demand for craft and technical workers, but an increase in demand for the number of graduates, who have an important role in supervising semi and unskilled labour (DfES 2003, p.39). The level 3 model requires a more limited number of graduates than the level 4 model. But it also suggests a greater degree of continuity, which allows for progression from technical to technological level of understanding through hierarchical programmes of study. Such a model assumes 'permeable' qualifications which allow technicians to progress to the technological level and beyond if they so wish. One feature of this model is that promotion to management function occurs as a result of further study and work experience at the technician level. Management is seen less as a generic skill and more one that is specific to the industry or function in which it is exercised. This model often makes use of a 'permeable' qualification system that allows progression from technical to technological levels within the industry-specific knowledge and builds specific managerial expertise through qualifications acquired after graduation.

The Level 4 model assumes the existence of technologists and researchers but, being based on a less highly skilled workforce at and below level 3, assumes a larger corps of managers with more generic managerial attributes.[xii] Since these cannot be assumed to have gained their managerial skill through the workplace, it can be inferred that there are some features of being a graduate that are thought to enable them to operate successfully as managers as a result of graduating. This is the economic backdrop of the interest in graduate attributes in some societies such as the US, the UK and Australia. This assumes, in the 'managerial' model of a knowledge economy, a generic skill of management which the education of graduates should enable them to rapidly acquire. One of the problems is that there is no clear idea about what the science of management should consist in or even whether it is properly called a discipline based on a well-established body of theoretical knowledge. Some commentators, like Drucker emphasise the importance of an all-round liberal kind of education. It is claimed that successful managers need a broad understanding of the world in they operate, together with skills that are applicable across as wide a range as possible of activities and situations. Thus the emphasis on graduate attributes can be seen as a way of updating the traditional manager's liberal education by making it more adaptable and more practical. Graduate attributes on this model arise from the wide knowledge and understanding of the society in which the firm operates that a liberal degree level education gives one, together with transferable skills that are, to a large degree, generic

Management is also seen, however, as the science of behavioural manipulation. If this is the case then a liberal education will not be sufficient to develop the attributes appropriate to a graduate, but will also require knowledge and techniques derived from psychology. These often play a large part in post-graduation management education. On the other hand, the technician model or level 3 of the knowledge economy suggests that management may be more industry-specific, allowing for the promotion of managers with technical and technological expertise, who then go on to acquire specific managerial knowledge. In either model, the development of generic graduate attributes might look attractive to an employer, as a way of shortening the managerial training process, but if some of these attributes are chimerical, there is little to be gained by seeking to develop them.

11. CONCLUSION: GRADUATE LEVEL EDUCATION AND CHANGING CONCEPTIONS OF LEARNING

Are we seeing a paradigm shift in conceptions of learning at undergraduate level? It is too early to say, but there is some evidence that currently popular cognitivist and behaviourist models find it difficult to accommodate the more social and collective learning which is at least implicit in the 'graduate attributes' model.[xiii] One may, of course, dispute whether these forms of learning are really anything more than aspirations. In some ways, the alternative route to degree level, via a technician qualification, seems more suited to the development of such workplace-applicable attributes, since it involves prolonged immersion in the social world of the workplace and hence development of them through a direct method. Furthermore, the sincerity of commitment to social and collective learning on the part of universities may be doubted given the reluctance of many institutions to really develop it as part of their assessment procedures.

On the other hand, the preoccupation with generic skills such as problem solving and thinking, suggests a continued adherence to a cognitivist 'thinking as an individual process' model in which these capacities are thought of primarily as attributes to be exercised individually. This diversity of practice and the persistence of individualist conceptions of learning make it difficult to claim, whatever new paradigms of learning may be emerging, that the notion of graduate attributes yet encompasses them. The interesting question is whether a model of graduate attributes can survive the different and somewhat contradictory approaches to learning that seem to be present in different conceptions of what graduate attributes are supposed to be.

If the primary vocational aim of degree-level education is to develop what I have called 'technological' as opposed to 'technical' ability, it is debateable whether this is really compatible with the development of 'graduate attributes', at least at the degree level. For on the one hand, the ability to think critically about one's subject matter, to solve problems within it and to be innovative are clearly, when taken together, technological abilities; they are acquired within the subject matter and are applicable within it. It is highly disputable whether they are readily applicable beyond that subject matter, without further training and/or experience. On the other hand, the communicative, numerical, IT and statistical skills developed in degree programmes are largely technical (unless the degree is actually a degree in that subject matter). As such they cannot be characterised as 'graduate attributes'. One might reply that where work at the technological level in a particular occupation involves teamwork, written communication and statistical ability, then these abilities will necessarily have to be developed to a technological level. But the point here is that they are developed beyond the technical to the technological level *at the workplace* or at least after the completion of a degree programme, and although their technical development in the classroom may be an unavoidable preliminary to their technological development at work, it can hardly be said that they are graduate attributes *per se* when the student graduates.

12. NOTES

[i] The work of Oakeshott (1962: 10-11), in which technical knowledge is seen as the mechanical putting into effect of rules, suggests that this is a low-level kind of knowledge. Some of Aristotle's discussion of *techne* seems to support this view, while in other places, the enactive and reflexive side of *techne* (or technique) is emphasised. In the latter interpretation, technical knowledge requires judgment, reflection and situational awareness, as well as knowledge of at least some of the theoretical rationale for a procedure. For a detailed discussion of Aristotle's views, Dunne see (1993: Ch.10).

[ii] For a useful categorisation of graduate occupations, together with an account of their relationship with degree subjects, see Elias and Purcell (2003).

[iii] Purcell et al, op.cit.

[iv] Endorsing their generic nature does not commit one to the view that they can be used without further training in the workplace. This is unlikely to be the case.

[v] Winch (1996: Ch. 2).

[vi] MacIntyre (1981: Ch. 3).

[vii] Hodgson (1999:Ch.7); Weil (2002: 95).

[viii] For a more detailed account of applied theoretical knowledge, see Clarke & Winch (2004).

[ix] This is not denied either by proponents of the desirability of teaching context-free thinking skills. See Siegel (1987: 37).

[x] We might well be suspicious of creativity in some occupations, creativity in accountants, for example.

[xi] These two models are ideal types to which different countries conform to a greater or lesser degree. Nevertheless, the literature does suggest a polarisation between these two broad models. By level 3 is meant educational achievement or technical skill that would normally result from full-time education or its part-time equivalent up to the age of 18. Level 4 denotes a qualification at degree level or equivalent.

^{xii} This model is most associated with the 'Anglo-Saxon' economies of the US, the UK and Australia. See Ashton and Green (op.cit.), Crouch, Finegold & Sako (1999), Brown, Green & Lauder (2001).
^{xiii} For more on workplace-related collective forms of learning, see Beckett & Hager (2002).

13. REFERENCES

Argyris, C. & Schön, D. (1974) *Organisational Learning*. New York: Addison-Wesley.

Ashton, D. & Green, F. (1996) *Education, Skills and the Global Economy*. Cheltenham: David Elgar.

Barrow, R. & Woods, R. (1975) *An Introduction to Philosophy of Education*. London: Methuen.

Beckett, D. & Hager, P. (2002) *Life, Work and Learning*. London: Routledge.

Bernstein, B. (1990) *Class, Codes and Control*. Vol. 4, London: Routledge.

Brown, P., Green, A. & Lauder, H.(2001) *High Skills: globaliation, competitiveness and skill* formation. Oxford: Oxford University Press.

Clarke, L. & Winch, C. (2004) 'Apprenticeship and Applied Theoretical Knowledge', in *Educational Philosophy and Theory*, Vol. 36, No. 5, pp. 509-521.

Crouch, C., Finegold, D. & Sako, M. (1999) *Are Skills The Answer?The Political Economy of Skill Creation in Advanced Industrial Countries*. Oxford: Oxford University Press.

DfES, (2003) *Education and Skills: The Economic Benefit*. London: DfES.

Drucker, P. 'The Manager of Tomorrow, in P.F. Drucker (ed.) (1993) *The Practice of Management*. New York: Harper and Brothers, pp. 370-378.

Dunne, J. (1993) *Back to the Rough Ground*, London, Notre Dame Press.

Elias, P., & Purcell, K. (2003) *Measuring Change in the Graduate Labour Market*. available at www2.warwick.ac.uk/fac/soc/ier/research/glmf/glmf1/

Fisher, A. (1988) *The Logic of Real Arguments*. Cambridge: Cambridge University Press.

Gingell, J. (2001) 'Against Creativity' *Irish Educational Studies*, Vol. 20, pp. 25-37.

Hacking, I. (2001) *An Introduction to Probability and Inductive Logic*. Cambridge: Cambridge University Press.

Hinchliffe, G. (2004) 'Work and Human Flourishing', in *Educational Philosophy and Theory*, special issue on learning in the workplace, Vol. 36, No. 5, pp. 535-547.

Hirst, P. (1974) *Knowledge and the Curriculum*. London: Routledge.

Hodgson, G. (1999) *Economics and Utopia*. London: Routledge.

Langhammer, M. (2002) *Using ICT as a Hook*. Belfast: Learndirect.

Levi, D. (2000) *In Defense of Informal Logic*. Dordrecht: Kluwer.

MacIntyre, A. (1981) *After Vtue* . London: Duckworth.

Oakeshott, M. (1962) *Rationalism in Politics* .London: Methuen.

Prais, S. (1995) *Productivity, Education and Training: an international perspective*. Cambridge: Cambridge University Press.

Revans, R.W. (1978) *The ABC of Action Learning*. Manchester: R.W.Revans.

Siegel, H. (1987) *Educating Reason*. New York: Routledge.

Smith, M. (2002) 'The School Leadership Initiative: An Ethically Flawed Project?', *Journal of Philosophy of Education*, Vol. 36, No. 1, pp. 21-40.

Toulmin, S. (1958) *The Uses of Argument*. Cambridge: Cambridge University Press.

Weil, S. (2002) *Oppression and Liberty*. London: Routledge.

Winch, C. (1996) *Qality and Education* . Oxford: Blackwell.

Winch, C. (1998) *The Philosophy of Human Learning*. London: Routledge.

CHAPTER 5

GEOFFREY HINCHLIFFE

GRADUATE EMPLOYABILITY AND LIFELONG LEARNING: A NEED FOR REALISM?

1. THE NATURE OF EMPLOYABILITY AND LIFELONG LEARNING

Conferences and seminars on graduate employability are coming thick and fast these days, though not many are attended by students themselves. This is just as well since only the most self-confident would not fail to be profoundly disheartened by what they are likely to hear at these events. For example, at a recent seminar in London (attended by graduate recruiters, practitioners, academics, NGO officials, employers and careers advisors) a prominent graduate recruiter gave a lengthy presentation on what attributes the modern graduate needs to have if they are to be regarded as employable. These include analytical skills, the ability to work in teams and fluent communication skills, both written and oral. In addition, our graduate must possess a sound awareness of relevant commercial drivers and demonstrate an ability to think in business terms. He or she must demonstrate an ability to take difficult decisions and show leadership potential, whilst at the same time convince a recruiter that they can listen sensitively, with due consideration to colleagues. They must also convey that they are not only comfortable with change but can initiate and 'champion' change (presumably in a sensitive way). In all, the presenter listed over twenty key abilities and attributes and each of these were fully described and broken down in separate paragraphs. The attributes of employability nowadays include intellectual abilities, performance skills, social skills and a range of personal qualities. How many employers themselves possess such a dazzling array of attributes, I wonder? Can we realistically expect young men and women in their early twenties to already possess (or have the potential to possess very quickly) all those skills and attributes which it takes *years* for any normal intelligent person to develop (and even then most of us have a few gaps[i]) ? How on earth have we got ourselves in

91

P. Hager and S. Holland (eds.), Graduate Attributes, Learning and Employability, 91–104.
© 2006 *Springer.*

such a position where expectations of new graduates are so absurdly inflated and so unrealistic?

I want to suggest, fairly briefly, one or two answers to this question before I go on to consider what a realistic approach to graduate employability could involve – and by 'realistic' I do not mean by this term deflationary expectations of what graduates can achieve but rather a more adequate concept of what 'employability' entails, particularly in the light of the demands of a knowledge economy. Talk of graduate *employability* marks an advance, of course, on the key skills discourse that dominated much of the 1990's: we no longer believe (if we ever seriously did) that a degree, supplemented by a few key skills, could characterise graduate employment requirements.[ii] Rather, the emphasis is on a range of abilities and skills, including cognitive abilities, knowledge and understanding which got somewhat neglected by the key skills discourse – this was rather unfortunate since it was just those cognitive and intellectual abilities that were supposed to distinguish the graduate from non-graduates. And by distinguishing employability (the potential for employment in its fullest sense) from employment skills (roughly those skills that are best learnt in context) universities are less likely to be seen as poor substitutes for on the job training. However, the emergence of the term 'employability' has come at a cost: we seem to want graduates with all the attributes of the expert without investing in the years it takes to develop them.

In a long-awaited but still important book, Philip Brown and Anthony Hesketh (2004) have analysed the recruitment policies of a number of larger companies that employ graduates in large numbers. It seems that some companies have to try harder each year to recruit (and attract) the kind of graduates they want, despite the fact that the number of graduates is increasing exponentially each year. The reason? Brown and Hesketh offer an explanation which draws on a particular concept of individuality that:

> privileges a Darwinian model of charismatic leadership where performance rather than knowledge or expertise is used to legitimate existing authority relations and the huge wage inequalities found in many American and British companies. *(p. 190)*

The authors are able to show, in convincing and entertaining detail, just how graduate recruitment policies – individual profiling, group activities, interviews and psychometric assessments – are used to pick out these potentially charismatic individuals and how these policies help to re-inforce the view that real 'stars' are thin on the ground but that only stars can drive companies forward – only 'stars' can really be the agents in the knowledge economy.[iii]   The authors also demonstrate that this view of the 'talented individual' is not only to be found in the private sector but also the public sector as well.

In order to convince recruiters that they are stars, graduates need to construct a narrative of employability which takes the form of a "reflective project of the self" (Brown & Hesketh 2004: 220). This requires a sustained personal narrative in which particular experiences – both academic and non-academic – are shown to have both helped form broader life-based aims and to have been in part formed by these broader aims. The aim is to present one's life as pretty much a seamless whole in which all setbacks become experiences which either re-inforce one's aims or appropriately modify them. The strategic-minded graduate had better leave one or two minor loose ends – to be convincing it's a good idea not to present one's life as an entirely seamless pattern. But the overall idea is clear: one must 'own' one's whole life as something which exists for the agent in a more or less transparent state: what's not transparent can't be owned and so is best left out altogether. This ideal of personal development has led Richard Smith (2004: 38) to speak of a "a culture of knowingness, a one-dimensional self-awareness that posits transparency as a ready ideal" and links this to a naïve Cartesianism and a non-problematic concept of agency. This concept of the self knows nothing of luck, of the ancient Greek *tuche* and knows nothing of Machiavelli's *fortuna:* this self makes its own luck, of course. And there is nothing in this self to discover since it's an empty vessel, waiting to be filled.

In some ways it is surprising that the transparent self still survives at all given the amount of criticism it has received throughout the twentieth century. But it has outlived a whole number of art movements (surrealism, abstract expressionism) as well as psychoanalysis. Its continuing existence has persisted not only in the face of numerous philosophical critiques (this is only to be expected): it has even survived being called into question in popular culture (for example in films such as John Ford's *The Searchers*, or *Last Tango in Paris*). The same company executives who extol the contemporary employability narrative of a transparent, non-problematic self most likely also think that *American Beauty* is a cracking good film.

Ideas of graduate employability are, then, fuelled by a concept of selfhood which places increasing demands on graduates to construct a narrative of employability before they have even got a proper job!

This concept of selfhood is further reinforced by the pedagogy of lifelong learning. The increasing prevalence of the term lifelong learning, compared to lifelong education, continuing education or adult education,[iv] marks a shift in which learning is seen as something that happens in many different kinds of contexts as well as within formal educational settings. It also, I suggest, marks a shift in emphasis from the *educator* to the *learner*. This is sometimes interpreted as a form of empowerment: the agent becomes the director of his or her learning which is managed (the business vocabulary is not accidental) according to the learner's needs (Fryer 1998: 7 provides a typical statement of this sentiment). But I want to suggest that something more subtle is happening as well, with the shift from educator to learner. We normally think of a pedagogy as a form of instruction with certain aims and methods directed by those with the appropriate authority. Furthermore, we assume a pedagogy implies some kind of curriculum which is delivered within an institutional setting. In this sense, a pedagogy may be libertarian, authoritarian or somewhere in between but in all these cases it is a set of methods and procedures which have their source in the teacher. These methods are the means through which the educational aims are achieved, that is the means through which, it is hoped, the learners absorb new knowledge, understanding, skills, character formation or whatever it is that is prescribed in the aims of the pedagogy. The methods and procedures remain the preserve of the teacher: they are the means, the vehicle by which the teaching/learning takes place.

But in lifelong learning it is the *learner* who takes on the mantle of pedagogy: the learner must become his or her own *teacher*. This can happen through personal development, self-reflection or through 'managing your own learning'. This does not mean that, in assuming a whole pedagogy, a learner always teaches herself: learning may or may not be self-directed but in either case it should always be self-managed. Above all, our learner must assume a learner identity: a person has to live out a pedagogy so that one is able to "acquire the self-image of a lifelong learner" (Knapper & Cropley 2000: 49). It is through the construction of this identity that one is able to become the bearer of a pedagogy – without a teacher, without an institutional setting and without a curriculum: the pedagogy consists precisely in those unwritten, ghostly prescriptions which are always self-prescriptions and because they have this self-prescribed nature are emblematic of one's own self-empowerment and, indeed, of one's own emancipation.[v]

Thus it is that employability prescriptions on the one hand and pedagogic prescriptions on the other pleasantly fuse: in order to maintain that 'narrative of employability' our bright young graduate has also to acquire the identity of a lifelong learner as well. (Life means life, by the way: one maintains one's learner identity to the grave. There is no experience that is not, at the same time, a learning experience and there is no time that one can shed the image of the 'learner'). The affiliation between learner identity and employability on the one hand and Foucault's conception of self-formation through training and discipline on the other, are too obvious to be spelt out at length. Lifelong learning has become, unwittingly perhaps for some – especially those who still cling to lifelong learning as a form of self-empowerment and self-emancipation – a weapon of market discipline and all the more effective for becoming a weapon of *self-discipline.*

Now, I want to suggest that this version of employability and lifelong learning, a kind of pedagogy of the self or auto-pedagogy, is unrealistic for two reasons. First of all, it places onerous burdens on individuals which, over a whole life, are only realistic if you have only yourself to worry about. As soon as one has domestic responsibilities, children, aged parents etc, etc. then there will be times – and these times may last months and years, not days and weeks – when one's own concerns become of lesser importance and when self-reflection and self-development become distant memories simply because one is too busy reflecting on, caring about and developing the lives of others. So much is (or ought to be) obvious and I shall spend no more time on this reason.

The second reason is less obvious and needs a certain amount of explanation. I shall first of all briefly examine the requirements of a knowledge economy and then spend a bit more time elaborating the context in which these requirements are played out. I shall then be in a position to suggest revisions to the pedagogy of lifelong learning and, as a consequence, suggest a more realistic approach to graduate employability.

2. KNOWLEDGE, SKILLS AND UNDERSTANDING

I want to emphasise something which may at first sight seem paradoxical: namely that we all carry, as individuals, a knowledge *deficit* – known unknowns as has been famously said. The more emphasis there is on knowledge as both an asset and commodity the less likely it is that an individual will be able to carry all the relevant knowledge inside his or her own head. In part, this is due to the sheer quantity of information and its complexity, both of which grow yearly.[vi] It is also due to the *context* and the *form* in which knowledge operates. The point has been well put by Geoffrey Hodgson (1999):

> Action always takes place in a material and natural integument but it deals more and more with intersubjective discourses concerning the interpretations, meanings and uses of information *(p. 185)*

Knowledge is embedded in different kinds of *situations* and only if one masters a discourse is one able to use such knowledge in new situations. It is more than likely to be only partially codified and remains in peoples heads (by the time it has been documented it is probably already out of date). Hodgson therefore emphasises the way in which knowledge involves "socially transmitted cognitive frames and a shared social language" (p. 200). Thus, as an individual, I carry a knowledge deficit partly because I can't possibly know everything that needs to be known but also, and crucially, because of the socially embedded nature of that knowledge. I can be a knowledge bearer as a *participant* in a discourse (or at the intersection of more than one discourse) but my participant status attests to my dependence on others.

It is not only in respect of knowledge and understanding that we are situation-dependent. Skilful behaviour depends crucially on the ability to 'read' situations so as to modify the performance accordingly. Of course, I can learn a skill in the sense that I can learn a series of techniques. For example, I may learn how to give presentations – all the way from their preparation right through to handling questions at the end. I may learn how to present information in an attractive way and I may also learn (and remember) the art of 'eye-skimming' the whole audience at regular intervals. But none of these techniques will tell me how to judge a particular audience's expectations at a particular time. Nor will these techniques tell me how they should be modified in the light of those expectations.[vii]   What is needed is therefore a situational understanding[viii] which allows the techniques (in this case of communication) to be modified accordingly. Moreover, it is only through situational understanding that any kind of skill transfer can take place: although some IT skills automatically transfer (Windows is the same in Singapore as it is in Yorkshire) the majority of skills that form part of employability need the agent's situational awareness for transfer to happen. This does not mean that situational awareness can take the place of skilful technique: but techniques consist of a repertoire which can be played and improvised – without the repertoire there can be no performance at all.[ix]

These thoughts may become clearer if we consider a so-called generic skill, problem solving. Now if there were such a definable skill as problem-solving (applicable to all problems) then whoever could market it would be a millionaire many times over. The closest one could ever get to such a skill would be a methodology which might be applied to a closely defined and related range of problems (for example, there are methodologies on the market which give a procedure for locating change factors in a malfunctioning process). On top of this there are also stages in problem solving that one can follow – roughly investigation/scoping the problem/proposing solutions/selecting a solution/testing, etc. But neither the closely defined methodology nor the project life cycle approach amount to the skill of problem solving. The one gives a technique, applicable over a small range of situations and the other simply identifies the stages that one needs to undergo if one is going to successfully address a problem.

What a practitioner needs is three attributes: first the background knowledge which enables her to understand the problem as a problem of a certain kind, second a repertoire of techniques which in the past have helped one investigate/select and test solutions and, finally, a situational awareness which enables her to understand the *precise* nature of the problem and therefore enables her to select from her repertoire of techniques. It is this awareness – or better, understanding – which also enables her to fashion new techniques or at least to re-fashion existing ones. Fortunately we now have, thanks to Donald Schön, a phrase that describes this process of complex thinking in action: reflection-in-action (Schön 1983).

In one sense the term 'problem solving' scarcely does justice to the often complex nature of this activity. But to the extent that we can recognise that integration of background knowledge, techniques and situational awareness, and to the extent we can say that some people are better at this activity than others then we can refer to it as 'problem solving'.[x]

It may be commented that people have always had to have situational understanding, except under conditions dominated by task-driven routine work and learning. But the point that Schön and others are trying to address is the changing nature of situations, characterised by uncertainty and instability where it is fruitless to rely on set procedures, no matter how complex. It is not that everything in situations constantly changes: it isn't the case that every situation is unique. The difficulty is working out just what it is that is the same and what knowledge can be relied upon.

2.1 The Nature of Situations

Theorists and researchers into professional development, lifelong learning and skill transferability have spent a great deal of time working out what kind of cognitive abilities are needed to deal with situations of risk and uncertainty. But they have spent much less time analysing what could be called the structural features of situations themselves. For example, Eraut has taken issue with Schön as to the precise meaning of 'reflection-in-action'. He is of the opinion that what

Schön characterises as reflection-in-action could just as well be called reflection *on* action and what Schön is really drawing our attention to is a process of deliberation (Eraut 1994: 142-9). In his discussion, Eraut concludes that 'metacognition' is a better term than reflection which he confesses he can make little sense of. But this seems to be taking us away from the nature of situational understanding back towards the traditional model of the professional who cautiously deliberates before deciding what to do. Schön's concept of reflection-*in*-action at least conveys something of the idea that reflection can take place as part of the process in which a person is trying to make sense of just what the situation is in which she finds herself. Eraut's point can be taken most usefully, perhaps, if we assume that a practitioner may undertake both types of reflection – if the reflection-in-action fails to satisfactorily resolve the nature of the situation then maybe a process of deliberation is called for.

In so far as there is a real dispute between these two theorists it is one which centres on the type of cognitive abilities of the agent. It seems as if we are still dealing with a concept of agency that is more or less self-transparent. The kind of agency that Schön describes in his many examples is one of the cool professional in complete control of a situation. We have the professional on the one hand and the situation on the other. The latter is subject to the gaze and the benign manipulation of the former. Situation and subject are still separate. That is what being a professional is all about.

Put philosophically, this view amounts to saying that individuals are logically prior to the situations in which they find themselves. And I want to suggest that this gets it precisely the wrong way round: situations are 'prior' to individuals. Note that I am *not* stating that individuals can be reduced to situations: I am not about to obliterate the existence of individuality. Rather I am saying that individuality is not a static given but something which is negotiated, constructed and fashioned: and then re-negotiated and re-fashioned again. It is not just that situations are unstable: concepts of our own individuality are potentially unstable as well.

This idea is difficult to make sense of but it is one of the leading themes of Heidegger's *Being and Time*, especially in the first division of that work. Heidegger is particularly concerned to show that the self is always a situated self with respect to others: the existence of others therefore becomes an integral aspect of the self's own existence. He describes this state of affairs as 'being-with'. This quote may help explain better what he is getting at:

> Does one not start out by making out and isolating the 'I' so that one must then seek some way of getting over to the Others from this isolated subject? To avoid this misunderstanding we must notice in what sense we are talking about 'the Others'.......... by 'Others' are rather those from whom, for the most part, one does *not* distinguish oneself – those among whom one is too. This Being-there-too with them does not have the ontological character of a being-present-at-hand-along-'with' them within a world. This 'with' is something of the character of Dasein; the 'too' means a sameness of   Being as circumspectively concernful Being-in the world. 'With' and 'too' are understood existentially, not categorially. By reason of this *with-like* Being-in-the-world, the world is always the one I share with Others. The world of Dasein is a *with-world*. Being-in is *Being-with-Others*.
> *(Heidegger 1962: 154-5)*

The essential point is that Dasein (loosely a 'self') is in a world which is shared with others and this sharedness means that I can never prise myself apart from those relations that help constitute who I am in the first place. That is what Heidegger means when he says that 'with' is to be understood 'existentially'. This approach also features in his analysis of communication :

> Communication is never anything like a conveying of experiences, such as opinions or wishes, from the interior of one subject into the interior of another. Dasein-with is already essentially manifest in a co-state-of-mind and a co-understanding. In discourse Being-with becomes explicitly '*shared*'; that is to say, it *is* already, but it is unshared as something that has not been taken hold of and appropriated.
> *(Heidegger 1962: 205)*

It is through communication that determinate situations arise out of the indeterminate condition of situatedness (the condition of being-with) by making being-with *explicitly* 'shared'. Situations may arrive ready-made, as it were, where the function of discourse is to make them apparent; or they may be brought into being through communication, through enquiry and dialogue. But in both cases, once the situation has been established then – to revert back to our practitioner once more – the agent is a participant in a situation that is shared.

It is an awareness of this shared nature that makes reflection-in-action possible: the point about this kind of reflection is that a situation is modified as a result of its operation: the situation is partly determined by the activity of this kind of reflection. If we have a situation in which all the participants are undertaking some kind of reflection-in-action then the character of that situation will transform itself through this activity. And it should not be thought that situations only exist through perception or hearing. Situations can exist inside the head which is why reflection of a more deliberative nature, even if physically separate and apart, may be still part of a situation. Situations, as we all know, can be virtual.

Thus situational understanding is not something that we should think of as undertaken by an autonomous, discrete self which is fully transparent to itself. Full transparency becomes impossible once we understand that, because we are in a permanent state of being-with, our identities can never be fully under our control (the use of violence or force to impose my identity on others merely acknowledges this lack of control). We can now also have a deeper understanding of what went wrong with Tony Blair at the meeting of the Womens Institute: he didn't have the grace to acknowledge his *shared* situation with those thousands of women.

3. TOWARDS A REVISED NOTION OF EMPLOYABILITY AND LIFELONG LEARNING

We can now see, I hope, why most current notions of graduate employability, whilst an improvement on the crude skills model of graduate employment requirements, place unrealistic demands on graduates. If we take the account of situational understanding I have presented along with Geoffrey Hodgson's account of why we usually carry a knowledge deficit we can start to see how it is that our conception of employability is inflationary – practically, professionally, economically and philosophically. In this situation, what is the job-seeking graduate to do ? Hesketh and Brown suggest graduates tend to divide into Players – who play the game laid down by recruiters – and Purists who want to be accepted for themselves alone. Until employer expectations become more realistic, graduates will have to learn to become Players.

A more realistic concept of employability would involve the recognition that graduates cannot possibly have all the knowledge, skills and abilities that are required of them. Part of their employability would involve precisely the awareness of the shared nature of these attributes and a certain – if I may say so – modesty about just what any individual can contribute. For situational understanding involves, in part, a recognition of the *limits* of what I might be able to achieve along with a recognition on my essential dependency on others. Employability would therefore place a high value on my ability to share knowledge and understanding. This does not undermine the need for leadership but it does imply a need for leadership which is enabling with respect to others and not merely strategic.

What implications do these reflections have for the pedagogy of lifelong learning? It will be recalled that I spoke of this pedagogy as having a peculiar character, whereby the individual, in assuming the identity of the learner, is obliged to be the owner and bearer of this pedagogy. This too, it was suggested, places hopelessly unrealistic and onerous demands on individuals. There are two alternatives here. The first would be to abandon completely the idea that any pedagogy can be owned in this way and revert back to the more traditional concept of pedagogy I outlined. This, I think, would be an unfortunate outcome. It would place in jeopardy the value of self-reflection, management of one's own learning and metacognition. And although these devices certainly can be viewed as contemporary methods and tools of disciplining the self they also provide the basis for maintaining a critical stance as far as learning is concerned. The other alternative would be to maintain the pedagogy of ownership but to insist that this ownership be shared. How could this work, and in particular how could it work with learning related to employability?

The insights of Lawrence Stenhouse can, I think, be still of great help to us even though they were formulated (or maybe even because they were) in a time, thirty years ago or so, when the pedagogy of the self was still in its infancy. Stenhouse was, of course, concerned primarily with the activity of teaching which he conceived of as a research activity. This went further than simply reflecting upon actual results in the light of planned objectives: he suggested that "all curricula are hypothetical procedures testable only in classrooms" (Stenhouse 1985: 68). Stenhouse went further than this in as much he made explicit the hypothetical nature of knowledge embedded in a curriculum : "all curricula are hypothetical realisations of theses about the nature of knowledge" (Stenhouse, 1985: 65). It was the provisional basis of the curriculum which laid the foundation for the research stance: "by a research stance I mean a disposition to examine one's own practice critically and systematically" (Stenhouse, 1975: 162-3). However, this stance was not that of an isolated individual because in the same passage just quoted he emphasises that "research is a co-operative and joint responsibility". What I want to suggest is that by 'teacher', read 'lifelong learner' and by curriculum, read "situated knowledge".

Stenhouse stresses two features that are of interest to us. First, the provisional and hypothetical nature of knowledge, which for him necessitates a research stance that can be seen as ideas underpinning a pedagogy of research. I do not mean by this the idea of the traditional researcher, armed with a scholarly apparatus of publications, research tools and methodologies. It is the research *stance* that is important here: the hypothetical and provisional nature of situations require that one's situational understanding is also subject to systematic revision. But secondly, this critical stance is one that can only be realised as a co-operative and shared endeavour. Recalling, once more, the characteristic presence of a knowledge deficit then we can see how this particular feature is not only desirable in itself but also a necessary one as well.

4. CONCLUSION

The idea of a revised pedagogy of lifelong learning and the revised notion of employability come together: the person who is eminently employable is the person who understands that learning is a critical and co-operative pursuit and who can use this understanding in practical domains of some complexity. Academia is usually strong on the critical side but somewhat neglects (not entirely, of course) the co-operation side of things: the achievement culture of the academy tends to be strongly individualised. In the workplace, co-operation is taken – usually – for granted: teamworking, to be sure is a buzz word but this should not mask its importance for us, nor its effective reality. On the other hand, a critical stance is not always appreciated in the workplace, to say the least. Would it not be nice, though, if we were to bring the two together, both in the workplace and the academy?

5. NOTES

[i] Take any public figure and you will find gaps. e.g., Blair: strong oral communicator, a bit fluffy on the analytical bit. Brown: strong analytical grasp, strong on detail but a bit mechanistic on the communication front – etc, etc.

[ii] The research conducted by Peter Knight and Manz Yorke (2004), together with the *SkillsPlus* research team, has done much to switch the focus of graduate employability away from key skills agenda towards cognitive skills and the development of self-efficacy: these can only be developed through a sustained engagement with a programme of learning.

[iii] The authors observe that, since the advent of Bill Gates, 'geeks' who add value to a company may also turn into stars. Geeks, of course, are to be distinguished from mere 'nerds' (see Brown and Hesketh 2004: 180-184).

[iv] These terms are discussed briefly by Rogers (2002: 29-33) and extensively by Wain (1987).

[v] For an entertaining, if slightly chilling, account of lifelong learning enthusiasts who argue in this vein, see Coffield (2000: Ch.1).

[vi] The Dean of the Medical School at the University of East Anglia stated that one of the reasons for switching to problem-based learning was the impossibility of any incipient medical practitioner being able to master a syllabus taught in conventional ways: a practical acknowledgement of a permanent knowledge deficit.

[vii] As Tony Blair famously found out when he (of all people) found himself being slow handclapped at the annual meeting of the Womens Institute at the Albert Hall in London. This consummate communicator misjudged his audience and what should have been, for him, an easy stroll, turned out to be a public embarrassment. One can survive setbacks though: a few weeks later, Blair went on to secure another election landslide victory.

[viii] Situational understanding is discussed by John Elliott (1993: 7-19) and also by Michael Eraut (1994: 124-7), amongst others.

[ix] Knight and Yorke seem to overstate the case in their attack on the skills agenda. In their dismissal of an over-reliance on the *language* of skills (2004: 31) the technique and performance associated with skills seems to get lost in their account, so that their substitute for skills – 'skillful practices' simply amounts to the skillful mastery of a particular practice or discourse. Knight and Yorke's concept of employability is just a shade too cognitivist for my liking and nowhere acknowledges that the mastery of a skillful practice in part depends on the mastery of certain techniques. It seems to forget Ryle's observation that knowing how can *precede* knowing that (Ryle 1949) and that self-efficacy (which they stress, rightly, as an important part of employability) can come about, in part, through successful performance (like giving a decent presentation). In case anyone has any doubts about the relevance of skills to graduate employability in the eyes of employers they need only to read any set of graduate job adverts. Skills discourse is highly prominent (communication and teamworking skills) with an emphasis on performance and results.

[x] Examples of problem solving are always difficult to give because 'real' problems are always complex and often require insider knowledge. But think of the software engineer who has the necessary background technical knowledge and a bunch of techniques which help him/her to figure out logic paths and data relationships. The situational understanding here could refer to client problems within a specific business environment within which the software operates.

6. REFERENCES

Brown, P. & Hesketh, A. (2004) *The Mismanagement of talent: employability and jobs in the knowledge economy*. Oxford: Oxford University Press.

Coffield, F. (ed.) (2000) *Differing Visions of a Learning Society: Research Findings*. Bristol: Policy Press.

Elliott, J. (1993) (ed.) *Reconstructing Teacher Education: Teacher Development*. London/Washington D.C: Falmer Press.

Eraut, M. (1994), *Developing Professional Knowledge and Competence*. London/Washington D.C.: Falmer Press.

Fryer, R.H. (1998) *Creating Learning Cultures*. London: Department of Education and Employment.

Heidegger, M. (1962) *Being and Time*. trans. J. Macquarrie & E. Robinson, Oxford: Blackwell.

Hodgson, G. (1999) *Economics and Utopia*. London: Routledge.

Knapper, C. & Cropley, A. (2000) *Lifelong Learning in Higher Education*, 3rd Edn. London: Kogan Page.

Knight, P. & Yorke, M. (2004) *Learning, Curriculum and Employability in Higher Education*. London: Routledge/Falmer.

Rogers, A. (2002) *Teaching Adults*, 3rd. Edn. Buckingham [England]; Philadelphia: Open University Press.

Ryle, G. (1949) *The Concept of Mind*. London/Harmondsworth: Penguin.

Schön, D. (1983) *The Reflective Practitioner*. New York: Basic Books.

Smith, R. (2004) 'Abstraction and Finitude: education, chance and democracy' in G. Jover & P. Villamor (eds.) *Voices of Philosophy of Education, Proceedings of the 9th Biennial Conference of the International Network of Philosophers of Education*, Madrid, Spain: Complutense University, pp. 34-45.

Stenhouse, L. (1975) *An Introduction to Curriculum Research and Development*. London: Heinemann.

Stenhouse, L (1985) *Research as a Basis for Teaching: Readings from the Work of Lawrence Stenhouse*, (eds.) J. Rudduck and D. Hopkins. London/Portsmouth, NH: Heinemann Educational Books.

Wain, K. (1987) *Philosophy of Lifelong Learning*. London: Croom Helm.

CHAPTER 6

ANDREW GONCZI

THE OECD: ITS ROLE IN THE KEY COMPETENCIES DEBATE AND IN THE PROMOTION OF LIFELONG LEARNING

1. INTRODUCTION

Over the past decade the OECD has had a prominent role in the debate about generic competencies and lifelong learning. Yet the nature of the organisation's involvement in education is rarely a matter for comment in the individual developed countries.

It is the argument of this chapter that through its publications, its projects and its testing/assessment programs the OECD has had a substantial impact on the nature of educational policy in individual countries. I also argue that in focussing on areas of education which have been neglected in the past in most countries, the OECD is also making a substantial contribution to the reform of education systems, particularly the refocusing of curriculum on a wider range of outcomes than has existed to date, and in the recognition of the importance of education outside the formal system.

The most prominent of the educational issues that the OECD has been focussing on in the last decade has been lifelong learning. The naming of the concept is itself instructive. Rather than lifelong education, the term which was chosen by the council of Europe when the issues were first discussed in the 1970s, lifelong *learning* suggests something wider. In fact the original concept as outlined in Faure's *Learning to be* (1972), was concerned with second chance education in formal institutions. By contrast, when the OECD Education Ministers committed themselves to 'lifelong learning for all' in 1996, they explicitly stated that this meant going beyond second and third chance education and that:

P. Hager and S. Holland (eds.), Graduate Attributes, Learning and Employability, 105–124.
© 2006 *Springer.*

> Everybody should be able, motivated and actively encouraged to learn throughout
> life. This view of learning embraces individual and social development of all kinds in
> all settings – formally in schools, vocational tertiary and adult education institutions
> and non formally, at home, at work and in the community. *(Lifelong learning
> for all, 1996: 15)*

The bulk of this chapter concentrates on the activities of the OECD, which have helped both directly and indirectly to clarify the concept of lifelong learning, and to assist the individual OECD countries to try to turn the rhetoric of their Ministers into educational policy. In order to do this it is first necessary to describe briefly the way the OECD is structured.

2.   THE NATURE OF THE OECD AND ITS WORK

The OECD groups 30 member countries who come together to discuss, develop and refine economic and social policies. 'They compare experiences, seek answers to common problems and work to co-ordinate domestic and international policies to help members and non-members deal with an increasingly globalised world' (OECD, http://www.oecd.org/about/). While these discussions may lead to formal or informal agreement, a major aim is to inform members across all areas of public policy. There are substantial interactions with 70 other countries with emerging market economies.

Exchanges between OECD governments flow from information and analysis provided by a Secretariat in Paris which undertakes and disseminates research, and collects and analyses and produces statistical data across a wide range of fields including education.

This work underpins discussion by member countries when they meet in specialised committees of the OECD.

2.1 Committees

The Secretariat in Paris carries out research and analysis at the request of the OECD's 30 member countries. The members meet and exchange information in committees (over 200, covering all policy areas including education) devoted to key issues, with decision-making power vested in the OECD Council which is made up of representatives of the member countries.

2.2 Secretariat

The 2,300 staff of the OECD Secretariat in Paris work directly or indirectly to support the activities of committees. Some 700 economists, lawyers, scientists and other professional staff, mainly based in a dozen substantive directorates, provide research and analysis.

The work of the Secretariat parallels the work of committees, with each directorate servicing one or more committees, as well as committees' working parties and sub-groups. But increasingly, OECD work is cutting across sector lines in cross-disciplinary or horizontal studies. The OECD's work on sustainable development, and its International Futures Program, which aims at identifying emerging policy issues at an early stage, are thoroughly multidisciplinary. Work on employment and unemployment has brought together macroeconomic specialists, experts on tax and enterprises, on technology, as well as labour market and social policy analysis. Environmental and economic analysis can no longer be examined in isolation. Trade and investment are inextricably linked. Biotechnology concerns policy for agriculture, industry, science, environment and development. Gauging the effects of globalisation will draw in virtually every field of policy analysis.

The OECD consists of various departments and directorates covering a whole range of public policy from the environment to the economy. Two directorates are involved with education: the Directorate for Education, Employment, Labour and Social Affairs which analyses education and training as it impacts on unemployment, and the Directorate for Education which 'helps member countries achieve high-quality learning for all that contributes to personal development, sustainable economic growth and social cohesion' (OECD, http://www.oecd.org/about/). In particular, EDU develops strategies for promoting lifelong learning in coherence with other socio-economic policies'. The Program for International Student Assessment (PISA) provides direct assessment of the levels of achievement of 15-year-olds every three years. Major policy messages from the work are published in the annual Education Policy Analysis (OECD, http://www.oecd.org/document). Investigations of long-range trends and innovations in education are the specific focus of the Centre for Educational Research and Innovation (CERI).

In summary, the OECD's way of working consists of a process that begins with data collection and analysis, and moves on to collective discussion of policy. Mutual examination by governments, multilateral surveillance and peer pressure to conform or reform are at the heart of OECD effectiveness.

3. WHY THE OECD HAS FOCUSSED ON LIFELONG LEARNING

In the publication *Lifelong learning for all,* which was the outcome of the meeting of OECD Education Ministers in 1996, the need for a new focus on lifelong learning was justified by a number of interacting social and economic forces. These included globalisation, technological change, changes in work, and the changing nature of the labour market. The primary argument was the increasing need for knowledge and skills in both the production and services sectors of OECD economies. In addition, the risk of polarisation between those fully engaged in acquisition of competencies, and those on the margins, was discussed, as was the likely impact of this on social cohesion.

Four strategies for developing lifelong learning were proposed: strengthening foundations for learning through improving early childhood education and rethinking the formal school system so that it can offer individualised programs; developing better links between learning and work – the transition process; rethinking roles and responsibilities of the various participants – governments, learners families, etc; and developing new ways of resourcing lifelong learning, at post compulsory levels in particular. There was particular emphasis on the disparity of income between those with post compulsory qualifications and those without, and on the way in which the benefits of lifelong learning are shared between the individual, the firm and the wider economy and society.

4. HOW SUCCESSFUL HAVE COUNTRIES BEEN IN ACHIEVING THE LIFELONG LEARNING GOALS?

In 2001 the Education Ministers met again to review progress, since 1996, in making lifelong learning a reality. The conclusion was that though some progress had been made, much work needed to be done to achieve the goals set out 5 years before.

The annual CERI policy analysis of 2001 undertook a stocktake of progress, concluding that few countries did well on the majority of measures. These measures included literacy levels, secondary retention rates, tertiary completion rates, adult rates of participation and literacy, and growth in public and private spending on learning.

A number of problems were identified in the stocktake. One of these was the lack of reliable data on some aspects of lifelong learning, e.g. adult achievement outside formal education. Another was the uncertainty about the kinds of competencies needed in the developing knowledge economy, and whether identified competencies were part of the traditional school curriculum. In addition, the lack of clarity about what works as a *system* of lifelong learning – how various elements of policy act together.

A number of things were clear however in 2001. Participation rates through schools have increased, as have participation rates in tertiary education. However participation in early childhood education was low, as was that of adults in non-formal education. As the OECD policy brief, *Lifelong learning* (2004: 3) points out the latest International Adult Literacy Survey (IALS) demonstrates that more than 25% of adults perform at the lowest level of skill.

It is also the case that there are a large number of secondary students who leave school without any qualifications. In fact participation rates mask the considerable difference between achievement of the top and bottom 25% of students in foundation skills such as reading – the difference amounts to between two and four years of schooling as the Program for International Student Assessment (PISA) revealed in 2000 (see below). In many countries low achievement is associated with low SES and disadvantage (e.g. Australia and UK) and high performance with high SES. However, the value of OECD comparisons is demonstrated by the fact that in other countries (e.g. Finland, Korea, Japan and Sweden) poor performance does not follow from disadvantage and low SES, and that high performance is possible on average, irrespective of family background. That is, high performance in schools is possible with equity. Since school achievement levels are a good predictor of success in life this is clearly an important finding and demonstrates the value of undertaking international comparisons. Participation in the workforce is highly correlated with school and tertiary education achievement. Employment rates for those without an upper secondary qualification are much lower than those with such qualifications. There is also a close relationship between earnings and level of qualification. While it is true that opportunities exist for learning beyond the school, for example in firms, it is also the case that the majority of those who access these opportunities have higher levels of school achievement. So good foundations at school are fundamental to lifelong learning and to future success as individuals.

In their new communiqué in 2001, *Investing in competencies for all,* the OECD Ministers reaffirmed the basic directions of 1996. However, they pointed out that there were many challenges ahead if lifelong learning was to become a reality: the need for basic education as the foundation on which other competencies need to be built; the need to identify the competencies needed for the knowledge economy and society; the need to address the inequities in education, including the digital divide; and the need to set high standards for schools.

An agenda for future work of the OECD was outlined. This agenda included the clarification of the competencies individuals need in the knowledge economy; the need to identify innovative policy options for the financing of lifelong learning; and further development of the indicators of performance, particularly the assessment of the preparedness of young people for adult life.
They concluded:

> Our shared vision is of increased levels of competence in our populations and of a more equitable distribution of this competence. Our task is to facilitate investment in competencies for all. Investment in education and training and other opportunities is an investment in the futures of our countries and peoples. *(p. 6)*

In the following sections, I will deal with two programs that have the potential to progress the agenda set out by the Ministers in 1996 and 2001 – the *DeSeCo* project and the continued growth and refinement of the PISA project. It will not be possible to deal with the vital issue of reform/innovation of the school sector, though it needs to be said that without this it will not be possible to implement a *system* of lifelong learning and 'competencies for all', but clearly this issue would be the subject of a chapter (or a book) in its own right.

5. THE *DESECO* PROJECT – 1997–2003

This project *Definition and selection of competencies: Theoretical and conceptual foundations* (*DeSeCo*, 2002), commenced in 1997 under the OECD's Education Indicators program (INES), led by the Swiss Federal Statistics Office. The project's aim was to clarify what competencies, apart from reading, writing and computing, are necessary for an individual to lead an overall successful life, and for society to face the challenges of the present and the future.

The origins of the program can be found in the same sorts of concerns that are articulated in *Lifelong learning for all* – the recognition of the changing nature of our global society, and the potential for both increased productivity and wealth on the one hand, and growing social inequality with the consequent impact on social harmony on the other.

The role of education as an engine of productivity and potentially of equality was taken as a given by the initiators of this project. It was recognised, however, that the nature of the curriculum had become a contested topic in the contemporary developed world, and that this was part of a wider governmental concern across the OECD about the quality of education and returns on educational investment. The impetus for this project, concluded in 2003, was the view amongst a growing number of educationalists and governments that curriculum and subject-based competencies were inadequate as a basis for a successful life in the contemporary era, and for the achievement of a harmonious society.

The aim of the project was to develop a conceptual framework within which individual 'key' (or generic) competencies appropriate to the contemporary world could be developed. This development was to take place within a lifelong learning perspective, with the associated aim of undertaking any future assessment of such competencies in an international setting. One advantage of this approach is that it provides a bridge between school-based assessment of key competencies and those assessing key competencies in adults, hence reinforcing the links between various phases of life and learning over the lifespan.

The project was guided by a number of questions:

- Is it possible to identify competencies which are needed for successful participation in a variety of fields of life?
- How can such competencies be theoretically justified?
- Are such competencies interdependent?
- To what extent are they valid from country to country?
- To what extent are they independent of age, gender, etc?
- Are different competencies needed in different phases of life?
- How can indicators of these competencies be developed?

The program of work was the most extensive ever undertaken to answer these and other questions. A number of activities were undertaken: an analysis of international studies on educational indicators; a study reviewing scholarly work on the concept of competence; expert papers on key competencies by academics from different disciplines and different countries (economics, psychology, anthropology, sociology, philosophy – from Switzerland, France, Germany, UK and the USA); and comments on these from practitioners and policy makers. These were all discussed at a symposium in 1999 and the papers and comments later published in a book (Rychen and Salganik 2001). Following this an analysis of country specific key competencies was undertaken and a second symposium convened in 2002. A strategy paper followed, plus a second book by the same authors (Rychen and Salganik 2003).

It is not possible in this chapter to do full justice to the richness of the material, which emerged out of this extensive project, but some of the key issues and insights from these perspectives can be highlighted.

5.1 The Wider Context Within Which DeSeCo Has Operated

Before examining some of the arguments and competencies which emerged from the various disciplines, it is necessary to place the *DeSeCo* project as a whole in its historical context – within the OECD's work on developing indicators of educational outcomes. This has been at the centre of the OECD's work, the attempt to provide data against which educational performance can be evaluated and can lead to improvement.

Salganik (2001) suggests that it is possible to categorise these developments as first and second generation work. In the original work there was an attempt to develop cross-curricular competencies, in addition to curriculum bounded knowledge and skills. In addition there was the widely discussed attempts to obtain cross-national measures of adult literacy. The latter work led to the first international comparable measures of the relationship between literacy skills and earnings. At the same time, there was a recognition that the then (1998) existing indicators, which relied on analysis of formal schools (e.g. attainment and costs), did not give a full picture of the meaning of ' human capital' defined as the skills, knowledge and competencies of individuals relevant to economic activity. It was acknowledged that there was a need to focus more directly on *individual* attributes which were developed in a variety of contexts beyond formal schooling

The second generation of studies culminated in a project for assessing life skill (ALL), and the Program for International Student Assessment (PISA) focused on the knowledge and competencies of 15 year olds, first implemented in 2001 and since in 2003. This is discussed below.

These projects, though not designed as a coordinated project, have led to the acceptance within the OECD Secretariat and increasingly in many of the OECD countries, that the desired outcomes of education are broader than subject related knowledge, and are acquired beyond formal schooling, and that these outcomes are a preparation of life in all its facets. In this aspect of its educational work the OECD Secretariat has been acting as a think tank seeking to influence public policy across the OECD.

The result should be that within a few years it is likely that the work preceding *DeSeCo*, and the work undertaken during it, will lead to information on learning outcomes which is much broader than anything we have had to date. These projects and *DeSeCo* itself mark a significant change in thinking about the nature of human capacities. It is a movement away from narrow cognitive emphases exemplified in the articulation and dominance of the IQ movement to capacities that are more related to real life and extend far beyond the cognitive.

5.2 The Multidisciplinary Nature of the Project

This approach was a response to the view of the project director that the topic of human competencies for a successful life is not a matter for educationalists alone. As Rychen puts it:

> [this topic] is situated at the forefront of research across the social sciences as it addresses issues fundamental to human behaviour and society's institutions with regard to the challenges of contemporary social problems and broad complex demands from different sectors. *(2001: 5)*

The breadth of this project can be seen as both a strength and a weakness. Its strength is that, arguably, it has enabled new perspectives and insights to be brought to bear on this topic which till now has been largely limited to the views of educationalists. It can also be argued that the breadth of the project has made it clear the competencies which have been identified cannot all be developed within formal educational institutions, let alone schools. In this way the project makes an indirect contribution to the wider lifelong learning agenda of the OECD.

The weakness, however, is that unsurprisingly, the variety of perspectives produced a large number of competencies with consensus limited to a few very broad areas. The attempt to go beyond the very broad areas meant a process of selection necessarily based on values. Furthermore, as one of the commentators on the academic papers suggests, 'attention will be directed, inevitably, to that which can be measured' (Harris 2001).

The fact, however, that there was a recognition in the project that decisions about the nature of the competencies and how they are developed and assessed are essentially political and ethical, mitigates these weaknesses. As Rychen puts it:

> Conceiving key competencies is inevitably influenced by what is valued in society and by the goals set for human and socio economic development... the challenge is to define key competencies broadly taking into account the plurality of values and life patterns. *(2001: 7)*

Notwithstanding the difficulties each of the contributors acknowledged, all but one of them was able to identify a set of competencies that from their normative perspective are the key to a successful life in contemporary democratic society.

From the philosophical perspective French academics Canto-Sperber and Dupuy develop their argument from their interests in cognitive science/philosophy of mind and moral and social philosophy. They argue that much educational thinking in the West is based on a limited conception of skill and competence which has emerged from behavioural and cognitive psychology and neuroscience. They argue that this approach conceptualised competence as being:

> The capacity to follow abstract rules or algorithms and bringing them to bear on basic data that result themselves from a decomposition of the environment into recognizable elements. *(2001: 68)*

This approach, they argue, is inadequate and fails to take into account such things as intuition and common sense (See Polanyi 1958, Oakeshott 1975).

This view is combined with a perspective from moral philosophy, specifically what they term 'value ethics' which involves an analysis of the possibility of living a good life and the kinds of values that make a life meaningful. In contrast to utilitarianism and Kantianism this shifts the emphasis from the intrinsic features of action (e.g. happiness for all in the case of utilitarianism to the agent him/herself and his/her beliefs, feeling, dispositions, etc.) That is, the focus is on the capacity to the agent to act rightly. In addition there is a need to ground these capacities within conceptions of society so that the subjective mental state is linked to the objective state of the world.

What emerges from their thinking is a constellation of five key competencies: for dealing with complexity; perceptive competencies; normative competencies; cooperative competencies; and narrative competencies.

How do these competency areas interact in the lives of individuals? Coping with complexity is thought of as a metacompetency. It consists of the capacity to recognize patterns and relationships between what has been experienced previously and new experiences. However, they argue that this is not sufficient to make one's way in the world because the limitations of human cognition make it impossible to take account of all details in all situations. Hence there is a need to discriminate between the relevant and irrelevant elements of a situation. In effect this is a kind of practical intelligence which enables a person to be sensitive to the context/situation and to adapt their actions to this context – these capacities are what they term, perceptive competencies.

However, there is also a need to think about the rightness of one's action. Such competencies depend on the beliefs and character of the agent and on their conception of the nature of the good life. In addition, there is the need for a capacity to distance themselves from the judgement, to look forward, to evaluate human actions and right and wrong and to manifest autonomy, amongst other things. These are what they refer to as normative competencies. The linking of the capacities of the agent with the wider world requires cooperative competencies. Here Canto-Sperber and Dupuy take a Rawlsian approach where society is seen as a cooperative venture for mutual advantage, but one marked by conflict as well as cooperation. The capacities which are needed here are the ability to trust and to put oneself in another's place.

Finally there is the need for narrative competencies – an area they feel is widely ignored. This is the ability to construct and conceive plans for one's life, both individual episodes and the whole of life. It is the capacity to makes stories of one's own life and the life of others, intelligible.

For the French sociologist, Phillipe Perrenoud (2001), the question of whether it is possible to develop key competencies both across and within cultures is highly problematic. He argues that this is a deeply ideological task particularly when one considers the notion of normality. Nevertheless, he suggests it is possible to advance the debate if one confines oneself to the developed world, though even then great care must be taken. The central question for Perrenoud is what are the competencies needed for actors to operate in various social fields as understood in the work of Bourdieu?

He points out that to be an actor in a field(s) there needs to be a familiarity with the rules, rights, language, etc. in the field. He hypothesises that there are a number of competencies which transverse all social fields which are needed to avoid being at the mercy of others who seek to fashion the field to their own ends. These are: the ability to identify, evaluate and defend one's own rights, resources, etc; to be able to develop strategies either individually or in groups; to be able to cooperate; to build democratic organizations; to resolve conflict; to be able to change the rules; and to negotiate social orders which allow peaceful co-existence.

He argues further that these competencies are developed through a process of socialisation, which encourages a limited autonomy. One of the aims of the education system should be to enhance this autonomy largely through developing a reflective approach emphasising critical thinking.

The approach taken by the American economists Levy and Murnane (2001) is a more empirical one than the other contributors, and one limited to the competencies required for successful life in a market economy, as measured by lifetime earning. They define competencies as skills, both cognitive and non-cognitive. They develop a list of competencies which are empirically demonstrated to lead to higher income. These are: basic literacy and numeracy; ability to communicate effectively; ability to work productively in groups; emotional intelligence – particularly the capacity to relate well to others; and the ability to use computers. They also point out that there is a premium paid to people with educational qualifications, though why is not clear.

Through the use of a variety of research methods such as studies of earnings inequality, wage functions (statistical analyses of data which affects wages), ethnographic studies of work, etc. they have established relationships (though not necessarily causal ones) between competencies and wages. They are not clear whether each of the competencies can be viewed as independent or about whether the various levels within each competency impact on earnings. They conclude that all these competencies can be learnt and that they are likely to be important to facets of life outside the capacity to earn a living.

5.3 Common Ground

All the multidisciplinary perspectives were reviewed by a number of academics and practitioners. Robert Kegan (2001), a developmental psychologist, argues that while there are differences between them, all the contributors argue for a level of mental complexity which is much higher than it has been in past decades. This mental complexity goes beyond a socialised mind to what he calls the self-authoring mind. What is meant by this is a level of autonomy which allows us to distance ourselves from the socialising process, though not at the expense of developing relationships with others and with wider communities. Kegan's conclusion, one implicit in all the contributions, is that we need to develop in adults an 'internal authority' which enables us reflect on their own values and society's prescriptions in an ongoing way. This, he claims, is a difficult task for the majority of people and that notions of competency for a post-modern world, which arguably is what is needed today, are currently beyond the competence of all but a small proportion of the population. The very fact that this is the case however, provides an intellectual justification for an emphasis on lifelong learning in educational policy.

5.4 Conclusions of the DeSeCo Project

The project concluded that the notion of competence is an important one and goes well beyond the notion of skill. Competent performance implies the mobilising of knowledge, cognitive and practical skills, as well as attitudes, emotions, values and motivations. Competencies become 'key' when they 'contribute to highly valued outcomes at the individual and societal level, are instrumental for meeting important complex demands and challenges in a wide variety of contexts and are important for all individuals', (*DeSeCo, Summary of the final report*, 2003a: 3).

They identified three main categories of competencies:

- Interacting in socially heterogeneous groups,
- Acting autonomously
- Using tools interactively

The specific competencies in the first category – the ability to relate well to others, to cooperate and to manage and resolve conflict, were seen to be vital to life in a globalised world and increasingly in individual multicultural societies. In the second category – the ability to act within the 'big picture', to form and conduct life plans, the ability to defend and assert one's rights, interests, needs and limits – are all vital in various aspects of life, work, family and civic society. The third category included the ability to use interactively language, symbols and texts, knowledge and information, and technology. This category had in mind reading, mathematical and scientific literacy, amongst other things.

Underpinning all these is a critical and reflective stance. The conclusion of the project was that if we are to understand the idea of key competencies, it is necessary to go beyond the outcomes of typical curriculum of formal institutions, which stress variously recalling knowledge and sometimes thinking abstractly, to the kind of capacity that is developed through the integration of formal and informal knowledge. These are capacities which can only be developed gradually over the lifespan.

Clearly this approach to the nature of competency provides a persuasive justification for lifelong learning, and in particular the need to provide opportunities for adults to develop and learn throughout their lives. In addition though, this approach also obviously has potential implications for the curriculum and structures of schools and tertiary institutions.

The project also supported the principle that the key competencies were interrelated and that these 'constellations of key competencies' (*DeSeCo,*

Summary of the final report, 2003a: 4) will vary with the contexts in which they are applied.

The implications of this work for future international assessment is significant. This will be dealt with after the next section which examines the current state of international assessments, and their contribution to our understanding of generic competencies. Irrespective of the future impact on international assessment, the *DeSeCo* project, through the development of the multidisciplinary competency framework itself, serves a number of purposes. As Scott Murray suggests (2003), it will enable researchers in a range of academic disciplines not known for cooperating, to discuss the issue of key competencies within a common structure. The project also enables those involved in school-based assessment to understand the context of assessing key competencies in adults and visa versa. This should have the effect of improving the assessments in both contexts.

6. PROGRAM FOR INTERNATIONAL STUDENT ASSESSMENT (AND ADULT LITERACY ASSESSMENT)

Prior to 2000, OECD studies of adult achievement and school student achievement were very different. Virtually all school achievement assessment focussed on curriculum knowledge that was common between countries. By contrast, adult achievement of literacy, as in the International Adult Literacy Survey (IALS) and the Adult Literacy and Life Skills survey, focussed on tasks of differing complexity and difficulty as the basis for measurement. However the Program of International Student Assessment (PISA) of 2000 and 2003 rests on the same theoretical basis at the IALS and ALL studies (see OECD (1999) *Measuring student knowledge and skills: A new framework of assessment*). PISA is an internationally standardised test which covers the domains of reading and mathematical and scientific literacy. It also covers an additional domain of problem solving. Emphasis is on the capacity to function in various situations within each domain.

The PISA program is a collaborative program which measures how well students at age 15, the end of compulsory schooling in most OECD countries, are prepared to meet the challenges of contemporary society. The assessment reflects the curriculum in the OECD, but is focused on the use of knowledge in the real world. The assessment reflects the capacity of students to engage in lifelong learning by using their school-developed knowledge in a variety of non-school settings. Thus, while PISA does assess curriculum knowledge, it also examined the capacity to reflect and apply knowledge.

The assessment takes place every three years, through the use of pen and paper tests. The survey was implemented in 43 countries in 2000/2 and 42 countries in 2003. Between 5,000 and 10,000 students from 150 plus schools are typically tested in each country. It is administered over a three-year cycle covering reading literacy (2000), mathematical literacy (2003) and scientific literacy (2006).

The reasons for adopting this approach are outlined in the PISA 2003 Assessment Framework (OECD, 2003b). In summary the OECD believes that certain broad general skills are essential to success in life beyond school. These include communication, adaptability, flexibility, problem solving, and the use of information technologies. These competencies are developed across the curriculum and assessment of them requires a cross-curriculum focus. In addition to the specific domains measured in PISA, the application of knowledge in adult life depends on the acquisition of broader concepts than knowledge acquisition in schools. In mathematics, for example, the capacity to reason quantitatively is more important than answering textbook questions.

It is obvious that students cannot learn everything in school that they need in adult life. Hence they need to develop the ability to learn in the future. This includes the ability to learn independently and in groups where people are dependent on each other. For this reason an assessment of the capacity to regulate students' own learning was included in the 2003 assessment as a core component.

The reason for outlining the basic elements of the PISA in this context is to point out the contribution it is beginning to make to an understanding of generic competencies as a basis for lifelong learning. In essence it could be argued that by focussing on these wider concepts it is directing and informing educational policy in OECD countries, moving them towards a need to consider the development of a wider range of human abilities than currently exists.

Of course the PISA test is not without its critics. Some have pointed out that the models underpinning this test (and the IALS) do not capture the ability of lower skilled students to accomplish tasks that require reading in non-standard ways (Scott Murray 2003). Others argue that the OECD has helped to produce a testing culture within countries which dominates all educational activities. Resources tend to follow test results (Schleicher 2003), which means other important outcomes valued by teachers are ignored.

However the counter arguments are very powerful. International assessment has moved the focus of public attention towards outcomes which makes educational institutions more accountable. The assessment of adults' competence provides data, which enables us to see how what is known in schools, translates to competence in later life. Much of the focus of educational policy to date has been on the transition from school to work, but it could be extended to other phases in life. Also by focussing on things that are not currently part of the mainstream of curriculum in many countries, the international assessments of the type PISA and the ALL represent are a force for reform in education systems, and specifically of advancing the lifelong learning agenda.

The findings of the *DeSeCo* project, moreover, have the potential to increase the range of what is currently being assessed, and to provide a fuller picture of what students have learnt and can achieve. Most of the current assessment concentrates only on the first of the *DeSeCo* categories – using tools interactively. There is now the basis at least to start work on assessments that cover the other two categories – acting autonomously and interacting in heterogeneous groups. Future PISA assessments will undoubtedly incorporate these latter categories, though much technical work remains to be done. In the longer term it will mean that international assessment will provide a far richer and multidimensional view of student outcomes than exists currently.

7. INTERNATIONAL ASSESSMENT AND EDUCATIONAL POLICY

The link between international assessment and educational policy in individual countries is, however, still not fully developed. Where clear comparisons can be drawn, OECD statistics and test results act as a benchmarking exercise which governments find difficult to ignore completely, particularly if they are taken up by parliamentary oppositions and understood by the wider public. However the OECD's effectiveness is based on the provision of data that is often not completely transparent and can be ignored by individual governments when the public is unable to understand the significance of them. The hope for the framework built by *DeSeCo* is that it can become the basis for better assessments in the future so that they become more transparent and clearer in their implications for the individual. That would result in a stronger relationship between assessments and public policy in education, and help to overcome the ever-present danger of undervaluing outcomes in education which are not covered by existing assessments.

8. CONCLUSION

Lifelong learning for all remains an ambitious aim for which a long-term strategy is needed. As a recent OECD policy brief *Lifelong learning* (OECD 2004: 4) points out there is still the need for further reform in five areas: need to improve access; ensuring foundation skills for all; recognising all forms of learning, not just formal education; ensuring collaboration between a wide range of partners; and resource allocation.

The OECD has been playing a role in addressing some of these issues, through its country reviews, its research, its projects, its assessment programs, its statistics and its more general publications. This chapter has focused on work in defining the competencies needed for a successful life and the international testing projects. There is no doubt that these programs have been a step forward in encouraging lifelong learning, though how significant a step remains to be seen. By developing and assessing a wider range of competencies than have traditionally been the domain of formal education, they have encouraged formal education to expand its curriculum and to focus on outcomes that have traditionally been ignored. It is to be hoped that this will motivate a greater proportion of young people to stay in formal education and to ensure they achieve skills which are the foundation of later learning. These curriculum and assessment reforms should in turn have an impact on the recognition of non-formal education and create links between various education sectors, and between educational systems and other parts of society. Much indeed remains to be done in many countries, but a start has been made in many of them. A major question, if continuing reform in the areas mentioned above is to be achieved, is availability of resources. In the OECD's 2000 publication *Where are the resources for lifelong learning?* the authors focussed on the rates of return to lifelong learning and suggested that this could be achieved in two ways – reducing costs and increasing efficiency, and by increasing the quality and benefits of outcome of lifelong learning. Cost saving and efficiencies are easy to suggest though their implementation is often difficult.

The most obvious strategies which have been used across OECD countries is by cutting teaching costs, coordination and rationalisation between sectors, such as merging schools, bringing vocational and general education together, by policies for the recognition of prior learning, by creating competition between the public and private sectors, and by the use of ICT. Less obvious strategies include the devolution of financial responsibility to the level of the provider which can provide incentives for cost reduction that do not exist when responsibility is at national or regional levels. Similarly, attempts have been made to provide incentives for increasing quality of provision along with cost effectiveness.

Clearly these policies of decentralisation, marketisation and doing more with less have had an impact on all areas of government policy across the OECD, not just education. However it is now being argued that these measures will not be sufficient to fund all the changes required if lifelong learning is to become a reality, and it is for that reason that all countries have been experimenting with the mobilisation of private resources to supplement public resources. There seems little doubt the influence of the OECD has been very significant in this area. The underpinning principle which guides these efforts is the sharing of benefits which sits alongside a view that individuals and firms generally under-invest in learning, given the benefits they receive. The attempt is to devise schemes which divide the costs of education and training equitably between the beneficiaries, without reducing opportunities for those with few resources.

There is still much to be done and many debates to be had, but first steps to lifelong learning for all have at least been taken.

9. REFERENCES

Canto-Sperber, M. & Dupuy, J. P. (2001) 'Competencies for the good life and the good society' in D. S. Rychen & L. H. Salganik (eds.) *Defining and selecting key competencies*. Seattle: Hogrefe & Huber, pp. 67-92.

Definitions and Selection of Key Competencies: Contributions to the Second DeSeCo Symposium, (2002) Geneva: Switzerland, 11-13 February, 2002.

Harris, B. (2001) 'Are all key competencies measurable? An education perspective' in D. S. Rychen & L. H. Salganik (eds.) *Defining and selecting key competencies*. Seattle: Hogrefe & Huber, pp. 222-227.

International Commission on the Development of Education (1972) *Learning to be: the world of education today and tomorrow*. E. Faure (et al) Paris: UNESCO

Kegan, R. (2001) 'Competencies as working epistemologies: Ways we want adults to know' in D. S. Rychen & L. H. Salganik (eds.) *Defining and selecting key competencies*. Seattle: Hogrefe & Huber, pp.192-204.

Levy, F. & Murnane, R. J. (2001) 'Key competencies critical to economic success' in D. S. Rychen & L. H. Salganik (eds.) *Defining and selecting key competencies*. Seattle: Hogrefe & Huber, pp. 151-173.

Oakeshott, M. (1975) *On human conduct.* Oxford: Clarendon Press.

OECD (Organisation for Economic Cooperation and Development) (1996) *Lifelong learning for all.* Meeting of the Education Committee at Ministerial Level, 16-17 January, 1996, Paris: OECD.

OECD (Organisation for Economic Cooperation and Development) (1999) *Measuring student knowledge and skills: a new framework for assessment.* Paris: OECD.

OECD (Organisation for Economic Cooperation and Development) (2000) *Where are the resources for lifelong learning ?* Paris: OECD.

OECD (Organisation for Economic Cooperation and Development) (2001) *Investing in competencies for all.* Communiqué, from the Meeting of the OECD Education Ministers,
3-4 April, 2001, Paris: OECD. Available at *www.oecd.org/media*

OECD (Organisation for Economic Cooperation and Development) (2003a) *Definition and selection of competencies: Theoretical and conceptual foundations*, *DeSeCo.* "Summary of the final report: Key Competencies for a successful life and a well-functioning society". Paris: OECD.Available at www.statistik.admin.ch/stat_ch/ber15/deseco/deseco_finalreport_summary.pdf

OECD (Organisation for Economic Cooperation and Development) (2003b) *The PISA 2003 Assessment Framework.* Paris: OECD. Available at www.pisa.oecd.org/

OECD (Organisation for Economic Cooperation and Development) (2004) *Lifelong learning.* Policy brief, February, 2004, Paris: OECD. Available at www.oecd.org/publications/Pol_brief

Perrenoud, P. (2001) 'The key to social fields: Competencies of an autonomous actor' in D.S. Rychen & L.H. Salganik (eds.) *Defining and selecting key competencies.* Seattle: Hogrefe & Huber, pp. 121-149,

Polanyi, M. (1958) *Personal knowledge: Towards a post-critical philosophy.* Chicago: University of Chicago Press.

Rychen, D. S (2001) 'Introduction' in D.S. Rychen & L.D.Salganik (eds.) *Defining and selecting key competencies.* Seattle: Hogrefe & Huber, pp.1-15.

Rychen, D. S. & Salganik, L.H. (eds.) (2001) *Defining and selecting key competencies.* Seattle: Hogrefe & Huber.

Rychen, D.S. & Salganik, L.H. (eds.) (2003) *Key competencies for a successful life and well-functioning society.* Cambridge: Mass., Gottingen: Hogrefe & Huber.

Schleicher, A. (2003) 'Developing a long-term strategy for international assessments' in
    D.S.Rychen & L. D.Salganik (eds.) *Key competencies for a successful life and
    well-functioning society*. Cambridge: Mass., Gottingen: Hogrefe & Huber, pp.161-186.

Scott Murray, T. (2003) 'Reflections on international competence assessments' in
    D.S.Rychen & L.D.Salganik (eds.) *Key competencies for a successful life and well-
    functioning society*. Cambridge: Mass., Gottingen: Hogrefe & Huber, pp.135-159.

CHAPTER 7

LESLEY SCANLON

GRADUATE ATTRIBUTES AND THE TRANSITION TO HIGHER EDUCATION

1. INTRODUCTION

In Australia the term 'graduate attributes' is used to refer to the generic skills, knowledge, dispositions and attitudes undergraduates develop during their university studies. In this chapter, however, I extend the context in which the term is used to include a university preparation course, the competency-based Tertiary Preparation Certificate (TPC). This course was developed and delivered by Technical and Further Education (TAFE) the largest provider of vocation education in New South Wales, Australia. The discussion focuses on students' perceptions and interactions with the graduate attributes and is based on the findings of a four year study of adult learners conducted by the author as a teacher-researcher (Scanlon 2002). [1]

This study produced some interesting findings not only in its identification of the graduate attributes acknowledged by students as significant in their transition to university but also in its identification of the teacher attributes critical in students' acquisition of these same graduate attributes. These two findings make the study significant in the context of lifelong learning because it is recognised, for example, by Candy, Crebert & O'Leary (1994) and Hager, Holland & Beckett (2002) that participation in lifelong learning is reliant upon generic abilities such as those examined here. This link between graduate attributes and lifelong learning is highlighted throughout the chapter. [2] The chapter is divided into four distinct sections. The first section focuses on the learning context and examines the nature of the course in which the study was conducted, identifies the graduate attributes which underpin the course, establishes a profile of the students in the study and explores the reasons why these students returned to formal education. The focus of the second section is a discussion of the graduate attributes identified

P. Hager and S. Holland (eds.), Graduate Attributes, Learning and Employability, 125–148.
© 2006 *Springer.*

by students as essential in their transition to university. The third section examines the teacher attributes identified by students as crucial in student acquisition of graduate attributes. Finally the chapter indicates the destinations of the students following the course and the changes to their student identities resulting from their acquisition of graduate attributes.

2. THE ADULT LEARNING CONTEXT

2.1 The Course

In Australia, Sheehan (2001: 5) argues there is 'no over-arching framework, no comprehensive and overall policy of lifelong learning', nonetheless, he suggests that formal and informal agencies are 'getting things done'. A good example of one of the ways in which things are being done is the TPC course. A course recognised by TAFE as having a key role in lifelong learning. This key role was signalled in the Prevocational *English & Humanities Journal* (1995: 28), which located the course in the context of lifelong learning and acknowledged that such courses are only the beginning of 'an ongoing lifelong process'.

To facilitate this learning across the life span each module in the course was underpinned with graduate attributes the acquisition of which the Humanities Journal (1995: 28) suggested would result in the development of 'lifelong learning skills', such as, a willingness to learn new ideas, flexibility, adaptability, responsiveness, open-mindedness and adaptability to change. There was, however, no attempt to develop a comprehensive profile of a lifelong learner, nor was reference made to the work of Candy, Crebert & O'Leary (1994: 43-44) whose much more extensive profile was developed the previous year for the National Board of Employment, Education and Training. Nonetheless, it is clear that TAFE intended the course to play a significant role in lifelong learning by providing mature age students with the opportunity to return to formal education and to make the transition to university.

The role of TAFE NSW in lifelong learning has changed over time much like Further Education in the United Kingdom. Originally TAFE provided initial trade training to early school leavers and a range of leisure courses for adults. More recently, as in the United Kingdom, TAFE has provided second chance education to adults through access courses and alternate pathways to university education. These pathways and links between educational institutions are important because Sheehan (2001) argues they provide the opportunities for learning across the life span. One of the most popular and successful alternate pathways in TAFE over the past 20 years has been the TPC course. Through this course adult students gain entry to university either through the competitive University Admission Index in which they compete with school leavers or through a variety of adult entry schemes.

There have been a number of significant changes in the past 20 years to the way the course has provided for the needs of adult learners. The original 1983 course was in effect two distinct courses one for students of Applied Science and the other for students of Arts, Humanities and Social Sciences. The two courses were integrated in 1989 providing students with a more flexible programme through wider subject choices. However, the most significant changes occurred in 1993 following the Australian Federal Government's identification and development of generic competencies and the subsequent adoption of competency-based education and training. As a result the course was not only reconstituted in a competency format but was also underpinned by a set of generic competencies, the Mayer Key Competencies.

It is these competencies which constitute the graduate attributes which are the focus of discussion in this chapter. I use the term 'graduate attributes' rather than 'Mayer Key Competencies', unless specific reference is made to the Mayer Committee's development of these competencies. There are two reasons for this: first, the term has wider currency outside of Australia; second, as Hager, Holland & Beckett (2002) suggest, 'attribute' better describes the skills, attitudes, dispositions and values which make up generic competencies.

2.2 The Attributes

These attributes, the Mayer Key Competencies, were developed in Australia as a result of a series of education policy initiatives by successive Federal Labor Governments in the period 1983–1996. These initiatives originated from government recognition that Australia had lost its competitive, international trading position. One explanation for the nation's perceived lack of international competitiveness, a lack similarly identified by nation states across the industrial world, was that the workforce was not sufficiently flexible or multi-skilled to enable Australia to operate competitively in the global market.

Successive Federal governments claimed that Australia's economic recovery must be tied to educational change, and that this change should take the form of competency-based education and training. The result was a plethora of policy documents which resulted in the reconstitution of education and training in a competency-based format. A key feature of the implementation of these educational changes was the identification and development in two key reports, commissioned by the Australia Education Council, *Young People's Participation in Post-compulsory Education and Training* (Finn Report) and *Putting General Education to Work: The Key Competencies Report* (Mayer Report) of a set of generic competencies, the Mayer Key Competencies:

- Collecting, analysing and organising ideas and information
- Communicating ideas and information
- Planning and organising activities
- Working with others and in teams
- Using mathematical ideas and techniques
- Solving problems
- Using technology

These competencies were of course not identified and developed in isolation and there are similarities between the competencies identified in Australia and similar generic lists developed at the same time in the United States, the United Kingdom and New Zealand (Harris *et al.* 1995).

Government interest in graduate attributes and the resurgence of interest in lifelong learning Field (2001: 10-11) argues can be located in the economic challenges resulting from globalisation and rapid technological change. A similar connection was recently made by the Department of Education, Science and Training in Australia (2003). Sheehan (2001: 4) points out, however, that OECD ministers recognised that lifelong learning is about more than economic survival. It is also about social inclusiveness, democratic engagement and personal fulfilment. In Australia it is now recognised that lifelong learning is also about 'the economic well-being of the individual' (Department of Education, Science and Training 2003: 2). The recent strategy paper from the Directorate for Education, Employment, Labour and Social Affairs Education Committee (*DeSeCo*) (2002: 12) similarly extended the economic focus to include individual rights and the conduct of personal projects. Within the same project Ouane (2002: 4) highlights an approach to competencies from the standpoint of the individual's empowerment and self-fulfilment and Rychen (2002: 5) argues that any set of key competencies must not only contribute to economic and social success but also enable individuals to live a successful life.

In Australia following the identification and development of the Mayer Key Competencies the Federal Government funded projects involving schools and TAFE were established to make recommendations on the teaching, assessment and reporting of the key competencies. At the same time educational institutions imported the competencies into curriculum documents as graduate attributes. It was these curriculum documents and these attributes with which students interacted when they returned to formal education in the TPC course. However, before examining how students interacted with the graduate attributes it is first essential to establish a profile of the students and to investigate their reasons for returning to formal education.

2.3 The Students

All of the students in the study came from within a 20 kilometre radius of the large urban TAFE college in NSW where the study was conducted and were thus representative of the socio-economic profile of this area. It was an area characterised by economic hardship reflected in high youth unemployment, a heavy reliance on social security benefits, and young single (female) parent families. 26 of the 35 students who were interview participants in the study were aged between 19 – 29 and of these 20 were female students. This high proportion of female students in the course can be explained not only by the area demographic but also because the college provided a number of alternate pathways to encourage women to return to formal education; the TPC course being one such pathway.

Within the group of 26 young students 11 of the 20 females were single parents. As a consequence the students in the study were heavily reliant on social security benefits. Overall 26 students received either single parent pensions or study assistance frequently supplemented by part-time work. Of the remaining nine students, five were married and did not work or receive social security benefits, relying on the income of their partners, while 4 students supported themselves solely through part-time work. All of the students in the study shared two things: school had not been a successful learning experience for them and none of the students completed their school education. Students with this kind of educational profile recent research (European Centre for the Development of Vocational Training (Cedefop) 2002, Crichton & Kinsel 2002) suggests are less likely to engage in post-school education.

2.3.1 Returning to formal education: 'Unfinished business'

The recent Danish Adult Education Research project found that the reasons why individuals return to formal education are complex. Based on the findings of this study Illeris (2003: 14) argues that the current rhetoric and expectation of learning across the life span has had an impact on the way adults now approach returning to formal learning. Its previously overt voluntary nature where students sought enlightenment, emancipation and empowerment has been replaced, it is argued, by force and persuasion in the sense that not engaging in formal learning is to risk 'social and economic marginalization'. The Danish project found that students' motives for returning to formal education are not straightforward but rather a mixture of social, personal and/or technical factors many of which are located in students' past learning experiences.

The significance of these experiences was highlighted by Cedefop (2002: 12) which identified the importance of early school experiences as the time when students discover learning as a positive way of spending time. It was suggested that early learning establishes the foundation for individuals to learn across the life span. Crichton and Kinsel (2002: 144) argue that if students are not successful at school they develop less complex social identities and view themselves in singular, mono-dimensional ways. As a result of this restrictive view they suggest that students cannot see beyond the present and are unable to perceive the need for education.

The current study on which the discussion in this chapter is based presents a very different view, however, and found that although students did not develop a positive attitude to learning at school and did see themselves in mono-dimensional terms in the sense of their learner identities, nonetheless, they were still able to look to the future and identify their need for further formal education. The study found that rather than positive early experiences and success at school it was the negative experiences of school combined with events in adult life which induced students to embark on a return to formal education and subsequent continued learning. These events or 'punctuation marks' generate learning needs for adults and are often associated with family and work structures (Merriam 1994: 76).

Significant punctuation marks for students in the study which induced them to return to formal education included, for example, 'placating a parent'. In these cases parents issued an ultimatum to unemployed young people 'do something or leave home', as one student expressed it. In other cases there were parents of young children who themselves wanted to be 'role models' for their children. Like the young mother who did not want to be 'just another single mum' but a mother who also studied. Another student also wanted to provide an example for his young children and emphasised the importance of not wasting their educational opportunities at school but at the same time encouraged them to pursue education across the lifespan, 'education's for your whole life', he told them.

For other students the punctuation marks were associated with employment. Some students found that without formal qualifications it was either difficult to obtain work or to obtain meaningful, well paid work, 'I found out how hard it was to get a job, that's why I came back'. For others it was not being promoted because of their lack of formal qualifications, 'when I missed out on promotion I wondered if I would get anywhere in the industry'. Still other students found being made redundant from long held jobs enabled them to establish the link, for the first time, between education and work when they unsuccessfully sought alternative employment. As one student put it, 'that's when I hit the wall.' For these students redundancy provided both the impetus and the opportunity to return to formal education.

A very powerful motive for all students in returning to formal education was the opportunity to renegotiate the learner identity they acquired at school and which had hitherto proved an obstacle to formal learning. Thirty years ago Ohliger (cited in Boshier 1998: 9) identified schools as formal institutions which have the proclivity of 'defining people as inadequate, insufficient, lacking and incomplete.' This was the experience of all of the students in the study and in order to forge a new identity students had to unlearn their negative past experiences and forge new learner identities through positive new experiences which formed the basis of their new learner reality. In adulthood students were determined to learn their way out of their restrictive school identities, such as being 'tagged as a slow learner' or being thought of as 'an idiot'.

What is evident in all these motives is a sense of unfinished business. It is as though the source of students' past unsuccessful learning, the school, was also the source for their return to formal learning. For this reason it is therefore important to consider the learning identities students acquired at school.

2.3.2 School learner identities
Students' school identities can be conceptualised as ideal type constructs which Hargreaves (1977: 280) argues act as powerful defining mechanisms in the way they describe and evaluate students. Once students appropriate these school identities they endure for as long as they remain plausible explanations of the institutional reality of students' learning. However, these identities are revisable and this is where lifelong learning plays a crucial role by providing new contexts in which adults have the opportunity to renegotiate their old learner identities. In

this way identities undergo change, elaboration or qualification as they are shaped through experiences (Heritage 1984: 53). What then were these learner identities that most students felt the need to renegotiate?

Only three distinct learner categories were identified in the study and these corresponded to students with poor, mediocre and good academic grades. This limited range of categories is not unusual for as Berger (1966: 107) points out there is a limited repertoire of types available to participants in all institutional situations. Students with low and medium academic grades suggested that as well as grades other factors were considered in allocating them to lower academic classes. These factors included family problems, such as, bereavement, separation or peripatetic families and student rebelliousness. The few students in the highest academic stream considered they were there solely on the basis of their academic grades.

The study found that commitment to lifelong learning may begin not because students are successful at school but rather because they are unsuccessful. As adults in the twenty-first century the students in the study identified the need to forge new learner identities and subsequently learn their way out of their marginalised school-based learner identities. Once students took the decision to return to formal education and initiated interaction with the curriculum attributes they subsequently identified the most useful attributes in their quest to begin the completion of their school education and for many to make the transition to university.

3. KEY ATTRIBUTES IN MAKING THE TRANSITION TO HIGHER EDUCATION

The curriculum context in which the students made their return to formal learning was underpinned by the graduate attributes identified earlier in the chapter. These attributes were identified by government committees and business as essential for individuals to engage successfully in the workplace and in life in general. However, within the curriculum context of the study students found only four of these attributes essential to both course completion and to making the transition to university: Collecting, Analysing and Organising Information; Communicating Ideas and Information; Planning and Organising Activities; and Working with Others and in Teams.

Before examining students' interaction with these specific attributes I want first to look at the way students, in a general sense, responded to the graduate attributes. They did so in three different ways: as vital for assessment, essential to work and as sensitising concepts. All of the students in the study recognised the essential link between assessment and certain graduate attributes. Of these students there were those who thought, 'if those things aren't going to be marked then I would say, "All right let's forget about them." ' That is, the only significant attributes were those which contributed to the students' final assessment grade. It was after all this assessment grade which determined students' entry to university.

There were other students with extensive employment experiences who saw the attributes 'as pretty much essential' to the workplace. Still other students saw the attributes as sensitising concepts in Blumer's (1969) sense of facilitating a heightened awareness of the task at hand. By this students meant that they were more aware of what they did when they were engaged in learning and in this way the attributes facilitated their acquisition of knowledge and skills. In this sense the graduate attributes provided students with a kind of metacognitive awareness. As well as these overall responses to the graduate attributes students also spoke about the significance of four of these attributes.

3.1 Collecting, Analysing and Organising Information

Student learning in the course was structured around individual research projects, thus, making collecting, analysing and organising information pivotal to each of the assessment activities. However, students did not speak about this attribute in any holistic sense but rather referred to each of the different elements separately. Therefore in the following discussion I have followed this same convention. I recognise, however, that the three elements are integrated in real life. Not only that but as Hager (1996) has noted separate attributes form complex clusters or in *DeSeCo* (2002: 14) terminology form 'competency constellations'.

3.1.1 Collecting information
Collecting information for course research assessments was a complex activity for students. One reason for this was that the college library did not have the range of academic sources students required. Therefore, students collected information from 11 different municipal libraries, 6 university libraries and the State Library of NSW. Another reason was students' past educational experiences in which information was transmitted to them by the teacher and therefore, they had limited experience collecting information and what experience they had was restricted to small school libraries.

Other reasons for the complexity of this attribute were related to the multiple demands on adult learners. Collecting information involved issues such as time, distance, transportation, budgetary constraints, employment schedules and family commitments. It must be remembered that the adult learners' world consists of many segments: the family, work and learning segments all of which have permeable boundaries (Merriam 1994: 74). Time was a major obstacle for all students because collecting information was a weekend activity, a time when family commitments were more intense and public transportation and library opening hours were more restricted. The availability of sufficient time to collect information was made even more difficult by the fact that students frequently travelled considerable distances and, as most students relied on public transport, this not only restricted the range of libraries from which they were able to collect information but also made some libraries inaccessible.

The majority of students had financial difficulties so that funds were not always available to travel to the college each day, therefore, travelling at weekends to libraries was frequently impossible. This financial obstacle was compounded by the fact that, when students found information, they either had to spend long periods of time in libraries taking notes, or incur the additional expense of photocopying information. Many students engaged in part-time employment to defray the costs of studying and this was another obstacle requiring the co-ordination of family, work and study timetables. Single parents found weekends particularly difficult because of the lack of child-minding facilities.

Once these obstacles had been negotiated students had to decide what information to collect; again a new decision. There were an array of decision making processes that students employed as they became more experienced, self directed learners. Initially the first reference point was the module teacher, however, as students became more experienced they consulted curriculum documents to ascertain learning outcomes and assessment criteria, some students chose topics with which they were already acquainted, others who were unfamiliar with their selected topic first consulted encyclopaedias before referring to specialist texts. Students commented on their gradually improving collection procedures as they progressed from collecting 'everything' to more selective collection.

3.1.2 Analysing information
The second element and the most challenging for students was analysis. Students employed a number of different but related ways of analysing information, such as, breaking down information, establishing links between different pieces of

information, and establishing the credibility of information. There were different variations of the breaking down metaphor, for example, 'picking things out' and 'filtering down'. Ultimately, however, the purpose of this distillation technique was to enable students to locate information essential to their individual research project. Students who referred to 'establishing links' described a range of techniques including using cardboard, paper and mind maps as displays on walls. The links that students sought to establish were, for example, between events, between interpretations of these events and between accumulated factual information. Finally there were a few students who through their own self-directed learning after leaving school and prior to the course incorporated the issue of credibility into their analysis. The students who referred to this issue also commented that at this point in their learning they did not have the requisite skills to know 'what else is out there' and how much it was 'beyond my capabilities'.

3.1.3 Organising information
Organising information was the final element in this attribute. Students identified three techniques: 'cut-and-paste', the closely related 'writing bits-and-pieces' technique, and the linear technique of 'writing it straight out'. The cut and paste technique referred to by the vast majority of students was the 'glue stick and scissors' technique with only a few students using computer technology. In these techniques students either created a piece of work which was then reorganised or they created their work under headings. The destructive element in the first technique if performed manually was initially confronting for students though it was widely adopted in time by most students. Writing 'bits and pieces' was a closely related technique and again manual or computer generated sections of work were reorganised and linked.

'Writing it straight out' was a linear approach to organisation and mirrored the technique with which students were most familiar at school. Some students talked about writing from what they called 'the top', that is, beginning with the introduction while others wrote from the 'bottom up', from the conclusion. Students emphasised that their focus was on establishing a flow. This technique, however, appears to have been the least successful and most students adopted an alternative process as they became more experienced.

Interacting with the different elements of this attribute was not only cognitively challenging for students but involved students in complex negotiations across the multiple segments of their life world.

3.2 Communicating Ideas and Information

Once students had collected, analysed and organised information the next most essential attribute for them in terms of assessment was communicating their ideas and information. Students identified with this attribute in terms of whether or not they saw themselves as writers or orators.

3.2.1 Writers

Students who saw themselves as writers fell into two distinct groups. The first group preferred writing as a medium of communication because it gave them a sense of control over the communication process. This sense of control arose from the fact that written communication gave them time to 'find the right word', to revise their arguments and to plan 'what goes where'. An associated reason for writing as the preferred medium of communication was that it was a permanent record upon which students could reflect. Students in the second group said they preferred to write because they experienced profound difficulties in oral communication. These difficulties resulted from nervousness, fear and 'the stress of presenting to one's peers'. For both groups of students, however, writing provided the satisfying opportunity for 'capturing that thought on paper.'

3.2.2 Orators

The orators similarly fell into two distinct groups. In the first group were students who enjoyed the physical aspects of face-to-face interaction, the opportunity to receive feed-back, and the challenge of constructing ideas 'on your feet'. The second group chose oral communication simply because they found academic writing too demanding. It is important to note that students who identified themselves as writers or those who acquired the requisite writing skills were at a distinct advantage in the course. The reason for this being that all assessments used to calculate students' university entrance scores were written essays or reports.

3.3 Planning and Organising Activities

In discussions of planning and organising activities students referred, as they did with collecting information, to the multiple contexts of their life worlds. The contexts students referred to included; the world of the family, the world of employment and the world of learning. Again, however, it was evident that it was course assessment that was the catalyst for these activities.

3.3.1 The family

The significance of the world of the family in planning and organising activities can be explained by two things, first, the high proportion of females in the course and second, the large number of single parent families. Being female made a difference because whether or not female students had partners family organisation was their responsibility and within the family it assumed precedence over their learning activities. Students' learning in these households was considered secondary and frequently irrelevant by other members of the family. For example, even students with children in their 20s, 'did a lot of work [study] from 10 p.m. to 2 a.m, a lot of us did that. We did everything else first'. Students spoke about family celebrations and family holidays taking priority over their learning needs requiring them to delay course completion for as much as a year.

The single parents in the course tended to have younger children and consequently the students' learning time at home was restricted. One student commented on the difficulties that resulted from not being able to spend sufficient time with her children, 'the children are not easy to control when you don't give them your full attention'. Another student said that her children want her to 'give up' but because studying was important to her, she said, 'I'd be resentful'.

It was not only time that was problematic in the family but also space. Organising a space was difficult for many students and none had their own designated learning spaces. Rather they used domestic spaces when they were vacated by other members of the family. For example, one student said her house 'has two toilets and I lock myself in one and study' another had a cardboard box which was used as a portable study area. Most students, however, used kitchen and dining room tables and garages.

3.3.2 Work

The world of work was also significant in many students' planning and organising. Most students who were social security recipients also did some paid worked to supplement these benefits. To accommodate work and study students frequently made major adjustments to their lives, for example, one student said, 'I stick to a plan. I work and my study now is my social life because it's going to be my future'. Other students worked in the evenings but most found that planning work schedules around study was too difficult and they frequently reduced both their work hours and module commitments. Other students attended classes during the day and worked in the evenings, however, few students were able to sustain this kind of schedule. One student found not having money 'sucks' and tried to work in the evening, however, this left her tired and distracted and she decided to stop work, have no money and do well at the course because, 'I've got the rest of my life to earn heaps of money.' A number of students found the course more demanding than they expected and reduced both their hours of work and the number of modules they were studying.

3.3.3 Learning

Within the learning world students talked about planning in terms of setting timetables and displaying these as reminders. For example, students commented on having 'timetables sticking out of every bit of my room'. Timetabling here referred both to hours of the day set aside for learning and also the semesterised planning of assignments. There were a number of students who had extensive employment histories and drew on these experiences to sustain them in their return to study, 'In a way I treat this like work. I'm not getting paid for it, but I treat it like a job'. Treating study like work in real terms meant being punctual, learning within set hours and completion of all assignments within the given time.

3.4 Working with Others and in Teams

Within the course students worked together in many informal ways, however, in discussions of team work students referred specifically to formal arrangements for assessments. There were compulsory team work assessments in all course modules. These teams were what Schutz (1970: 83) calls 'voluntary groups'; that is, institutionally situated teams whose composition and group roles are defined by members of the group, not by the institution in which they are situated. These teams were in a constant process of evolution in which individuals defined their own unique situation in the group in order to realise their own personal interests. It was therefore necessary to adjust individual goals so that common goals could be achieved (Schutz 1970: 84).

3.4.1 Teams as learning supports

The significance of working in teams to achieve common objectives has been identified by business interests and ensconced in government policy documents as a key attribute for work participation. However, while some students in this study found teamwork supportive of learning the majority found it problematic and distracting. The students who found working in teams a supportive learning experience said things like 'you're not swimming by yourself' and made reference to the multiple contributions made by team members. Other students found the team a sounding board for their ideas. Students agreed that the key to productive teamwork was open communication and joint decision making. Ultimately, however, teamwork as a positive learning experience 'depends on the sort of people'.

3.4.2 Teams as distractions

It must be said, however, that most students found team work problematic for a number of reasons. The first was the difficulty of ensuring equitable responsibilities between team members. Students often felt that they 'were the only one doing anything'. Another reason was that students felt that their ideas were stolen by other team members or 'my ideas got corrupted with all their ideas'. For these students teams were really only individuals seemingly working together for assessment purposes, but in reality were a group of people working as individuals.

Still another reason why students found teams problematic was absenteeism. One of the reasons for this was that team work was principally an assessment requirement in the first semester and it was in the first semester that some students felt overwhelmed and withdrew from the course. The effect of this was that other students found their team 'did a disappearing act'. Absenteeism was also a problem because students' work and family commitments made scheduling meetings outside of class extremely difficult, 'people work and do things and it's just about impossible'. The final reason was the inability of some students to work together, students expressed their amazement 'at just how easily personalities can clash', a clash which was frequently the result of 'a one-eyed vision'. An interesting finding from students' comments on working in teams was that whether students considered teamwork a positive learning experience or whether they found it problematic all students agreed that they would rather work alone. The reason for this was that working in formal teams was simply 'too risky'.

Within the context of the course only four of the seven graduate attributes identified earlier in the chapter were recognised by students as critical in their transition to university. The reason for this is clear, these attributes were seen by students to be more closely associated with assessment than were the other attributes. In the study students, however, did more than identify significant graduate attributes they also identified the key attributes required of teachers if they were to assist students in their acquisition of graduate attributes.

4. ACQUIRING GRADUATE ATTRIBUTES: THE SIGNIFICANCE
OF OTHERS

It is evident from the above discussion that if students are to acquire graduate attributes it is not sufficient to identify and incorporate these attributes into curriculum documents they must also be integral to assessment. If, however, graduate attributes are to be operationalised, that is applied to new situations and tasks, Oates (2001: 3, 14–5) argues, it is dependent on pedagogical practices, such as, the inclusion of a wide range of learning contexts, problem-based learning, self-directed learning and self-reflection. A decade ago Candy, Crebert & O'Leary (1994) identified a similar range of pedagogical practices required to promote lifelong learning. Recently Cedofop (2002: 9) noted the significance of 'human-based pedagogies and face-to-face interaction' as keys to successful learning. In general terms the pedagogical practices recommended for the acquisition of graduate attributes and to encourage lifelong learning must not be didactic or directive (Sheehan 2001: 9).

The need for non-didactic and non-directive pedagogy was reiterated by students in the present study. These students had a very clear idea of the kinds of teachers they required to assist them in their acquisition of graduate attributes; teachers markedly different from those they experienced at school. The teachers that students identified from their school experiences fell into two dominant types: those who 'threw facts' at students and those who 'somehow had too much power' over students. Of course it must be remembered that these students were not successful at school and indeed did not finish school.

The principal teacher attributes students considered essential in their own acquisition of graduate attributes included: expertise, enthusiasm, communication and empathy. [A more detailed discussion of these attributes appears in Scanlon (2004)]. Taken alone, none of these attributes were sufficient, instead students expected individual teachers to have a synthesis of these attributes. The following examination of teacher attributes reveals the complex nature of the needs of adult learners and the significance of teachers in assisting students acquire graduate attributes.

4.1 Expertise

Students revealed an holistic notion of expertise which they considered encompassed: subject expertise, pedagogy expertise and curriculum expertise. Subject expertise was very much taken for granted by students in that they expected teachers to 'know their subject' and 'to know what they're talking about'. This kind of expertise, however, was not valued by students if teachers did not have pedagogical expertise, that is, if they could not plan and implement structured, effective classroom learning. Students expected teachers 'to be prepared for class'; 'to be flexible, the ones I appreciate most are not set in their ways' and to engage in student-centred pedagogical practices, 'I don't want to be spoon-fed anymore'.

The third kind of expertise was related to curriculum interpretation. For the first time students worked directly with curriculum documents the correct interpretation of which was critical if they were to successfully complete the course. Students found these documents extremely daunting because of the arcane language; it was 'too complicated', 'hard to understand' and 'complex jargon' and this ensured that the teacher played the central role in curriculum interpretation. Students explained teachers' curriculum interpreting processes in terms of the teacher, 'explained', 'went through', 'interpreted', 'simplified' and 'clarified' the language of the curriculum. In these interpretive efforts, one student explained, teachers 'give us their version of it' and another commented, teachers 'write their own little thing about it'.

4.2 Enthusiasm

The enthusiastic teacher was the teacher with spirit and vivacity who was able to transport students into a new world of learning different from the world they experienced at school. Students lived complex lives fulfilling multiple roles and meeting multiple demands in the many segments of their life-world and because of this they expressed the need to be enthused by their teachers. Teachers could do this by not 'teaching by the book, by making it interesting'. Such teachers injected a physical element into the lesson by moving around and using their voice, and they select interesting ways of doing things. Students had little patience with the teacher who taught report writing by asking students to 'report on the room'. One student's response, 'Can't you think of anything more interesting?' Multiple demands on students, as well as multiple distractions from outside the learning world, meant that teachers had to engage students through their own enthusiasm.

4.3 Communication

Effective communication fostered the inclusion of all students and teachers in the learning process. It was about ensuring that all students and teachers were involved in the educational conversation. A lack of inclusive communication had a serious impact on students' learning and students could feel excluded from class because they 'were not being listened to.' Other students withdrew from modules because the teacher was not an effective communicator. Teachers exhibited a lack of communication when they became 'edgy' if they were asked 'too many questions', which led students to wonder why people like this became teachers.

Communication between teachers was as important as communication between teachers and students because students were confused by the number of different modules they were required to study and the number of teachers with whom they interacted. This confusion increased when there was a lack of communication between the module teachers. As one student observed, 'One teacher wants something one way, the other wants it another way' and another said, 'It's a nightmare trying to clarify what the teachers want'.

4.4 Empathy

Adult students expected empathetic teachers. That is, teachers who could effectively interact with students and understand the difficulties adults faced when they return to formal education. Students expected that teachers did not 'talk down to them' and that they respected students for not 'just sitting on the dole. We're trying to do something to get a future for ourselves.' The teacher who failed to show empathy was seen to be the teacher 'who had forgotten what it was like to be a student. Forgets how hard it is.'

The above identification of teacher attributes is a clear indication of the kinds of teachers and pedagogical practices students required of teachers in their acquisition of graduate attributes. These teachers were markedly different from the teachers students encountered through their school learning experiences. It can be argued, moreover, that they are the kinds of teachers more likely to have the skills and dispositions to engage in the pedagogical practices identified in the literature (Candy, Crebert & O'Leary 1994; Sheehan 2001; Cedofop 2002) as encouraging the acquisition of graduate attributes and thus forming the basis for future engagement in lifelong learning.

5. DISCUSSION

The students in this study returned to formal education largely because they were unsuccessful learners at school and felt the need to renegotiate the learner identities they acquired there. As we have seen there were also events in their family and work situations which prompted their return to formal education. What made it possible for these students to do this was also partly their identification of TAFE, much as Gallacher *et al.* (2002: 496) found in the United Kingdom, as the 'local Tech'. That is, the institution where they elected to learn was seen to be supportive, non-threatening and not like school. Moreover, the teachers in this institution were also markedly different from the teachers students encountered in school.

Once enrolled in the course students actively sought new learner identities and developed strategies by which to determine the development of these identities. For example, some students elected what were for them the most challenging research projects as a means of saying 'Can I do it?', as one student put it. There was also recognition of the need to be active within the classroom by becoming energetic in seeking knowledge, 'you have to open your mouth and say something'. Another way students actively pursued knowledge was by spending extended time at college to compensate for what were frequently difficult learning situations at home. Active pursuit of an improved learner identity characterised the students in the course and links back to their return to formal education to attend to 'unfinished business' and to learn their way out of their marginal learner status.

Realisation of a change in their learner identities manifested itself differently to different students. For a few students it was quite sudden such as the student who received his first satisfactory assessment grade which he said, 'knocked me blooming right out of the water.' However, for most students it was a gradual change process in which some began to realise, 'that they were capable of learning and getting ahead', others began to 'feel a lot better about myself', still others spoke about gaining 'more confidence overall'. The increased positive approach to learning was accompanied by a determination on the part of students 'to get somewhere' in the sense of becoming a better learner. This was more than an end point destination for as one student said, 'I don't think you ever reach good learning. It's like walking towards it and it steps away. But you realise that you're walking into better learning.'

I suggested earlier in the chapter that the course was intended to play a key role in learning across the lifespan and that graduate attributes of the kind in the course are considered central to the pursuit of lifelong learning. It is further argued by Sheehan (2001: 11) that lifelong learning should not only enable learners to arrive at a new place but more importantly 'to travel with a different view' and have new expanded options. It is evident that the students in the study clearly travelled with a different view not only of themselves but of their place in the world. It was this change of view which enabled them to see expanded options and to arrive at a new place. The one option not previously available to these students was transition to university and this was the new place at which many students in the study arrived.

The table below shows the destinations of 28 of the 35 students in the study on their completion of the course. There are 28 students because it was these students who spoke most about their learner identities at school and for whom most of their destinations are known.

Table 1. Post-course student destinations

Grades	University	TAFE	Work	Parenting	Unknown	Total
Poor	8	3	2	1	2	16
Mediocre	6	1	0	0	1	8
High	4	0	0	0	0	4

The most significant indicator of students' new learner identities and the new places at which they arrived is that at least half of the 16 students who had poor academic grades at school made the transition to university. This is indicative of a new view because it was well known by these students that being tagged at school as slow learners meant not only that they did not finish school but that they certainly did not go to university. Of the remaining students in this category almost half continued formal education in TAFE, two students returned to full-time employment and one student, as she intended, returned to full-time parenting, the destinations of three students is unknown.

Overall, the table shows that university was the most popular destination for students with 18 students making that transition. The sample of students is very small and care must of course be taken in drawing conclusions from such a sample, but the table does indicate that students who enrolled in the course with middle to good academic profiles were more likely to continue on to study at university than were the students deemed to be academically poor. This trend is evident in that at least 75% of the middle range students (one destination unknown) and 100% of the academic students gained entrance to university. Nonetheless, that at least 50% of the academically poor students made the transition to university is a significant consequence of their acquisition of graduate attributes and their subsequent revised learner identities.

The acquisition of graduate attributes and engagement in lifelong learning are considered two hallmarks of active participation in life and work in the twenty-first century. Participation in a full, successful life in a complex changing world Ridgeway (2001: 209) argues is also closely related to certain personality attributes. One of these attributes and one that is significant to this study is 'a strong, positive self-concept that allows the individual to act confidently.' Hager, Holland & Beckett (2002: 4) similarly identify personal attributes as significant in gaining and retaining employment. The growth in self concept Weinart (2001: 55) argues cannot be overestimated as a product of lifelong learning. The findings of this current study suggest that once students successfully renegotiated their learner identities they gained a new confidence in themselves as learners and as their destinations reveal certainly travelled with a different view. That this is only the beginning of a longer journey is well summed up by one student.

> I'm finished. I'm happy, content, relieved, proud and somewhat sad. I will miss my experiences in the course. I will miss the getting to know you stages with my classmates. I will miss the person I was six months ago. Just who will I eventually become?

6. NOTES

[1]. As a teacher-researcher I taught all the course humanities modules – Historical studies, Political studies, Multicultural Australia, Australia's Asia-Pacific Relations – during the period of the research. I collected the data on which the chapter is based both as an observer of and participant in students' acquisition of graduate attributes. The students' voices in the chapter were collected as recorded conversations.
[2]. The completion of this chapter was facilitated by a teaching relief grant from the Faculty of Education, University of Sydney.

7. REFERENCES

Australian Education Council (1991) *Young People's Participation in Post-compulsory Education and Training.* Report of the Australian Education Council Review Committee. Canberra: Australian Government Publishing Service.

Australian Education Council and Ministers of Vocational Education, Employment and Training (1992) *Putting General Education to Work: The key competencies report.* Melbourne: Australian Education Council and Ministers of Vocational Education and Training.
Berger, P. (1966) 'Identity as a problem in the sociology of knowledge', *European Journal of Sociology*, Vol. 7, No. 1, pp. 105-115.

Blumer, H. (1969) *Symbolic Interactionism: Perspective and Method*. Englewood Cliffs, New Jersey: Prentice Hall.

Boshier, R. (1998) 'Edgar Faure after 25 years: down but not out', in J. Holford, P. Jarvis & C. Griffin *International Perspectives on Lifelong Learning*. London: Kogan Page, pp. 3-20.

Candy, P.C., Crebert, G. & O'Leary J. (1994) *Developing lifelong learners through undergraduate education*. Commissioned report No 28. Canberra: National Board of Employment, Education and Training.

Crichton, S. & Kinsel, E. (2002) 'The Importance of self and development of identity in learning'. Paper presented at the *International Lifelong Learning Conference*, Yeppon: Queensland, Australia 16-19 June, 2002.

Department of Education, Science and Training (DEST) (2003) *Lifelong Learning and Teacher Education*. Canberra: DEST. Available at www.dest.gov.au.highered/eippubs/eip03_4defau.

Directorate for Education, Employment, Labour and Social Affairs Education Committee (*DeSeCo*) (2002) *Definition and Selection of Competences: Theoretical and Conceptual Foundations*. DEELSA/ED/CERI/CD(2002). Paris: OECD.

European Centre for the Development of Vocational Training (Cedefop) (2002). *Consultation process on the European Commission's Memorandum on lifelong learning: analysis of national reports*. Cedefop panorama series, No. 23. Luxembourg: European centre for the development of vocational training.

Field, J. (2001) 'Lifelong education' *International Journal of Lifelong Learning*, Vol. 20, Nos. 1/2, pp. 3-15.

Gallacher, J., Crossan, B., Field, J. & Merrill, B. (2002) Learning careers and social space: exploring fragile identities of adult returners in the new further education, *International Journal of Lifelong Learning*, Vol. 21. No. 6, pp. 493-509.

Hager, P. (1996) *Conceptualising the Key Competencies*. Draft discussion paper. Sydney: University of Technology

Hager, P., Holland, S. & Beckett, D. (2002*) Enhancing the Learning and employability of graduates: the role of generic skills*. Business and Higher Education Round Table Position Paper No. 9. Melbourne: Business and Higher Education Round Table

Hargreaves, D. H. (1977) 'The process of typification in classroom interaction: Models and methods', *British Journal of Psychology*. Vol. 47, pp. 274-284.

Harris, R., Guthrie, H., Hobart, B. & Lundberg, D. (1995) *Competency-Based Education and Training: Between a rock and a whirlpool*. Macmillan: Melbourne.

Heritage, J. (1984) *Garfinkle and Ethnomethodology*. Cambridge: Polity Press.

Holford, P., Jarvis, P. & Griffin, C. (1998) *International   Perspectives on Lifelong Learning*. London: Kogan Page

Illeris, K. (2003) 'Adult education as experienced by learners', *International Journal of Lifelong Learning*, Vol. 22, No. 1, pp. 12-23.

Merriam, S. B. (1994) 'Learning and Life Experience: The Connection in Adulthood', in J. D. Sinnott. *Interdisciplinary Handbook of Adult Lifespan Learning*. Westport, Connecticut: Greenwood Press.

Oates, T. (2001) *Key skills/key competencies – avoiding the pitfalls of current initiatives*. Additional *DeSeCo* expert options. Geneva: Swiss Federal Statistical Office.

Ouane, A. (2002) *Defining and selecting key competencies in lifelong learning. DeSeCo* symposium. Geneva. 11-13 February, 2002. Geneva: Swiss Federal Statistical Office.

Prevocational Programs Training Division (1995) *English & Humanities Journal*, TPC Issue. Sydney: NSW Technical and Further Education.

Ridgeway, C. (2001) 'Joining and functioning in groups, self-concept and emotion management', in D. S. Rychen & L. H. Salganik (eds.) *Defining and Selecting Key Competencies*. Seattle: Hogrefe & Huber, pp. 205-211.

Rychen, D. S. (2002) *A frame of reference for defining and selecting key competencies in an international context. DeSeCo* symposium. Geneva. 11-13 February, 2002. Geneva: Swiss Federal Statistical Office.

Rychen, D. S. (2001) 'Introduction', in D. S.Rychen & L. H. Salganik (eds.) *Defining and Selecting Key Competencies*. Seattle: Hogrefe & Huber, pp. 1-15.

Rychen, D. S. & Salganik, L. H. (eds.) (2001) *Defining and Selecting Key Competencies*. Seattle: Hogrefe & Huber.

Scanlon, L. A. (2002) *Student experiences of learning generic competencies: an interactionist account*. Unpublished PhD. University of Technology, Sydney

Scanlon, L. A. (2004) ' "She just blends and comes down to our level and communicates with us like we're people": students' perceptions of quality teaching and learning.' *Change* Vol. 7, No. 1, pp. 93-108.

Schutz, A. (1970) *On Phenomenology and Social Relations*. Chicago: University of Chicago Press.

Sheehan, P. (2001) *The critical importance of lifelong learning*. Business and Higher Education Round Table Position Paper No. 4. Melbourne: Business and Higher Education Round Table

Sinnott, J. D. (1994) *Interdisciplinary Handbook of Adult Lifespan Learning*. Westport, Connecticut: Greenwood Press.

Weinart, F. E. (2001) 'Concept of competence: a conceptual clarification', in D. S. Rychen & L. H. Salganik (eds.) *Defining and Selecting Key Competencies*. Seattle: Hogrefe & Huber, pp. 45-65.

CHAPTER 8

SIMON BARRIE

ACADEMICS' UNDERSTANDINGS OF GENERIC GRADUATE ATTRIBUTES: A CONCEPTUAL BASIS FOR LIFELONG LEARNING

1. INTRODUCTION

Lifelong learning is a commonly espoused quality of university graduates (Candy, Crebert & O'Leary 1994). However even a cursory consideration of the literature reveals a bewildering array of definitions and assumed meanings attached to the term. Such confusion is of course not limited to this particular graduate quality. There have been repeated calls (see for example Clanchy & Ballard 1995; Holmes 2000) for basic definitional work and a clarification of the theoretical and conceptual basis for such graduate attributes, skills or capabilities, (just to mention a few of the terms used to describe these sorts of learning outcomes). However, while policy statements listing graduate qualities have proliferated and the vocabulary used has come to have the appearance of a shared common usage, the extent to which the underlying meaning of terms like lifelong learning is shared, remains questionable.

This chapter discusses how a phenomenographically derived description of academics' conceptions of graduate attributes has been applied to the task of revising one university's statement of generic graduate attributes, with a particular focus on the graduate attribute of lifelong learning. In doing so the chapter considers the different understandings academics hold of lifelong learning as a graduate attribute and how these are reflected in different approaches to university curricula.

Rather than seeking to impose a single 'correct' definition, the chapter describes an approach that recognises the reality of such disparate understandings and incorporates these in a university's statement of graduate attributes. Using this perspective, it was possible for the University's existing conglomerate list of

149

P. Hager and S. Holland (eds.), Graduate Attributes, Learning and Employability, 149–167.
© 2006 *Springer*.

different types of generic graduate attribtues to be re-organised, rather than redeveloped from scratch, and the role of the different types of initiatives already in place to be recognised. The chapter explores how the revised policy achieves this by explicitly accommodating two significantly different conceptualisations of lifelong learning.

The approach brings to the surface the buried, but significant, underlying assumptions academics hold regarding the place of a graduate attribute like lifelong learning in more traditional, 'knowledge based' curricula. Of the various conceptions of graduate attributes described in this chapter, the most complex conception of lifelong learning is as 'a learner's attitude and stance towards herself'. This is an example of a conception of generic graduate attributes that has the potential to go beyond the limiting notions inherent in many previous formulations of 'generic skills' (Barnett 1997).

2. AUSTRALIAN UNIVERSITIES AND LIFELONG LEARNING: INITIATING CHANGE

Australian universities' policy statements have claimed lifelong learning and other generic attributes on behalf of their graduates for over a decade, and in some cases for much longer. Consider the attributes of graduates proposed by Reverend Dr. John Wooley (1862), Foundation Principal and Professor of Logic and Classics, in his speech at the inauguration of the University of Sydney; a description of graduate qualities that has many features in common with present day descriptions of lifelong learning (Candy, Crebert & O'Leary 1994).

> Our undergraduates ... will we may reasonably hope, possess a well cultivated and vigorous understanding; they will have formed the habit of thinking at once with modesty and independence; they will not be in the danger of mistaking one branch of science for the whole circle of knowledge, nor of unduly exaggerating the importance of those studies which they select as their own. Above all they will have attained the truest and most useful result of human knowledge, the consciousness and confession of their comparative ignorance. *(Wooley 1862: 21)*

Such rhetoric may have become commonplace in contemporary Australian university policy, however the current climate of accountability is set to bring additional scrutiny to bear on such claims of graduate outcomes including lifelong learning. At the very least it seems reasonable to expect that universities might provide evidence that they have appropriate strategies in place to realise claims that their graduates are lifelong learners and possibly even to provide evidence of the actual achievement of such outcomes. However, two recent significant national reports on generic attributes in higher education in Australia (Hager, Holland & Beckett 2002, Bowden *et al.* 2000) have pointed to the need for significant curriculum reform to fulfil universities' current claims of generic graduate attributes. A recent national survey of Australian employers (DETYA 2000) also suggests that from the perspective of this group university graduates may not have fully developed some of the espoused attributes. The perceived need for curriculum reform is further illustrated in many universities recent initiatives in this area (B-HERT 2003).

So, in light of questions as to the evidence of universities achieving such outcomes like lifelong learning, what indications are there that universities are systematically developing such attributes through their curricula and teaching? Internationally, reviews of university initiatives in the UK have found that despite the existence of some excellent practices these are isolated initiatives and the overall picture in regard to graduate attributes and the higher education curriculum is one of patchy uptake and implementation. Somewhat surprisingly this is the case despite a decade of extensive government funding in the UK through agencies such as the Higher education Funding Council of England.

The overall picture of personal and transferable skills in the UK higher education sector is not very encouraging. Certainly there is little evidence of effective practice on any large scale. There is however considerable evidence to suggest that, sometimes major, development programs have had only limited success (Drummond, Nixon & Wiltshire 1998: 23).

While there has been no similar comprehensive national evaluation of university initiatives in regard to generic attributes in Australia and certainly there has not been the level of additional funding from government, the picture of generic skills initiatives in Australian universities appears to be similarly 'patchy'. Many lifelong learning initiatives reported in the literature (see for example Fallows & Steven 2000) while often representing effective practice in a single subject, tend not to have explicitly targeted policy development to achieve systemic changes in institutional teaching and learning culture. Perhaps more significantly from the perspective of this chapter, initiatives have rarely focussed on research-based development of either policy or practice. Instead most academic development and curricula reform initiatives appear to have accepted the prima facie case for existing statements of graduate attributes like lifelong learning and the assumptions inherent in such statements regarding the fundamental nature of these sorts of university learning outcomes. This appears to be the case even in the relatively few university-wide curriculum development initiatives that have been implemented systematically (B-HERT 2003). Indeed there has been little in the way of a critical appraisal by the higher education community of the theoretical or conceptual underpinning of the whole notion of generic attributes (Holmes 2000). This is surprising given the apparent variability in acceptance by academics and students of the idea of generic attributes as a central outcome of a university education and the apparent variability with which such attributes are actually incorporated as an integral component of university curricula.

> Despite innovative initiatives, the complexity associated with the development of these skills coupled to their permeation throughout courses ....leads to a level of confusion which is unacceptable. *(Kemp & Seagraves 1995: 327)*

The lack of a coherent conceptual underpinning to the idea of generic attributes has been commented on by many researchers and there have been repeated calls for such basic preliminary work (Bennet, Dunne & Carre 1999; Clanchy & Ballard 1995; Holmes 2000). However this issue has remained largely un-addressed and it seems likely that in the absence of an appreciation of the conceptual underpinning of generic attributes, current attempts by Australian universities to implement systematic policy development and curricula reform to develop lifelong learning and other generic attributes will continue to meet with varying degrees of success and achieve only 'patchy' outcomes.

3. A RESEARCH BASED FRAMEWORK FOR A SHARED VISION OF LIFELONG LEARNING

In recent years many Australian universities have initiated generic graduate attributes projects which have included a focus on lifelong learning (Hager, Holland & Beckett 2002, B-HERT 2003). However, as noted previously these initiatives, while marking a serious attempt at systemic reform, do not address the lack of a research-based theoretical or conceptual underpinning to the notion of generic graduate attributes.

> (Graduate attributes initiatives) Have had little impact so far, in part because of teachers' scepticism of the message, the messenger and its vocabulary and in part because the skills demanded lack clarity, consistency and a recognisable theoretical base. Any attempt to acquire enhanced understandings of practice through which to inform staff and course development initiatives thus requires the conceptualisation and development of models of generic skills. *(Bennett, Dunne & Carre 1999: 90)*

Recent research (Barrie 2003) into academics' understandings of generic graduate attributes in the context of the undergraduate university curriculum has highlighted the reality of such disparate views. In providing an empirically derived description of the variability in academics' understandings of generic attributes it provides one possible conceptual basis from which to consider generic attributes. This conceptual basis provides a framework for articulating generic graduate attribute outcomes in policy and for understanding how the range of existing isolated initiatives within a university might be combined and integrated in an overall strategy.

The research focussed on the activities of university teachers charged with developing graduate attributes as part of the usual undergraduate experience. It identified a hierarchy of four, increasingly complex understandings of generic graduate attributes as outcomes of a university education. These empirically derived understandings, or conceptions, identified using phenomenographic analysis of interview data (Marton & Booth 1997), vary along several dimensions. For instance, the conceptions of generic graduate attributes vary in terms of the fundamental nature of the outcomes, ranging from atomistic low level technical and personal skills to more complex, holistic, interwoven abilities and aptitudes for learning. They also differ in terms of the relationship between these outcomes and discipline knowledge, and the transformative potential (for knowledge and the individual) of such attributes. Amongst other things, these variations have consequences for the degree of specialisation of generic attributes in different discipline settings and for academics' perceptions of the relevance, and hence value, of including such attributes amongst university learning outcomes.

The research described academics' understandings (conceptions) of graduate attributes as learning outcomes in terms of a hierarchy of four empirically derived and increasingly complex categories:

Precursory
Complementary
Translation
Enabling

At the simplest level of the hierarchy, generic graduate attributes can be conceived of as basic *Precursory* abilities which provide a foundation upon which the discipline knowledge of a university education can be built. However, other academics express a different understanding of graduate attributes, one that goes beyond this conception to encompass university learned, general functional abilities and personal skills that can usefully *Complement* the discipline specific learning outcomes of a university education. Other academics understand generic attributes to be more than useful additional general skills. Rather they are specialized variants of such general skills that are essential in the application of discipline knowledge and the *Translation* of university learning to unfamiliar settings, thus usefully transforming the products of university learning. Some academics express a still more complex understanding of generic attributes as *Enabling* abilities and aptitudes that lie at the heart of all scholarly learning and knowledge, with the potential to transform the knowledge they are part of and to support the creation of new knowledge and transform the individual (for a detailed description of these four phenomenographic categories see Barrie 2003: 105-117).

The four qualitatively distinct categories are hierarchical, with *Enabling* outcomes subsuming and being supported by *Translation* outcomes, which in turn are supported by *Complementary* and *Precursory* outcomes. Such a hierarchy is logical, not only in terms of the features of the empirically derived categories of description but pragmatically. As with most dimensions of human capability and knowledge, graduate attributes would not be expected to spring into being fully fledged. Such outcomes are more likely to be the result of staged process of development and achievement with the increasingly complex outcomes benefiting from different strategies at different stages in the process of acquisition.

Related to the four understandings of generic attributes as outcomes, the research also identified six different understandings of the process of teaching and learning such attributes.

Remedial
Associated
Teaching Content
Teaching Process
Engagement
Participatory

Interestingly, in light of the prevalence of claims of generic attributes in institutional policy, some academics do not express an understanding of the teaching of generic attributes as being part of usual university teaching at all. Instead the development of graduate attributes is understood to be the responsibility of earlier educational experiences. From the perspective offered by conceptions in this category, the only role for the university in teaching graduate attributes is in terms of *Remedial* teaching for those students who have not already developed these skills. Other academics clearly do understand the development of graduate attributes to be part of the university's teaching role. For some academics this role is fulfilled through the provision of an additional separate curriculum in *Association* with the usual university curriculum. This is not a remedial curriculum rather it is a curriculum for all students. However, academics can also understand graduate attributes to be acquired as part of the taught content of usual university courses. Rather than an additional curriculum the graduate attributes curriculum is included as an integral part of the usual *Teaching content* of the discipline. Another understanding of the development of graduate attributes, is in terms of the *Teaching process* of usual university courses rather than the teaching content of the usual university course. Academics can express yet another perspective, one that understands the development of graduate attributes not as a part of *what* is taught, or the *way* it is taught, but rather in terms of the way the student *Engages* in learning in her or his usual university course. Some academics expressed yet another understanding. Rather than perceiving the development of graduate attributes to be through the way a student learns in a course it is through the way the student *Participates* in the broader learning experiences of university life (Barrie 2003: 135-136). As was the case with the conceptions of what graduate attributes are, the conceptions of how they might be developed are also hierarchical with the increasingly complex and increasingly student focussed, understandings of the teaching and learning of such attributes subsuming and incorporating elements of less complex conceptions.

This phenomenographic perspective on generic attributes provides one possible theoretical or conceptual perspective upon which a university's generic attributes initiatives might be based.

4. POSITIONING LIFELONG LEARNING IN A RESEARCH BASED POLICY FRAMEWORK

Lifelong learning is a common inclusion in most Australian universities' policy statements specifying the generic attributes of graduates (Candy, Crebert & O'Leary 1994). However, the same study reported a notable lack of actual practices that supported the development of such a graduate attribute. From the perspective offered by the research summarised in the preceding discussion it would seem that the academic members of the university community might have a variety of different understandings as to the nature of this graduate quality and its place amongst the more familiar discipline knowledge learning outcomes. That is, despite possibly espousing a shared agreement that lifelong learning is a desirable outcome, academics might not share an understanding of what lifelong learning might be.

> While there is evidence of a single emerging language, this exists in terms of common words not common meaning. *(Hirsh & Bevan 1988)*

This understanding of the structure of the variation in academics' conceptions of generic attributes, which was provided by the research described in the preceding section, has recently been applied to the task of revising the University of Sydney's statement of generic attributes of graduates (ITL 2003). Unlike the initial development of many such statements of generic attributes the approach to policy revision was research-based, a feature that has been argued as being essential in scholarly academic development work, particularly in research intensive universities (Prosser & Barrie 2003). Like many Australian universities the University had in place a policy statement describing various skills and abilities of graduates. Also like many of its counterparts the University's list of attributes had been developed in consultation with employers and the academic community. Indeed the attributes it listed were virtually indistinguishable from those of other Australian institutions. They were a collection of 'popular' yet often poorly specified skills, with an assumption that the various stakeholders held a shared understanding of what, for example an attribute like 'communication skills' might mean.

Rather than simply revising the existing list of attributes to include any additional contemporary or 'fashionable' attributes (for example 'proficiency with emerging communication and information technologies' is a recent addition to many universities' lists), the very nature of the graduate skills 'shopping list' was critically examined from the perspective offered by the research described in the preceding section.

On examination it became apparent that the existing list of graduate attributes was a conglomerate of the various types of outcome described in the hierarchical categories identified by the research, ranging from complex overarching abilities to low level technical skills. Not only did the list treat all the items on the list as being of an equal level of complexity, it treated these various skills as if they were unrelated to each other or to discipline knowledge. For instance, 'personal autonomy' was considered to be separate to 'critical thinking' which was separate to discipline knowledge. This ignores the idea the graduates need to think critically about 'something' (rather than in a vacuum) and that this critical ability might have something to do with intellectual autonomy.

Instead of this atomistic listing of skills and attributes of different levels of complexity, a two tiered structure was implemented reflecting the two most complex conceptions of generic attributes (as learning outcomes) identified in the research; the *Enabling* and *Translation* conceptions. In effect the list was reorganised to reflect the hierarchical and increasingly complex nature of graduate attributes in these two conceptions. Lower level skills and abilities representing the two lower levels of the hierarchy (the *Precursor* and *Complementary* conceptions) were removed from the list in favour of the more complex transformative attributes these basic skills provided the foundation for. This did not mean these less complex skills were considered unimportant as steps towards achieving higher level outcomes, rather it reflected the universities stance that such low level skills were not, on their own, sufficient as graduate outcomes.

We will first consider the overall policy structure at one university before looking in more detail at lifelong learning and the implications of this approach to policy for this popular generic attribute.

In line with the University's mission the revised policy identifies three holistic overarching attributes as important outcomes of University education: Scholarship, Global Citizenship and Lifelong Learning. In terms of the hierarchy of understandings identified in the research, these outcomes are analogous to the top level *Enabling* conception of graduate attributes. In this conception, generic attributes are interwoven networks of clusters of skills abilities and attributes that sit at the very heart of discipline knowledge and human capability. These are defined as follows:

> **Scholarship: An attitude or stance towards knowledge:** Graduates of the University will have a scholarly attitude to knowledge and understanding. As Scholars, the University's graduates will be leaders in the production of new knowledge and understanding through inquiry, critique and synthesis. They will be able to apply their knowledge to solve consequential problems and communicate their knowledge confidently and effectively.

> **Global Citizenship: An attitude or stance towards the world:** Graduates of the University will be Global Citizens, who will aspire to contribute to society in a full and meaningful way through their roles as members of local, national and global communities.

> **Lifelong Learning: An attitude or stance towards themselves:** Graduates of the University will be Lifelong Learners committed to and capable of

continuous learning and reflection for the purpose of furthering their
understanding of the world and their place in it.

The University's mission was a key factor in identifying these particular,
overarching attributes. As well as restructuring the list to better reflect the
underlying conceptual basis of generic attributes, the revision sought to more
clearly articulate the unique outcomes of a research-intensive undergraduate
education. In doing so the revision sought to differentiate the generic outcomes of
a research intensive university education from those which might be expected
from universities of a different type. For instance how might being taught by
leading researchers result in different generic outcomes to those developed
through a university education whose strength was primarily in its focus on
technology or in its links with the world of work? Interestingly these three
outcomes also echo the domains proposed by Barnett as part of his reformulation
of the notion of critical thinking; knowledge, the self and the world (Barnett
1997).

The policy recognises the development of these three overarching *Enabling*
graduate attributes as being supported by the development of the sort of graduate
attributes described by the lower level of the hierarchy, the *Translation* conception
of graduate attributes. At the *Translation* level, graduate attributes are understood
as disciplinary based clusters of personal attributes, cognitive abilities and skills of
application. It is these clusters that inter-link to form the networks of clusters
described in the *Enabling* conception. In the policy, these skills and abilities are
organised into five key clusters which embody the *Translation* level of the
conceptual hierarchy:

> **Research and Inquiry**: Graduates of the University will be able to create new
> knowledge and understanding through the process of research and inquiry.

> **Information Literacy**: Graduates of the University will be able to use
> information effectively in a range of contexts.

> **Personal and Intellectual Autonomy**: Graduates of the University will be
> able to work independently and sustainably, in a way that is informed by
> openness, curiosity and a desire to meet new challenges.

> **Ethical, Social and Professional Understanding**: Graduates of the University
> will hold personal values and beliefs consistent with their role as responsible
> members of local, national, international and professional communities.

Communication: Graduates of the University will recognise and value communication as a tool for negotiating and creating new understanding, interacting with others, and furthering their own learning.

The University's policy does not specify the details of the skills in each of the five clusters. This is because a key feature of the *Translation* conception of generic attributes is the interaction between discipline knowledge and generic attributes. This interaction shapes generic attributes to suit particular applied contexts and epistemologies. So rather than specifying the skills in each cluster for the entire institution the policy only provides an indicative list of the abilities that might comprise these clusters. Reflecting the highly discipline specific qualities of the translation level conception of generic attributes, each faculty of the institution has developed its own interpretation of the attributes which constitute each of the five clusters in their particular disciplinary context. We will touch on this process of interpretation further in the next section through a consideration of the implications of this approach to policy for the specific attribute of lifelong learning (see Barrie, Jain & Carew 2003 for a full discussion of this process).

5. CONTEXTUALISING THE LEARNING OF LIFELONG LEARNING

In the context of such a policy framework, these research findings provide one way of understanding how an academic community might approach the teaching and learning of a graduate attribute such as lifelong learning. The challenge was to consider how policy and practice might usefully take account of the variety of understandings of a generic attribute such as lifelong learning suggested by the research. The approach to policy revision described in the preceding section has attempted to take this variation into account. In particular the approach accommodates the different relationships between lifelong learning and disciplinary knowledge that these variations in understanding entail. The approach also explicitly recognises a role for the range of teaching and learning strategies associated with these different understandings of lifelong learning.

The revised policy specifies lifelong learning as a graduate attribute in terms of the *Enabling* conception. Here lifelong learning is understood to be an outcome of a particular type; an interwoven network of clusters of abilities, the development of which is fostered by particular teaching and learning experiences; those characterised by learner *engagement* in courses and *participation* in the broader social experience of belonging to a university community. At this level of the hierarchy, lifelong learning is described as an individuals attitude or stance towards themselves as a learner. This is a conception of a university education that has much in common with Barnett's (1997) re-conceptualisation of the purpose of a university education and as such avoids the evolutionary blind alley he warns is represented by traditional formulations of generic skills (Barnett 1997). The espoused aim in this conception of lifelong learning is for graduates of the University to be committed to, and capable of, continuous learning and reflection so as to further their understanding of the world and their place in it. In this conception the way a learner *engages* in his or her course and *participates* in university life is important. In this conception, lifelong learning qualities are so central to discipline knowledge and university learning that they may be largely implicit in curricula and teaching, and all but invisible to students. However, it is far more explicit in the other lower level conceptions of graduate attributes.

The hierarchical approach to policy has the potential to incorporate these other conceptions of lifelong learning in addition to the more complex *Enabling* conception. Various authors have claimed that graduate attributes are best developed in the context of discipline knowledge (Bowden *et al.* 2000, Barrie & Jones 1998). In light of this and the point noted earlier about the highly implicit nature of graduate attributes in the *Enabling* conception, then the specification of more explicit discipline-based *Translation* conceptions of lifelong learning, as a step towards the achievement of the more implicit higher-level *Enabling* outcome might be appropriate. At the *Translation* level of the hierarchy, a graduate attribute such as lifelong learning is understood in terms of the various clusters of specific, discipline based attributes and skills that together make up the more complex outcome that is the higher level conception of this attribute.

Lifelong learning at the *Translation* level of the hierarchy is described in terms of the five clusters of skills. While aspects of all the five clusters contribute to the quality of lifelong learning, it is those related to personal and intellectual autonomy and the cluster of skills related to information literacy which are most relevant. These two clusters are described as:

Personal and Intellectual Autonomy: Graduates of the University will be able to work independently and sustainably, in a way that is informed by openness, curiosity and a desire to meet new challenges.

The indicative (non-disciplinary) list of skills identified in the policy suggest that this cluster of skills might be understood in a discipline in terms of the following:

- be intellectually curious and able to sustain intellectual interest
- be capable of rigorous and independent thinking
- be open to new ideas, methods and ways of thinking
- be able to respond effectively to unfamiliar problems in unfamiliar contexts
- be able to identify processes and strategies to learn and meet new challenges
- be independent learners who take responsibility for their own learning, and are committed to continuous reflection, self-evaluation and self-improvement
- have a personal vision and goals and be able to work towards these in a sustainable way

Information Literacy: Graduates of the University will be able to use information effectively in a range of contexts.

This cluster of skills might be understood as:

- recognise the extent of information needed
- locate needed information efficiently and effectively
- evaluate information and its sources
- use information in critical thinking and problem solving contexts to construct knowledge
- understand economic, legal, social and cultural issues in the use of information
- use contemporary media and technology to access and manage information

One of the features of the *Translation* conception is that the more explicit skills that comprise these clusters will vary from discipline to discipline. For example in terms of lifelong learning different disciplines might require a familiarity with different specialised library data bases and search conventions as well as different disciplinary writing conventions, research methodologies and ethics protocols.

This disciplinary contextualisation reflects the degree of interconnectedness that exists between the generic attributes and discipline knowledge in this conception. At the *Translation* level of the hierarchy, lifelong learning is positioned as a parallel yet intimately related set of learning outcomes to disciplinary knowledge. By virtue of this close relationship lifelong learning skills are shaped by (and in turn shape) discipline knowledge. As such it is an expectation of the revised policy that the different disciplines will explicitly constitute the skill clusters that comprise lifelong learning differently in the context of their particular discipline knowledges.

As an example of this consider the following draft interpretations of each of the two primary lifelong learning skill clusters in quite different discipline contexts:

Information Literacy: Graduates of the **Sydney Conservatorium of Music** will be able to use information effectively in a range of contexts.

- be able to recognise the extent of information needed for professional and informed music performance, composition, teaching and research
- locate needed information efficiently and effectively using a variety of printed, audiovisual and online sources
- evaluate information and its sources
- use information in critical thinking and problem solving contexts to construct knowledge and improve music composition, performance and teaching
- understand economic, legal, social and cultural issues in the use of printed, audiovisual and online information
- use contemporary technology and audiovisual media to access and manage information

Information Literacy: Graduates of the **Faculty of Engineering** will be able to use information effectively in a range of contexts.

- An appreciation of the various forms of information within the engineering discipline including technical books and reports, research articles, customer requirements, company standards and an appreciation of the main legal definitions.
- An ability to identify, utilise and locate appropriate information resources including literature, electronic media and through personal interaction with both technical and non-technical audiences.
- An ability to gather, manage, integrate and critique information attained from various sources in order ascertain the relevant

information required for the identification, formulation and solution of a problem within the engineering context.

Personal and Intellectual Autonomy: Graduates of the **Faculty of Engineering** will be able to work independently and sustainably, in a way that is informed by openness, curiosity and a desire to meet new challenges.

- An appreciation for the role of creative thinking within engineering and the ability to undertake and indulge in the process of it.
- An ability to function effectively as an individual even within the context of teamwork, and to understand the importance of the individual role.
- An appreciation of the personal skills involving openness and curiosity both within the engineering discipline and outside of it, and the importance of relating the engineering discipline to the whole.
- A desire to ensure quality work and professional practice through the process of self-reflection.
- An appreciation of the endless bounty of knowledge both within the discipline and outside of it, and that effective engineering comes through the process of continual personal growth in terms of openness and curiosity towards this knowledge.

Personal and Intellectual Autonomy: Graduates of the **Faculty of Nursing** will be able to work independently and sustainably, in a way that is informed by openness, curiosity and a desire to meet new challenges.

- Accepts accountability and responsibility for own actions within nursing practice.
- Acts to enhance the professional development of self and others.
- Open to new ideas, methods and ways of thinking.
- Independent learners who take responsibility for their own learning and development.
- Reflective practitioners who have as their aim self-improvement

Such *Translation* level disciplinary contextualisation makes the teaching and assessment of such an attribute like lifelong learning a much more feasible undertaking. It still recognises the holistic nature of the *Enabling* conception towards which these skill clusters might contribute yet makes explicit and relevant the teaching and assessing of such an outcome in the context of different university courses.

However, what of the other lower level conceptions of lifelong learning that the hierarchy of conceptions of graduate attributes would suggest exist? Such a layered policy can also accommodate a role for *Complementary* and *Precursor* strategies as providing valuable non-discipline based support for all students and specialised support for students who lack the basic university-level entry skills relevant to lifelong learning. *Complementary* conceptions of graduate attributes would position lifelong learning in terms of the more atomisitic general technical and personal skills that can usefully complement the discipline specific learning outcomes of a university education. Skills such as general library and information searching skills (for example basic boolean internet search protocols, academic referencing conventions or generic critical thinking strategies) are incorporated as a foundation to more complex conceptions of lifelong learning. At a more basic level still, the *Precursor* conception of lifelong learning skills might be constituted in terms of bridging courses for students who lack foundation literacy and library skills.

6. CONCLUSION

Australian universities' approaches to describing and fostering the development of graduate attributes such as lifelong learning have not always been based in a conceptual understanding of such outcomes of a university education. Much of the literature on lifelong learning and similar generic graduate attributes presupposes a shared understanding on the part of the university community as to the place of such generic learning outcomes amongst the more familiar discipline based knowledge outcomes. However, recent research has found that academics hold qualitatively different understandings or conceptions of such outcomes (Barrie 2003).

This chapter has considered how a phenomenographically derived description of academics' conceptions of graduate attributes has been applied to the task of revising one university's statement of generic attributes of graduates. The application of the research findings to the task of revising and implementing a university's policy statement on graduate attributes is an example of research-led academic development (Prosser & Barrie 2003). Using the perspective provided by the research, it was possible for the University's existing conglomerate list of different types of generic skills to be re-organised, rather than redeveloped from scratch and the role of the different types of initiatives already in place to be recognised. Inherent in the resultant hierarchical, multi-layered policy statement of graduate attribute outcomes is the accommodation of a range of understandings of lifelong learning as an outcome representing increasingly complex skills or abilities as well as the different relationships between discipline knowledge and lifelong learning.

The revised policy achieves this by explicitly accommodating two significantly different conceptualisations of lifelong learning. The first of these is an outcome that is a cluster of discipline specific personal attributes, cognitive abilities and skills of application. The second of these is in terms of a trans-disciplinary outcome that represents interwoven networks of these clusters embedded within and between the different 'knowldeges' of all disciplines. This second, higher level conception has much in common with the reformulation of traditional notions of knowledge and wisdom which Barnett (1997) argues to be necessary in light of the present day purposes of the university. As such, this conception might provide a way of thinking about generic graduate attributes, such as lifelong learning, which avoids the limitations Barnett (1997) perceives in previous 'generic skills' approaches. However, while the revised policy specifies lifelong learning in terms of these higher level *Translation* and *Enabling* conceptions it does not negate the potentially valuable role of more 'generic skills' based courses. The underlying conceptual framework accommodates a role for such strategies in providing the necessary foundations for students' achievement of more complex graduate outcomes.

The research-based policy approach and associated academic development process (ITL 2003) described in this chapter are possibly more time consuming and require more initial effort than many other university's approaches to generic skills development. However, the process, while still in its early stages at the time of writing this chapter, appears to be allowing a different and much improved level of dialogue between members of the academic community as part of their efforts to foster the development of lifelong learning as a graduate attribute.

7. REFERENCES

Barnett, R. (1997) *Higher Education: A Critical Business*. Buckingham: SRHE & Open University Press.

Barrie, S.C. (2003) Conceptions of Generic Graduate Attributes: A phenomenographic investigation of academics' understandings of generic graduate attributes in the context of contemporary university courses and teaching. Doctoral Thesis. University of Technology Sydney.

Barrie, S.C (in press) 'Understanding what we mean by the generic attributes of graduates'. *Higher Education.*

Barrie, S.C. & Jones, J. (1999) 'Integration of academic writing skills in university courses: A model for generic attributes curriculum development', in Rust, C. & Gibbs, G. (eds.), *Improving Student Learning.* Oxford: The Oxford Centre for Staff Development, pp. 479-489.

Barrie S.C., Jain, P. & Carew A. (2003) 'Generic Graduate Attributes: A research based framework for a shared vision', *Staff and Educational Development International,* Vol. 7, No. 3, pp. 191-199.

Bennett, N., Dunne, E. & Carre, C. (1999) 'Patterns of core and generic skill provision in higher education', *Higher Education,* Vol. 37, pp. 71-93.

B-HERT (2003) Developing Generic Skills: Examples of Best Practice. *B-HERT News 16, April 2003.* Available at www.bhert.com/documents/B-HERTNEWSNo.16_001.pdf

Bowden, J., Hart, G., King, B., Trigwell, K. & Watts, O. (2000). *Generic Capabilities of ATN University Graduates.* Canberra: Australian Government Department of Education, Training and Youth Affairs. Available at www.clt.uts.edu.au/ATN.grad.cap.project.index.html

Candy, P., Crebert, G. & O'Leary, J. (1994) *Developing Lifelong Learners Through Undergraduate Education.* Commissioned Report No. 28, National Board of Employment Education and Training. Canberra: Australian Government Publishing Service.

Clanchy, J. & Ballard, B. (1995'Generic skills in the context of higher education', *Higher Education Research and Development,* Vol. 14, No. 2, pp. 155-166.

Department of Education, Training and Youth Affairs (DETYA) (2000). *Employer Satisfaction with Graduate Skills: Research Report 99/7,* Feb 2000 Evaluations and Investigations Program, Higher Education Division. Canberra: DETYA.

Drummond, I., Nixon, I. & Wiltshire, J. (1998) 'Personal transferable skills in higher education: the problems of implementing good practice', *Quality Assurance in Education,* Vol. 6, No. 1, pp.19-27.

Fallows, S. & Steven, C. (2000) 'The skills agenda', in S. Fallows & C. Steven (eds.), *Integrating Key skills in Higher Education.* London: Kogan Page, pp. 17-33.

Hager, P., Holland, S. & Beckett, D. (2002) *Enhancing the Learning and Employability of Graduates: The role of Generic Skills.* Business / Higher Education Round Table Position Paper No.9. Melbourne, Australia.

Hirsh, W. & Bevan, S. (1988) *What makes a manager: in search of a language for management skills*. Institute of Manpower Studies Report 144. Brighton: Institute of Manpower Studies.

Holmes, L. (2000) 'Questioning the skills agenda', in S. Fallows & C. Steven (eds.), *Integrating Key Skills in Higher Education*. London: Kogan, pp. 201-214.

ITL (2003) *Generic Graduate Attributes Project*. The Institute for Teaching and Learning, Sydney: The University of Sydney. Available at www.itl.usyd.edu.au/GraduateAttributes/

Kemp, I.J. & Seagraves, L. (1995) 'Transferable skills – can higher education deliver?' *Studies in Higher Education*, Vol. 20, No. 3, pp. 315-328.

Marton, F. & Booth, S. *(*1997*) Learning and Awareness*. New Jersey: Lawrence Erlbaum.

Prosser, M. and Barrie, S.C. (2003) 'Using a student-focused learning perspective to strategically align academic development with institutional quality assurance', in R. Blackwell & P. Blackmore (eds.) *Towards Strategic Staff Development in Higher Education*. Buckingham: Open University Press, pp. 191-202.

Wooley, C. (1862) cited in P. Candy, G. Crebert & J. O'Leary (1994). *Developing Lifelong Learners through Undergraduate Education*. Commissioned Report No. 28 National Board of Employment Education and Training. Canberra: Australian Government Publishing Service.

CHAPTER 9

MARK ATLAY

SKILLS DEVELOPMENT: TEN YEARS OF EVOLUTION FROM INSTITUTIONAL SPECIFICATION TO A MORE STUDENT-CENTRED APPROACH

1. INSTITUTIONAL CONTEXT

The University of Luton was established in 1993 from a local College of Technology. From its inception it has been committed to vocational education and providing educational opportunity for all who might benefit. Since 1993 the University's profile has changed considerably with an initial rapid expansion in student numbers followed by a reduction in home undergraduate recruitment counterbalanced by increased international and postgraduate students. Currently the student population is around 14,000 in three faculties: Creative Arts, Technologies and Science; Health and Social Sciences; and the Luton Business School. The annual in-take of UK students into full-time undergraduate provision is around 1500, the majority of whom are local to the university. The student population is ethnically diverse with a significant proportion (45%) over 21.

From its inception the University has been fully committed to modularity. Programmes are organized within undergraduate and postgraduate schemes which use a common credit and regulatory framework. In the early years students could choose from single and combined (major, joint and minor) awards at undergraduate level in most areas of provision but there has been a recent move away from providing such a wide choice since it has proved difficult to manage the students' experience effectively – both in terms of student development through the curriculum and student support and communication. In order to ensure consistency, within a modular framework with students studying across subjects, there has been a large element of central specification of curriculum policy with local implementation. This has been true of skills development where there has been an institutional framework within which all programme areas are expected to work since 1994.

169

P. Hager and S. Holland (eds.), Graduate Attributes, Learning and Employability, 169–186.
© 2006 *Springer*.

2. CORE CURRICULUM ELEMENTS: SKILLS AND EMPLOYABILITY

Responding to the needs of its diverse student body has governed institutional thinking about the nature of the curriculum. Two inter-related issues have been identified as being important to the University and its widening access and vocational mission: skills development and employability.

The basis of the University's emphasis on skills development can be found in its interaction with its diverse student population. Many of the University's students have been out of mainstream education for a number of years, few of their peer group will have studied beyond 18 and they are often the first family member to attend higher education. Responding to their needs has required education and development – on all sides. Whilst students are intelligent and able to balance the many competing demands of their everyday lives (including the growing need to work whilst studying), they are often not used to conversing and communicating in a way which academics recognize as being appropriate to study and assessment in a higher education context. The initial reaction is to blame the colleges and the secondary schools who in turn blame the primary schools and the primary schools the parents. The University has attempted to address this issue through an emphasis on skills development throughout the curriculum making it the responsibility of all academic staff with appropriate specialist support where necessary.

Whilst the importance of addressing skills throughout the curriculum has been largely, although not completely, uncontested (Atlay & Harris 2000); the extent to which the University should be responding to the perceived employment needs of the public sector, industry, commerce and the professions has been more controversial. There were those that were comfortable with the notion of a vocational curriculum whilst others favoured a more liberal arts approach. The reality has been that during the past five years students have largely voted with their feet. Courses in areas such as English and History have closed due to declining student numbers whilst vocationally related courses (such as social work, applied media and business studies) have expanded. Financial considerations are important when students are considering whether to enter full-time higher education and vocationally relevant education is seen as providing easier access to employment. Short term debt needs to be off-set by a long-term ambition for the higher earnings that a degree brings. In such a context, where there is heavy marketing of the benefits that higher education brings, there is a moral obligation on the University to ensure that students are prepared for graduate employment – 'employability' has thus become a key curriculum driver.

Knight & Yorke (2003) define employability as 'a set of achievements, understandings and personal attributes that make individuals more likely to gain employment and be successful in their chosen occupations'. Most of these *achievements, understandings and personal attributes* are not just important for employment – they are essential for academic development within the university and for day to day life beyond.

Employer needs have been identified in a number of reports and although each may use different terminology they emphasize students being prepared to function effectively in the knowledge economy – being able to rapidly fit into the workplace culture, work in teams, exhibit good interpersonal skills, communicate well, and take responsibility for an area of work (see, for example, Harvey et al. 1997).

3. THE CURRICULUM MODEL 1993–2000

The University sought to address skills development through a range of actions. Firstly, it required a clear specification of the curriculum and its expectations. The premise here is that learning is supported if students are clear about what they are working towards. From its inception the University based its curriculum model around specifying intended learning outcomes. These more clearly articulate what it is that students should be able to do by the end of the module or programme – a process which has also assisted staff thinking about their curriculum. The process of constructive alignment (Biggs 2003) then helps to ensure that students' learning is structured to achieve the intended outcomes and that it is these outcomes which are tested through the assessment process.

Secondly, the University's experience suggested that perceived skills deficiencies could not be dealt with through isolated skills modules but required concerted action across the curriculum. Thus skills were identified as part of the learning outcomes associated with each module. To do this, in the period up to 2000, the University worked with its own set of 'transferable skills' (or 'generic graduate attributes' as referred to in other chapters of this book) covering the following areas:

- Information retrieval and handling
- Communication and presentation
- Planning and problem solving
- Social development and interaction

Each skill area was broken down further into four or five sub-skills. These were defined at two levels; an initial entry level where the focus was on the skills required for further study and at undergraduate levels 2 and 3 where the emphasis was more on the skills required for employment and life beyond the University (Atlay & Harris 2000; Fallows & Steven 2000).

During the early phase of development the University progressed through debates about which skills, the relationship between subject specific and transferable skills, whether skills are transferable and whether they should be (or could be) assessed. The University has found explicitly identifying skills extremely useful in making its curriculum explicit to staff, students and visiting assessors. External scrutiny by the UK's Quality Assurance Agency (QAA) has consistently praised the University's provision and the value-added nature of the educational experience it provides its students. At the end of this phase the University came to view skills as best described as 'enabling': enabling students to access the curriculum, enabling them to engage with the curriculum and enabling the expression of their knowledge, understanding and wider abilities.

4. THE EVOLVING NATIONAL SETTING

In the UK the recognition that the attributes of a graduate extend beyond the confines of knowledge of their subject has a lengthy history which can be traced back to the 19th century (see Drew 1998, for a detailed discussion of skills development in the UK). In more recent times, the Dearing report into higher education in the UK (NCIHE 1997) had amongst its recommendations 'that institutions of higher education begin immediately to develop, for each programme they offer, a programme specification which identifies potential stopping-off points and gives the intended outcomes of the programme in terms of:

- the knowledge and understanding that a student will be expected to have upon completion;
- key skills: communication, numeracy, the use of information technology and learning how to learn;
- cognitive skills, such as an understanding of methodologies or ability in critical analysis;
- subject specific skills, such as laboratory skills.'

Since the publication of the Dearing report a number of actions have been taken at a national level building on work which was already underway to more explicitly define 'graduateness'. These include aspects related to skills. The QAA, in conjunction with subject experts drawn from across the sector, has overseen:

- at the qualification level – the development of a Framework for Higher Education Qualifications (FHEQ) to more tightly define the relative outcomes of different awards (QAA 2001a)
- at the subject level – the development of a series of subject benchmark statements which 'provide a means for the academic community to describe the nature and characteristics of programmes in a specific subject. They also represent general expectations about the standards for the award of qualifications at a given level and articulate the attributes and capabilities that those possessing such qualifications should be able to demonstrate' (QAA 2000–2004)

Furthermore, deriving from a recommendation in the Dearing report, national expectations were established for students' Progress Files which 'should consist of two elements: a transcript recording student achievement ... and a means by which students can monitor, build and reflect upon their personal development'.

'Guidelines for HE progress files', were developed on behalf of the sector by the Committee of Vice Chancellors and Principals (now, Universities UK and including Universities Scotland), the Standing Conference of Principals (SCOP), the QAA and the Learning and Teaching Support Network (LTSN). These suggested that the Personal Development Planning (PDP) element of the policy objectives should be operational across the whole HE system and for all HE awards by 2005/06 (QAA 2001b).

The Progress File concept contains:

- the transcript: a record of an individual's learning and achievement, provided by the institution;
- an individual's personal records of learning and achievements, progress reviews and plans that are used to clarify personal goals and can provide a resource from which material is selected to produce personal statements (e.g. CVs etc) for employers, admissions tutors and others;
- structured and supported processes to develop the capacity of individuals to reflect upon their own learning and achievement, and to plan for their own personal educational and career development – the term Personal Development Planning (PDP) is used to denote this process.

Progress Files aim to help make the outcomes, or results, of learning in higher education more explicit, identify the achievements of learning, and support the concept that learning is a lifetime activity. PDP is seen as 'a structured and supported process undertaken by an individual to reflect upon their own learning, performance and/or achievement and to plan for their personal, educational and career development'. The Guidelines identify the primary objective for PDP as being 'to improve the capacity of individuals to understand what and how they are learning, and to review, plan and take responsibility for their own learning, helping students:

- become more effective, independent and confident self-directed learners;
- understand how they are learning and relate their learning to a wider context;
- improve their general skills for study and career management;
- articulate personal goals and evaluate progress towards their achievement;
- and encourage a positive attitude to learning throughout life.'

5. EVOLVING THE UNIVERSITY'S CURRICULUM MODEL

5.1 Issues for Consideration

The actions the University of Luton had already taken meant that it was in a good position to respond to the developing national agenda. In 2000 it established a working group to undertake a review of its approach to skills in the curriculum in the light of developments in the sector and the emerging national expectations in relation to Progress files and PDP. The working group identified a range of issues that needed to be addressed:

- The initial curriculum model, whilst valuable in explicitly addressing skills development, was seen as often mechanistic – leading to a tick-box approach if poorly applied.
- The need to be able to recognize students' learning in a wider range of settings: the university, employment, volunteering, on work experience etc.
- The importance of placing greater emphasis on students' responsibility for improving their own learning (this was seen by many as the most important skill for a number of reasons; it was an essential part of being a graduate, it stressed a move from dependence to independence in the curriculum, and it recognised the reality of a university with a limited and diminishing unit of resource trying to respond to the increasingly varied needs of its diverse student body).
- Increasing the employability of its graduates – in an ever competitive graduate labour market and with the increasing use of data to produce 'employability' league tables.

- Assisting students to recognise and appreciate the skills and attributes they had developed so that they could represent these to potential employers.
- The need to address student motivation and self-efficacy.

Fundamental to the review was a desire to move to a more student-centred approach and the importance of considering student development as a programme rather than module issue (Knight 2000; Knight & Yorke 2002).

5.2 Refreshing Skills

Two approaches to refreshing and invigorating the skills curriculum were considered; revising the existing skills definitions or using the national definitions of skills as defined by the Qualifications and Curriculum Agency (QCA 2001, 2004) and used in secondary and post-compulsory education. The QCA skills are in the following areas:

- Communication;
- Application of Number;
- Information technology;
- Working with Others;
- Problem Solving; and
- Improving Own Learning and Performance.

The QCA skills were examined by selected programme teams from across the University and found broadly to meet subject and institutional needs (see Atlay 2003, for a more detailed discussion of the advantages and disadvantages of the use of these skills descriptors). After consultation it was decided to utilize the QCA descriptors to provide the framework around which skills could be identified – but not to assess to QCA requirements (a process which was viewed as overly bureaucratic, resource intensive and of limited educational value).

5.3 Enhancing Employability

From 1996 the University provided careers development as part of the curriculum through an optional Career Development Module (CDM) run by the University's Careers Advisers. This was received positively by students:

'Students felt they had benefited immensely from the CDM. Not only have they been able to distinguish what skills truly are, what skills they themselves posses and what they require to qualify for their career – they have already begun developing those skills'. (Independent focus group report.)

The University wished to build career development skills into the core curriculum for all students. However, it recognised that this could not be accomplished through the existing Careers Advisers but would require an approach which involved the careers specialists working with academic staff in embedding the career development skills into the curriculum. Thus, in addition to the QCA list of skills, the University added its own skill descriptors on career development, modelled on similar lines to the QCA skills, to reflect the central requirement for these skills to be embedded in the curriculum (See Table 1).

Table 1: University of Luton defined Career Development Skills

	Career Development	Evidence must show you can
CD4.1	Develop a strategy for planning and implementing your career choice(s), based on: Realistic self-assessment Awareness of Opportunities Decision-making skills using reliable information Action-planning skills	Identify, assess and articulate your skills, abilities, personal attributes, interests, values, experiences and circumstances, and relate these to career opportunities; Establish opportunities for developing career development skills and clearly identify the outcomes you hope to achieve; Identify relevant sources and research the information needed for planning purposes.
CD4.2	Monitor, progress and adapt your strategy, as necessary, to implement your plan. This will involve: A CV reflecting your self-assessment in relation to a Job's requirements A focussed Job Application form Self-presentation skills to cope with interviews and assessment centres	Identify what employers are seeking in terms of academic, personal and professional achievement; Promote yourself effectively on paper and in person, emphasising strengths and experiences relevant to a particular job opportunity; and Monitor and critically reflect on your use of career development skills, adapting your strategy as necessary to produce the quality of outcomes required
CD4.3	Evaluate your overall strategy and present a plan for future career development	Demonstrate a realistic match between career aspirations and personal characteristics, knowledge and experience; Plan for the further development of skills, knowledge and experience to meet career aspirations; and Assess the effectiveness of your strategy, including factors that had an impact on the outcomes, and identify ways of further extending your career development skills.

5.4 Emphasising Personal Development Planning

The University decided to integrate its revised approach to skills development with its plans for Progress files and PDP since it believed that these initiatives could be mutually supportive. Four main advantages of this approach were identified.

5.4.1 Metacognition

PDP processes could provide a means of structuring a curriculum which was student-centred and placed an emphasis on students taking responsibility for their own learning and performance – the core skill. PDP processes align with emphasising the importance of metacognition (Knight & Yorke 2003) and with the concept of meta-learning (Jackson 2004).

5.4.2 Self-efficacy and ipsative assessment

Progress Files could help address issues of self-efficacy through providing a record of positive achievement and a vehicle for ipsative assessment. Ipsative assessment is the measurement of distance travelled (sometimes called value-added) – the progress made by the individual student. One of the advantages of this approach is that it can be used to build student confidence and self efficacy which are important characteristics when dealing with students often with poorer prior educational attainment and experiences. Comparing outcomes at the beginning and at other stages of the programme (through PDP and portfolio-based approaches) can reinforce attainment as well as identifying areas for improvement. Ipsative assessment represents a further move away from a deficiency model of assessment – the tendency to provide feedback solely in terms of what still needs to be done hence reinforcing inabilities and undermining self-confidence. Furthermore, whilst much institutional attention is often directed at weaker students (since they are 'at risk'), an ipsative approach can be used to stretch students of all abilities. Thus ipsative assessment as part of PDP processes linked to target-setting, reflection and improving own learning and performance can play an important role in motivating all students to higher levels of attainment.

5.3.3 Flexibility

Progress Files could provide a place for reflection on various learning opportunities and experiences related to employability including work and life experiences beyond the curriculum. Thus it could provide a means of identifying, reviewing and reflecting on a wide range of attributes and of developing life-long learning skills.

5.3.4 Mirroring professional requirements

Most professional bodies and many employers have schemes for continuing professional development (CPD) built around processes which mimic aspects of PDP: reviewing effectiveness, identifying actions for improvement, undertaking development and reviewing the outcomes. Thus an emphasis on PDP processes should prepare students for CPD enabling them to gain the maximum value from such review processes.

6. THE REVISED CURRICULUM MODEL

UK universities are implementing Progress File expectations in a variety of ways. Some view PDP processes as an additional part of the student experience often linked to the personal tutorial system. In such approaches, PDP is often viewed as an additional support mechanism for the learner or as a vehicle for aspects of career development. For the University of Luton, PDP was seen as integral to the learning process. Furthermore, from its own previous experiences of experimenting with Progress Files in the early 1990's it believed that PDP processes were not likely to be taken seriously (by students and staff) unless they were part of the mainstream curriculum – and assessed.

The University adopted a strategy whereby there are specific modules at each level of the undergraduate scheme which serve to support personal development planning and progress file requirements – the PDP spine.

At level 1 all students have a personal, professional and academic development module (PPAD; pronounced rather unfortunately as P-PAD) which is subject based but serves a number of purposes including:

- providing an extended induction;
- identifying routes through the modular credit scheme;
- diagnostic testing;
- personal development planning;
- career awareness; and
- identifying the attributes of the typical graduate on completion and how the curriculum will help and assist the students to attain these.

The PPAD module is where students start the process of reflection and portfolio building and thus it is a natural place to discuss the importance of skills development with students, to undertake an initial skills assessment and to start students considering how they can improve their skills.

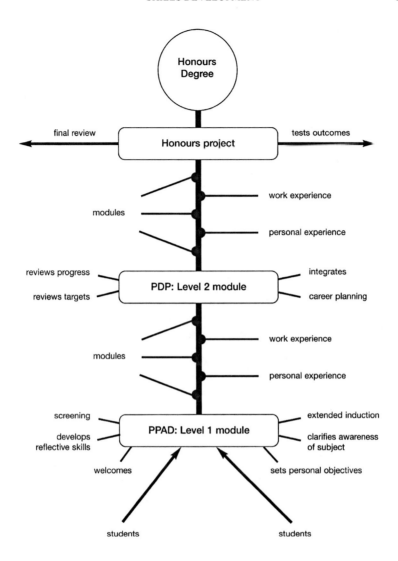

Figure 1. The PDP spine

This is then built on as part of the level 2 curriculum in a module, usually around research methods and preparation for the final honours dissertation, which also has an emphasis on career planning skills and reviewing progress – it is here that the career development skills are usually covered.

In the level 3 curriculum, normally as part of the dissertation module, students review their progress and can be assessed for their skills against the standards required for the programme. The basis of this assessment is likely to be an activity based on the student's ability to 'plan, do and review' their skills development. Detailed assessment of the Progress File is not a requirement.

Students have a responsibility for collecting information for their Progress Files themselves from the work they submit for assessment (thus encouraging them to collect and read assignment feedback) and from other activities within or without the University. Staff responsibilities are for ensuring that appropriate supportive material is generated, reviewing the student's Progress File as part of the assessment of the PPAD and level 2 PDP modules and undertaking any final assessment.

Programme teams identify, by reference to the appropriate subject benchmark statement and the QCA descriptors, the expected skills which graduates are expected to achieve. These are often defined and assessed through the dissertation but also potentially using the student's Progress File as a more detailed record of skills attainment both within and beyond the curriculum. Programme teams have a responsibility for ensuring the modules which the students study provide the opportunity to develop skills to the required level.

7. IMPLEMENTATION

The University trialled its approach to PPAD modules in three curriculum areas during 2002–03. This then became part of the level 1 curriculum in all areas during 2003–04 along with the PDP element at level 2, and is currently being implemented as part of the final year. One of the key features of the University's approach has been to allow each subject area to take broad institutional requirements and work with them in the context of the needs of their own subject and their students. This approach to change has allowed for variation in implementation to reflect the needs of the subjects.

In *Law* the approach to PDP involves specialist modules and a student portfolio, which they complete in their own time, with input from Careers and Learning Resources. The process is supported by all staff who act as personal tutors.

In *Sport and Leisure* the programme manager and Careers Adviser received project funding from the University to develop a level 2 module which involves the University's Virtual Learning Environment, CMS On-line and employer input.

In *Computing* the Career Development Module was adapted for use with international as well as home students. In preparing the proposal for their final year project, students are required to make links between the project and their career aspirations. A Careers Adviser and a member of academic staff act as supervisors.

In *Psychology*, professional body requirements make it difficult to create the space for specific modules. Here the PDP and careers processes have been mapped against the Psychology curriculum and students are provided with a specialist handbook which also examines the psychological underpinning to PDP processes.

In *Media* a commitment to employability runs throughout the undergraduate curriculum. Guest speakers (employers, agents, alumni) contribute to PDP modules to bring the world of work into the classroom. An annual careers event 'Going professional' is provided and a longitudinal graduate survey is underway covering aspirations, applications, actual jobs, work-related skill, and reflections on the curriculum.

In *Design* the level 1 PPAD module was adapted so that it ran as an intensive induction across the first three weeks of the curriculum. In level 2, professional practitioners are used to augment the curriculum and to provide a context for students' work.

Social Studies have taken and adapted the Career Development Module for their own use at level 2. Students write a report on an employment role and a self-evaluation against that role. PDP processes now feature throughout the curriculum not just in the PDP spine.

In *Business and Marketing*, a PDP approach is adopted in all modules since it is seen as promoting deep learning. At level 1 students are engaged in a range of experiential learning activities from which they reflect on their own strengths and weaknesses – a process which starts in induction week.

8. EVALUATION

A major meta-analysis undertaken to support the implementation of Progress Files in the UK (Gough *et al.* 2003) suggests that the PDP approach can have an impact on student learning but also notes that this area is, as yet, under researched. Case and Gunstone (2002) have identified some factors which militate against developing a meta-cognitive approach including increased workload and time-pressured assessments. Undoubtedly ten years of skills development at the University of Luton has had a major impact on the curriculum – but has it had any impact on student learning or self-efficacy? As noted earlier, external scrutiny of the University's provision has been very positive but are there any hard facts to support the conclusion that the PDP approach can be effective?

In principle evaluating the impact of educational intervention such as that discussed above in the context of a modular scheme with a common regulatory framework ought to be possible through a number of indicators such as student attainment, pass rates and retention. Furthermore module evaluations, which give a measure of student satisfaction for each module, can be used to compare student' perceptions. However, interpretation of comparative data needs to be treated with some caution for a number of reasons:

- there is considerable variation in the nature of the student body across the various discipline areas (ethnicity, prior attainment, prior educational experiences etc.);
- each discipline has its own culture – some lend themselves to a metacognitive approach whilst for others the introduction of PDP is more problematic;
- not all staff teaching the modules may be fully committed to the introduction of an approach which stresses metacognitive processing;
- innovation and change is not always immediately effective – staff and students need time to come to terms with the new curriculum. In the early phase innovation, experimentation and change need to be encouraged; and
- the wider curriculum was undergoing extensive change at the time of the introduction of the approach making it difficult to directly link cause and effect.

Student performance on the sixteen level 1 PPAD modules is shown in the following table with data for 2001–02 (prior to piloting PPAD modules) taken as a baseline for comparison. The University uses a 16 point grading scale where an A+ grade equates to a 16 and a bare pass is a D- (grade point 5). A module average of 9.5 is in the middle of the lower second class range (8.0–10.9).

Table 2. Student performance

	N	Average	Pass 1st time %	Pass after referral %
PPAD Modules 2003–04	909	9.5	84.0	88.6
Other semester 1 level 1 modules 2003–04	5438	9.3	85.7	88.1
All level 1 modules 2001–02	13812	9.1	80.7	82.2

The data shows that in 2003–04, the first year of full implementation, students performed slightly better on PPAD modules than other level 1 modules whereas pass rates are little different. Further work is required to investigate whether this difference is consistent and real, and to elucidate the reasons behind the differences. It may be that, in line with the findings of Case and Gunstone (2002), a metacognitive approach assists certain students but still fails students who adopt an information-processing approach.

PPAD modules have no additional academic staff resource, although they do often call on support staff (careers advisers and learning resources staff for example) to provide specialist input. Class size is not a factor here since the average class size for the PPAD modules was 53 whereas for the other level 1 modules it was 37 – the difference arises because some cognate areas share PPAD modules and there may be elements of option choice in some level 1 curricula. The increased performance of modules with higher student numbers is not an argument for higher class sizes; however, it does suggest that the metacognitive approach can help support students even where there are large class sizes.

The data shows that there has been a significant improvement in student performance since the emphasis on PDP processes was introduced both in terms of average module grades and, more markedly, pass rates. There has been no significant change in the nature of the student intake over this period but the University has been taking a range of actions to improve student performance at level 1 of which the PDP approach is part and it is difficult to identify the specific factors which have contributed to improved student performance. However, initial indications are that the PDP approach is having a benefit for the University's students and work is continuing on evaluating this impact through the monitoring of student performance and through focus group work and in-depth interviews with students. It remains to be seen whether this improvement in performance can be sustained.

9. CONCLUSION

Jackson & Ward (2004) note that 'success, whether defined in academic, personal or career-related terms, involves more than innate ability and exposure to good teaching. It requires the personal qualities of initiative, persistence, belief in self and self-direction'. The University's curriculum model is seeking to develop and recognise these attributes and places PDP processes central to learner development. Its experience of working with students from diverse backgrounds and with relatively low prior academic attainment is that generally it is not their intellectual ability which is hindering their academic progress but social expectations, motivation and relatively poor academic skills. The University's emphasis on skills development, through its curriculum and the additional support that it provides, is part of assisting the academic development of these students. Given their relatively low starting point there is clearly high 'added value' in the number of good degrees which such students subsequently achieve. Initial evaluation of the approach supports the advantages that it can bring.

Staff and students are becoming increasingly aware of the language of skills and their application to the teaching and learning process. However, implementation and understanding of the revised approach to skills and metacognitive processes is still somewhat patchy across the University but should become more consistent as staff become more familiar with what is expected. Implementation is being closely monitored and key practitioners are encouraged to meet to share experiences of implementing the revised curriculum involving an integrated approach to skills, personal development profiling and progress filing. There is still much to learn and the impact on students will be monitored closely. In recognition of its work in this area, the University of Luton has recently been recognised as a Centre for Excellence in Teaching and Learning by the UK Funding Council (Hefce 2005). The associated additional funding will be used to further support the development of an undergraduate curriculum model based on the explicit development of skills and emphasising personal development planning, and to examine the impact of this approach on student learning and employability.

10. REFERENCES

Atlay, M. T, & Harris, R. (2000) 'An Institutional Approach to Developing Students' "Transferable" Skills, *Innovations in Education and Training International*, Vol. 37. No.1, pp. 76-84.

Atlay, M.T. (2003) 'Refreshing and Revising – An Instiutional Approach to Skills Development', *Staff and Educational Development International*, Vol. 7, No. 3, pp. 181-190.

Biggs, J. (2003) *Teaching for Quality Learning at University.* 2nd Ed. Buckingham: Society for Research into Higher Education/Open University Press.

Case, J. & Gunstone, R. (2002) 'Metacognitive Development as a Shift in Approach to Learning: an in-depth study', *Studies in Higher Education*, Vol. 27, No. 4, pp. 459-470.

Drew, S. (1998) *Key Skills in Higher Education: Background and Rationale.* SEDA Special No. 6, Birmingham, UK: Staff and Educational Development Association.

Fallows, S. & Steven, C. (2000) *Integrating key skills in higher education: employability, transferable skills and learning for life*. London: Kogan Page.

Gough, D.A., Kiwan, D., Sutcliffe, K, Simpson, D. & Houghton, N. (2003) *A systematic map and synthesis review of the effectiveness of personal development planning for improving student learning*. London: EPPI-Centre, Social Science Research Unit.

Harvey, L., Moon, S. & Geall, V. with Bower R. (1997) *Graduates' Work: Organisational change and students' attributes*. Birmingham: Centre for Research into Quality, UCE, and the Association of Graduate Recruiters.

Hayden, M. (2003) 'Generic Graduate Skills and Attributes – A review', *Staff and Educational Development* International, Vol. 7, No. 3, pp. 259-272.

Hefce (2005) *Centres for Excellence in Teaching and Learning* (CETLs). Available at www.hefce.ac.uk/learning/TInits/cetl/

Jackson, N. (2004) 'Developing the concept of meta-learning', *Innovations in Education and Teaching International* Vol. 41, No. 4, pp. 391-403.

Jackson, N. & Ward, R. (2004) 'A fresh perspective on progress files – a way of representing complex learning and achievement in higher education', *Assessment and Evaluation in Higher Education* , Vol. 29. No. 4, pp. 423-447.

Knight, P. (2000) The value of a programme-wide approach to assessment', *Assessment and Evaluation in Higher Education*, Vol. 25, No. 3, pp. 237-51.

Knight, P.T. and Yorke, M. (2003) *Assessment, Learning and Employability*. Place??SRHE and OU Press.

Knight P.T. and Yorke M (2002) 'Employability through the curriculum', *Tertiary Education and Management* Vol. 8, No. 4, pp. 261-76.

National Committee of Inquiry into Higher Education (NCIHE) (1997) *Higher Education in the Learning Society*. 'The Dearing Report', Place? HMSO. Available at www.leeds.ac.uk/educol/ncihe/

QAA (2001a) *The framework for higher education qualifications in England, Wales and Northern Ireland*. Available at www.qaa.ac.uk/crntwork/progspec/contents.htm

QAA (2001b) *Guidelines for Progress Files*. Place? UK: Quality Assurance Agency. Available at www.qaa.ac.uk/crntwork/progfileHE/contents.htm

QAA (2000–2004) Subject *benchmark statements*. Place? UK: Quality Assurance Agency. Available at www.qaa.ac.uk/crntwork/benchmark/honours.htm

QCA (2001) *Guidance on wider Key Skills – levels 1–4.* London: Qualifications and Curriculum Authority. Available at www.qca.org.uk/603.html

QCA (2004) *Key Skills Standards 2004.* London: Qualifications and Curriculum Authority. Available at www.qca.org.uk/6507.html

CHAPTER 10

CATHERINE DOWN

LIFELONG LEARNING, GRADUATE CAPABILITIES AND WORKPLACE LEARNING

1. INTRODUCTION

Given the rate of technological change, an increasingly global marketplace and a shift from economies based on manufacturing and primary produce to knowledge economies, effective workplace learning becomes a key factor in a nation's wealth and well-being.

Learning through our work is increasingly essential if we are to keep pace with technological and organisational change and to contribute to the intellectual and social capital of our workplaces. Whilst it might be argued that not all of our work results in learning – routine repetitive tasks once mastered are unlikely to result in new learning – much of it does. A lot of this new learning is in response to new or contingent situations where we must adapt what we know and can do to resolve an issue, solve a problem or learn to adapt our work in response to new organisational structures, functions, systems or technology.

Our workplace learning is situated learning and it is the 'situatedness' (Lave & Wenger 1991) of this learning and the learner which determines what is learnt and how it is learnt. New skills and knowledge are not learnt through memorising or internalising, instead, they enacted by the learner as part of work practice.

This chapter looks at how workplace learning is currently understood and how effective workplace learning can be fostered.

The chapter begins with a discussion of some of the characteristics of workplace practice and learning which are problematical and the need for the development of appropriate frameworks with which we can explain our work and our learning through work. The dual nature – group and individual – of workplace learning is discussed, along with those organisational structures which control or

187

P. Hager and S. Holland (eds.), Graduate Attributes, Learning and Employability, 187–205.
© 2006 *Springer.*

enable our access to workplace learning. Recent research data is used to illustrate this discussion.

From there, the chapter turns to an overview of some key research perspectives, which inform our understanding of effective workplace learning. The research of the situated cognitivists, the machine-human interactionists and the socio-historical advocates has enabled us to view workplace learning through a number of lenses which each contribute to our understanding. In addition, research into organisational learning, although largely phenomenological, provides us with further understanding of the nature of workplace learning. Again, examples of recent research data are used to illustrate the possible applicability of these theories.

Finally, the chapter looks at our readiness for workplace learning and those capabilities or attributes which provide us with the necessary tools to ensure effective workplace learning. In order to focus on practice, this is illustrated through recent data and research findings.

2.   RESEARCH DATA AND FINDINGS

Throughout this chapter, I will draw on three key research projects in which I was/am the lead researcher to illustrate the points made. These are:

2.1 Strategic Evaluation of the Qualitative Impact of the Introduction of Training Packages on Vocational Education and Training Clients

Down (2002) was a national evaluation, commissioned by the Australian National Training Authority (ANTA), to study the impact on its clients of the introduction of Training Packages. These specificy the outcomes, assessment and qualification of vocational education and training programs in Australia. It involved a series of focus groups and interviews with 217 participants drawn from state and territory training authorities (STAs), registered training organisations (RTOs), industry personnel and students.

The data collected within this project gives us a rich tapestry of understandings of work and of the learning which occurs within and around it.

2.2 The Applied Technology Project

This current project (despite its oxymoronic title) has been designed to identify and construct a flexible framework for post-trade development in order to enable tradespeople to learn about and innovatively work with technology which was not invented at the time they undertook their initial training programs.

It currently covers a wide range of industry sectors from precision engineering, plumbing and gasfitting, fashion and textiles, building and construction and waste management, although it is not limited to these areas.

The participants in this project include industry workers and managers, vocational education and training teacher, industry trainers, vendors of technology and IT&C experts.

2.3 Situated Learning, Polycontextual Boundary Crossing and Transfer: Perceptions of Practitioners as to How Competence is Transferred Across Different Work Contexts

This is a research project which is still in progress. It looks at the theories and frameworks that training practitioners use to understand the transfer of what people know and can do across different workplace contexts.

The participants in this project are all practitioners involved in vocational education and training and are drawn from higher education, TAFE institutes, private providers, industry training, industry advisory bodies, consultants and government authorities

All three projects provided opportunities to capture qualitative commentary from participants regarding their workplace learning in times of change and repositioning.

3. CHARACTERISTICS OF POST-INDUSTRIAL WORKPLACES

Ronald Barnett (Barnett 1999, 2002) argues that we live and work under conditions of supercomplexity, characterised by contestability, challengeability, uncertainty and unpredictability . This makes the frameworks we use for understanding the world, for acting within it and for relating to others, both fragile and problematic. It is, therefore necessary for us to work at learning within the workplace. It is not sufficient to assume that learning about work will happen; it requires both deliberation and effort. The supercomplexity of the work contexts means that we must continually reconstruct the frameworks we use to make sense of our worlds in the light of unfolding events and practices within the workplace.

Beck (1992) describes the current age as the 'risk society', whilst Bauman (1996) prefers the term 'age of contingency'. Both terms accurately describe the conditions under which we work and learn. This was recognised by participants discussing the introduction of training packages in Australian vocational education and training when they commented that:

> There have been some hiccoughs in the system but that has to be expected in a period of innovation. You have to take risks, to try things, to find out what is and is not possible within a work situation. ... When you start working with a new organisation, it is always a risk ... *(RTO trainer participant)*

The contradictions which characterise our contemporary workplaces were also recognised by participants in the strategic evaluation project. For example as one participant noted:

> Because the need to deliver - to make the money roll in - is so important, there isn't time, not just for the development of staff, but the development of how to creatively use the packages as well. *(Small private RTO manager)*

> Teachers know that what makes for good teaching is the quality of teaching and learning interactions. But there is growing pressure to go on-line or to use self-paced booklets to cut costs. *(RTO teacher)*

Ann Whyte argues that in the real world of work, it is the paradoxes that dominate our actions and our understanding. Learning to navigate and find a balance between these paradoxes constitutes a large part of our workplace learning. Whyte (2002) identifies these paradoxes as being able to be both:

- competitive *and* cooperative
- me-first *and* you-first
- short term winners *and* long-term strategists
- voracious consumers and gentle community builders
- valued workers and poorly paid
- keen to work and disinterested in jobs

This is not by any means an exhaustive list and our learning with respect to such paradoxes and contradictions is for the duration of our working life. It is through the construction and reconstruction of the meanings of such contradictory forces that we establish our working identity. Barnett (1999) notes that learning through work presents personal challenges as well as intellectual ones. The concept of learning through work (and, indeed, the concept of lifelong learning) is essentially yet another paradox in a world where learning is associated with youth and uncertainty. To admit to being a learner sends 'mixed messages ... [about] ... one's organisational persona. Self images of maturity, self-reliance and authority

suddenly contrast with those of dependency and of lack of understanding.'
(Barnett 1999: 35).

Essential to our workplace performance and our learning through work are the
affordances or the opportunities for learning provided within the work context and
the agency which we are able to use to create or take advantage of learning
opportunities.

> How affordances are constituted in workplaces, are shaped by workplace hierarchies,
> group affiliations, personal relations, workplace cliques and cultural practices, as well
> as the kinds of activities in which individuals are able or requested to engage. *(Billett
> 2000: 31)*

In describing the highly contested nature of the workplace, Billet identifies
contingent workers as being particularly vulnerable:

> Contingent workers (i.e. those who are part-time and contractual) struggle to be kept
> informed (Tam 1997), to be granted opportunities to expand their role and to be
> supported by guidance from experienced full-time employees. Accordingly, the
> invitational qualities of the workplace are far from being benign or evenly
> distributed. *(Billett 2000: 31)*

The disparity in affordances and the limited effectiveness of individual agency
was reflected by these comments from participants in the strategic evaluation
project:

> It has been hard enough for us to get our head round the changes involved in Training
> Packages but what about our sessional teachers? What do they know about the
> changes involved. They are lucky if they've seen a small section of a Training
> Package let alone the whole thing. How can they possibly keep up with the changes?
> *(RTO teacher/manager, Down 2002: 33)*

> With virtually no staff development that really lets us explore Training Packages and
> how they affect us, we are supposed to implement this change within three months of
> the Training Package being endorsed. We have twice as many sessionals than
> permanent staff – and they have virtually no access to meaningful information.
> So will the bureaucrats please tell us how we are to cope! *(RTO manager, Down
> 2002: 33)*

Kim Kirsner (2002) notes that studies of surgeons in Canada found that
surgical skill was positively correlated with practice in carrying out a particular
operation. That is, the more experience surgeons had, the better they became at
that operation. The surprising finding was that as their performance improved their

ability to pass the examinations that gave them entry into their profession actually declined until, decades later, they were struggling to answer many basic questions.

Other studies with fire-fighters, nurses and others have confirmed such findings. Because we learn from our work experience by enacting our learning within our practice, it is implicit (or tacit) knowledge and becomes, over time, unconsciously embedded in our practice. We mimic the practice of our mentors and models without necessarily giving conscious thought as to why we are doing it.

Whilst such tacit knowledge enhances our performance, it remains unspoken and, therefore, cannot be shared with others. It is only by reflecting on our work practice that we can unpack it and transform such implicit knowledge into explicit knowledge. This is important if we are to work collaboratively or to teach or train others. It was acknowledged by respondents in my situated learning research. For example, one of them wrote:

> It is only through reflection of what we do, that we can identify how our practice is changing, what is new and what we no longer do. By rationalising these changes we add to our theoretical understandings of learning and our work. *(Down 2003b: 13)*

Workplace learning is thus seen as a purposeful, dynamic activity in which we interact with the work context – its people, culture, organisational history, work systems, processes, procedures, physical nature and emotional ambience – in order to better understand and work within it. As we do so, we construct and reconstruct our working identities and understandings. Workplace learning requires effort and workplaces are by no means benign environments. Our ancestors roamed through hostile forests and plains to hunt and gather food. Yet after a busy and emotionally tense day at work, many of us might reflect that our progenitors had it easy compared with our daily dealings with the 'dinosaurs' and other perils of the modern workplace.

4. THEORETICAL UNDERSTANDINGS

The recognition of situated learning has derived from three sources of research endeavour. The first of these is the "situated cognition" or "situated action" movement (Marton & Booth 1997: 11) , which centres around studies of learning and thinking in everyday situations outside of educational institutions. Key figures in this area are Jean Lave, Etienne Wenger, and John Seely Brown (Marton & Booth 1997) among others.

The second area of research endeavour which has contributed to our understanding of situated learning is that of computer scientists seeking alternative models to explain human-computer interactions, such as Clancey (1992) and Suchman (1987). Both these research areas place emphasis on researcher observation as a means of explaining human action in terms of their social or cultural situatedness.

The third area is that of the sociocultural or socio-historical school of psychology developed originally by Vygotsky and his followers. Known sometimes as "activity theory" (Engestrom 1999), this third area provides a powerful methodology for the study of change in terms of the social and cultural context in which it occurs. As Marton & Booth (1997) explain, Vygotskian psychology seeks to understand and explain consciousness (the inner) in terms of society (the outer) which is the reverse of the cognitivistic approach which explains the outer (acts, behaviour, etc.) in terms of the inner (mental representations).

Scholars within these research fields seek to establish the primacy of their understandings. For those of us who must daily negotiate the perilous environment of our workplaces and those of our students, it is, perhaps, more appropriate that we look at the key contributions that each of these three schools of thought has given to our understanding of learning through work.

4.1 Situated Action

Situated cognitivists recognise that it is the engagement of the learner with the context which is the driving force of learning through work (or other activity). In this approach there is an:

> ... implied emphasis on comprehensive understanding involving the whole person rather than "receiving" a body of factual knowledge about the world; on activity in and with the world; and on the view that agent, activity and the world mutually constitute each other. *(Lave & Wenger 1991: 33).*

In general, situated learning is generally understood as the learning which occurs when the learner sets out to acquire the necessary skills, knowledge and attitudes which will enable him/her to be part of a community of practice. This community of practice could be domestic, social or vocational. It is, what Lave & Wenger (1991) describe as legitimate peripheral participation which:

> provides a way to speak about the relations between newcomers and old-timers, and about activities, identities, artefacts and communities of knowledge and practice. It

> concerns the process by which newcomers become part of a community of practice.
> A person's intentions to learn are engaged and the meaning of learning is configured
> through the process of becoming a full participant in a sociocultural practice. This
> social process includes, indeed it subsumes, the learning of knowledgeable skills.
> *(1991: 29).*

Thus, we learn through purposeful activity with and within the workplace and this shapes our learning. Our learning is continuous and includes microgenic (or moment-by-moment) learning (Rogoff 1990). In the case of problem solving or learning over a much greater time span, we continually renegotiate the meaning of work and our place within it.

The key contribution that the situated cognitivists make to our understanding of learning through work is that we learn through practice, through engagement with our work context and through the enactment of and reflection on work practices. Reflection on our work and, thus, on our learning enables us to bring to the surface much of the tacit knowledge we have developed through our unconscious actions in response to our work and our work context. This was recognised by one participant in the strategic evaluation project when he commented:

> There isn't time anymore for the project team to sit down and talk and reflect
> together about what is going wrong, what is working, how we might improve. We
> make our individual reflections and judgements about what is going on, but as an
> individual, I'm not seeing the whole picture ... I think that diminishes the quality and
> holistic nature of our work. *(RTO participant)*

Whilst the situated cognitivists recognise that situated learning is the result of the learner interacting with the context, it is the learner who is central to the process. The context remains a shadowy, unexplained entity. To understand about the role of the context then we need to turn to socio-historical activity theory.

4.2 Human-machine Interactions

Studies of human interactions with intelligent machines emphasis that microgenic learning is continuous and that micro-adjustments to the interaction occur without deliberation (Clancey 1992: 3). Thus, any interaction is being simultaneously mediated by those involved. The ability to do this in a purposeful way so that a particular goal is reached is one of the essential learning skills necessary for effective workplace and social interaction and learning.

4.3 Socio-historical Activity Theory

The key contribution made to our understanding of situated learning from socio-historical research is that of the changing and dynamic nature of the context of learning. In the socio-historical school of thought, the context is also central to the learning and is itself dynamic and plays an active role in shaping the learning.

This means that in situated learning, we need to understand that the context is dynamic and shapes the learning. So we develop an understanding of the process of situated learning by an analysis of the context as well as the learner's role and actions within it. Thus, learning (formal or informal) does not derive from a series of learning experiences and assessment tasks, but though the learner actively interacting with the contexts (social, physical, intellectual and emotional) and situations (work, domestic and social) in order to better understand and to work within them.

Basically, activity theory focuses on both the process nature of change and its interactional nature. Any change process involves multiple human interactions and a chain of knowledge transactions, mediations and constructions of new understandings. The acceptance of the change and its translation into appropriate practice is achieved only when all concerned have fully integrated the change. Such integration occurs only after the change has been unpacked and repacked for different purposes, and this process characteristically involves periods of denial, efforts to neutralise the change, anger at the loss of past practice and, finally acceptance (Marris 1975)

The tool used by socio-historical theorists and researchers to analyse what is happening within the workplace is activity theory. This theory is founded on five principles.

The first principle of activity theory is that 'a collective, artefact-mediated and object-oriented activity system ... is taken as the prime unit of analysis', (Engestrom 1999: 4). This is illustrated in Figure 1.

The second principle is the multi-voicedness of activity systems, which, necessarily, frames a community of individuals with multiple-points of view, traditions and interests. The third principle is historicity as activity systems take shape and get transformed over a period of time. Hence, their problems and potentials can only be understood against their own history. The fourth principle is concerned with the central role of contradictions as sources of change and development whilst the fifth principle asserts that activity systems undergo expansive transformations when the object and motive of the activity "are reconceptualised to embrace a radically wider horizon of possibilities than in the previous mode of the activity (Engestrom 1999: 5)

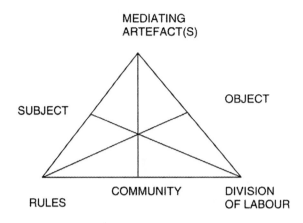

Figure 1. An Activity Unit
(Engestrom 1999: 4)

The analysis of the large amount of data collected in the strategic evaluation project was done using activity theory to analyse not only what people were saying, but why they might be saying such things. This involved analysing situations about which the participants were speaking and constructing the probable activity unit for this situation. An example of this is shown below (Figure 2).

This then enabled the completion of a grid comprised of the four questions:

- What is changing?
- Who is involved in this change?
- Why is it changing?
- How is it changing?

These questions are answered in terms of the five principles of activity theory: the activity unit; multi-voicedness; historicity; contradictions and paradoxes; and expansive learning. An example of part of an analysis is shown on the following page (Table 1). Such analyses enabled the interactional nature of the change and the consequent learning which was being reported upon. It enabled the context to become central to the analysis and to view the participants as actors within this dynamic, reflexive context.

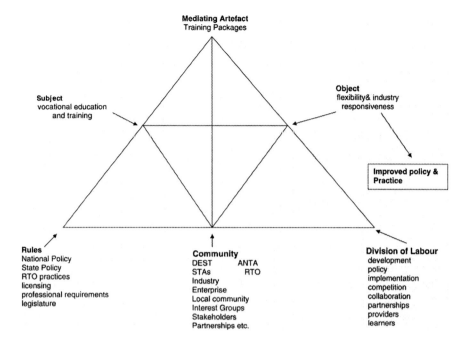

Figure 2: Example of an Activity Unit

5. SUPPORTING SITUATED LEARNING

If we think about the perspectives outlined above, we realise that situated learning cannot be taught in the traditional sense of teaching, not can in be prescribed in curriculum. Because it is based on an individual's interaction with the context he/she inhabits, the strategies undertaken by the learner are variable from one learner to another as are the outcomes of learning.

Thus, situated learning cannot be prescribed. However, as it is the main source of our informal learning in the workplace and in our domestic and social lives, then the role of teachers and other formal learning programs, with respect to situated learning is threefold, that is:

- ensuring that the learner develops the necessary skills to actively interact with and, therefore, learn from work and life contexts;
- appropriately supporting or facilitating situated learning;
- recognising the outcomes of situated learning through processes such as the recognition of prior learning or the recognition of current competence.

It is, perhaps, the first of these which is most relevant to this discussion. Universities, and other tertiary education institutions are beginning to focus on graduate capabilities or attributes These can be described as those attributes/capabilities which learners will have developed by the end of their programs of study and which will enable them to work effectively in their chosen occupation.

This focus originates from the needs of industry and the professions to have their new entrants work-ready or, at least, to be able to function effectively in their future workplaces. This emphasis on employability is integral to government policy and funding arrangements and makes explicit and demonstratable what was currently assumed. No longer is the hidden curriculum of the personal organisational, knowledge management, information and communication literacy, environmental sustainability, creativity and contingency management skills assumed to develop as a consequence of teaching and learning. It needs to be deliberately built into the curriculum and able to be assessed and reported upon.

The move towards such learning is described by Gibson, when he states that:

> QUT [Queensland University of Technology], like most other [Australian] universities has in recent times been giving greater attention to what students actually learn during the course of their studies, and how learning occurs in different contexts. In particular, there are classes of skills and capabilities developed by students which are not specific to a particular discipline or profession. *(Gibson 2003: 4)*

This concept is also being implemented by most other Australian Universities as part of their curriculum renewals programs. As one of the participants explains:

> ... the development of a capability based curriculum requires that program teams identify, through consultation with all stakeholders, the holistic, integrated capability that is the desired outcomes from the program of study. This integrated capability refers to the ability to act in previously unencountered situations relevant to the professional and civic contexts the student will encounter upon graduation and requires the ability to discern what is salient in novel situations and to design and take appropriate actions. *(Lines 2003: 13)*

By defining and attempting to assess such capabilities, higher education is taking its first tentative steps towards outcomes-based forms of assessment. That is, have the teaching programs achieved what they set out to do with regard to these capabilities? Do the learning activities of the curriculum deliberately and actively provide students with opportunities to learn and enhance such capabilities? Do the objectives of the program correlate with and include the development of these attributes?

This extract from an activity theory analysis relates to the introduction of Training Packages as the specification of the outcomes, outcomes, assessment and qualification of vocational education and training programs Previously a form of competency-based curriculum had been used.

Table 1. Change from curriculum to Training Packages

	Historicity	Multi-voicedness	Contradictions	Expansive cycles
What is changing?	For most VET practitioners, the development of curriculum and learning resources has been something which has been done for them. Such development has, for the last twenty years or so, occurred at either the national, state or local RTO level and has been performed by specialists in educational development. Thus, although many of our more experienced	Many of the research participants saw this change in responsibility for educational development as an essential step in enabling the VET community to access the potential which Training Packages offer. They see it as a chance to re-professionalise VET and to build up the capacity of practitioners for innovative, responsive and flexible practice.	One of the key contradictions in this issue is the apparent separation of the current resource development initiatives, which have been funded by the Department of Education, Science and Technology to support the implementation of Training Packages. Many of the participants in the research project believed that this effort was, at best stopgap, and at worst detrimental as it was a move	The Triple C project (a collaborative learning project, funded by the Australian National Training Authority, and involving practitioners from a range of vocational education and training organisations) was an opportunity to find a resolution to this issue. It involved groups of teachers, working in virtual communities, to develop resources which would help other teachers and trainers to implement Training Packages. As a professional development

	Historicity	Multi-voicedness	Contradictions	Expansive cycles
	teachers would have learnt about educational development in their initial professional teacher programs, they have not had to use these skills on a day-to-day basis. This has resulted in one-size-fits-all approaches in antithesis to the flexibility, customisation and contextualisation demanded by industry.	Others believe that it is a waste of energy as VET practitioners in separate organisations and locations each reinvent the wheel. These participants felt that centralised resources were needed. Clearly, a balance between these two points of view is needed if we are to find an effective way forward.	back to centralised resource provision and was, in the main, carried out by consultants and those with specific expertise in educational development and instructional design rather than by the teachers and trainers themselves. Some participants noted that the separation was exacerbated by a lack of consultation as to what was really needed and an undue emphasis on the quality of the format rather than the educational flexibility, quality and usefulness.	model the trial program was a success and enabled the sharing of experience and insights whilst at the same time honing teachers' expertise in their understanding and use of Training Packages, their use of information and communication technologies and their competence in educational development and instructional design.

Consequently, it has been found to be almost impossible to define such attributes on an institutional basis, as distinct disciplines or industry fields have not only different objectives in terms of what their successful students should know and be able to do, but they also use language in different ways and with different meanings. Thus 'employability' for an Arts graduate means something very different to 'employability' for a graduate of a Bachelor of Engineering (ICT systems) as the former refers to a wide range of occupational fields and thus implies adaptability and on-going learning whist the latter refers to a defined occupational field with the specific skills required for occupations required within that field.

Common graduate capabilities which are being specified at faculty and school level within tertiary education institutions include:

- knowledgeability;
- employability;
- creative thinking;
- critical analysis skills;
- information literacy;
- environmental sustainability literacy;
- leadership and global and domestic citizenship.

In vocational education and training systems, the importance of generic skills, such as communication, problem solving, planning and organising, innovation, working with others, employability and self-management, are being foregrounded in policy discussions. A number of research projects have been funded, at Federal and State/ Territory level to explore and gain consensus on the recognition of employability skills. The most notable of these is the joint program undertaken by the Australian Chamber of Commerce and Industry and the Business Council of Australia to define the employability skills (ACCI & BCA 2002) and consequential projects funded by the Australian National Training Authority and the Australian Department of Education, Science and Technology to develop models for discussion (including Down 2003a; Curtin 2004; Julian 2004).

In addition, the applied technology project has identified that there are two levels to the question of generic capability: firstly, what capabilities have been developed by individuals and, secondly, and far more importantly, how learners learn to use these capabilities effectively within the workplace.

The definition of such capabilities is being drawn from industry and educators. However, if these skills and attributes are to enable graduates of formal training programs to participate fully in the workforce and to commit to learning through work as well as within formal programs on a lifelong basis, then it is important that such graduate capabilities are grounded in an understanding of our situated learning within work contexts.

Thus an understanding and reflective experience of learning through work is necessary to ensure that we provide our workplace entrants with the skills they need to negotiate work. In order to do this we need to unpack the concept of situated learning through work to determine the capabilities they need to be able to learn through work, to interact with the context of work: its people; its social and political structures; organisation; common goals; its competitiveness and the forms this takes; and its changeability.

Michael Eraut and his colleagues from Sussex University have identified five ways in which learning through work was facilitated. These are:

- induction and integration
- exposure and osmosis
- self-directed learning
- structured personal support for learning
- performance management
     (Eraut *et al.* 2002: 129-130)

In any workplace, access to the first, fourth and fifth of these is an affordance and consequently not necessarily available to all workers. The quality of these affordances and the learning which results from them is variable and significant affected by the climate of the workplace (Eraut *et al.* 2002: 130). Access to the second and third of these mechanisms is dependent on the agency and the individuals' existing competence and capabilities.

So the questions which must be asked of those working to define and assess the graduate capabilities of their learners is 'Do such capabilities enable the learner to learn from their work and workplaces?', and 'Do the students have the necessary attitude to learn from work?' The most important of all is whether we are producing self-directed learners who have the necessary skills and attributes to effectively interact with and reflect on the context of their work. That is, are the graduates of our tertiary institutions prepared for work and the forms of learning embedded within this activity.

6. CONCLUSIONS

Most of our lifelong learning will occur within work, domestic and social contexts with the work (paid or unpaid) being the predominant context. The role of tertiary institutions to ensure that their students develop the appropriate learning and research skills and other generic capabilities to equip them for workplace learning is a vital one. The interest currently being taken in defining and assessing graduate attributes/capabilities is a step in the right direction but it is still only a small step and it is being largely made in isolation from an understanding of the relationship between learning and work.

Barnett points out that contemporary workplaces are increasingly characterised by conditions of supercomplexity. That is:

> We live in a framework where our very frameworks for comprehending the world, for acting in it and for relating to each other are entirely problematical. We live in a world characterised by contestability, changeability, uncertainty and unpredictability.
>
> … Only be taking work and learning seriously … can we address the age of supercomplexity in which we find ourselves. *(Barnett 1999: 29)*

If tertiary institutions are serious about ensuring that their graduates have the necessary skill, knowledge and attributes to take their place in our society and workplaces, then addressing their preparedness for the supercomplexity of contemporary workplaces in this age of contingency is essential. This can only be done through acknowledgement of the reflexive nature of work and learning and ensuring that our students are prepared for the workplaces they will and do inhabit.

7. REFERENCES

Australian Chamber of Commerce and Industry (ACCI) & the Business Council of
Australia (BCA) (2002) *Employability Skills for the Future.* Canberra: Training Reform
Section, Department of Education, Science and Training.

Barnett, R. (1999) 'Learning to work and working to learn', in D. Boud & J. Garrick (eds.)
Understanding Learning at Work. London & New York: Routledge, pp. 29-44.

Barnett, R. (2002) 'Learning to work and working to learn', in F. Reeve, M. Cartwright &
R. Edwards (eds.) *Supporting Lifelong Learning: Organizing learning.* London & New
York: Routledge & Falmer, Vol. 2, pp. 7-20.

Bauman, Z. (1996) 'Morality in the age of contingency', in P. Heelas, S. Lash & P. Morris
(eds.) *Detraditionalization: Critical reflections on authority and identity.* Oxford:
Blackwell, pp. 49-58.

Beck, U. (1992) *Risk Society: Towards a new modernity.* London: Sage Publications.

Billett, S. (2000) 'Co-participation at work: Knowing and working knowledge', in *Working
Knowledge: Productive Learning at Work,* Conference Proceedings. Sydney, NSW:
University of Technology, Sydney, pp. 29-35.

Clancey, W. J. (1992) '"Situated" means coordinating without deliberation.' Paper
presented at McDonell Foundation Conference *The Science of Cognition.* Sante Fe:
New Mexico.

Curtin, P. (2004) 'Employability skills for the future', in (ed.) J. Gibb, *Generic skills in
vocational education and training: research readings.* Adelaide: National Centre for
Vocational Education Research, 2004, pp. 38-52.

Down, C. M. (2002) *Strategic evaluation of the qualitative impact of the introduction of
Training Packages on vocational education and training clients.* Melbourne: Australian
National Training Authority.

Down, C. M. (2003a) 'Employability Skills: Revisiting the Key Competencies or a new
way forward', *Proceedings of the 11th Annual International Conference on Post-
Compulsory Education and Training.* Gold Coast, Queensland, Australia: Centre for
Learning Research, Faculty of Education, Griffith University, Vol. 1, pp. 171-178.

Down, C. M. (2003b) 'The impact of training packages: What might we learn about
substantial system-wide change processes?' *International Journal of Training
Research,* Vol. 1, No. 2, pp. 1-20.

Down, C. M. (2005). *Situated Learning, Polycontextual Boundary Crossing and Transfer:
Perceptions of practitioners as to how competence is transferred across different work
contexts.* PhD thesis. RMIT University.

Engestrom, Y. (1999) 'Expansive Learning at Work: Toward an Activity-Theoretical Reconceptualization', *7th Annual International Conference on Post-Compulsory Education and Training*. Gold Coast, Queensland, Australia: Centre for Learning and Work Research, Griffith University, pp. 1-26.

Eraut, M., Alderton, J., Cole & Senker P. (2002) 'Learning from other people at work,' in R. Harrison *et al.* (eds.) *Supporting Lifelong Learning: Perspectives on learning.* London & New York: Routledge/Falmer. Vol. 1, pp. 127-145.

Gibson, D. (2003) 'A framework for developing and assessing generic capabilities in QUT Law graduates.' *B-HERT News,* No. 16, pp. 4-5.

Julian, T. (2004) 'Employability skills: Balancing the equation,' in J. Gibb (ed.) *Generic skills in vocational education and training: research readings.* Adelaide: National Centre for Vocational Education Research, pp. 84-94.

Kirsner, K. (2002) 'Implicit knowledge,' in. R. McDonald, J. Figgis and L. Doyle (eds.) *Fresh Thinking About learning and Learners: A Blue Skies project.* Brisbane: Australian National Training Authority, pp. 18-23.

Lave, J. & Wenger, E. (1991) *Situated Learning: Legitimate peripheral participation.* Cambridge: Cambridge University Press.

Lines, R. (2003) 'RMIT University - Initiatives in developing and renewing curricula to a capability based approach,' *B-HERT News,* No. 16, pp. 13-14.

Marris, P. (1975_Loss and Change. New York: Anchor Press/ Doubleday.

Marton, F. & Booth, S.(1997) *Learning and Awareness.* Mahwah, New Jersey: Lawrence Erlbaum Associates.

Rogoff, B. (1990) *Apprenticeship In Thinking: Cognitive development in social context.* Oxford: Oxford University Press.

Suchman, L. A. (1987) *Plans and Situated Actions: The problem of human-machine communication.* Cambridge: Cambridge University Press.

Tam, M. (1997) *Part-time Employment: A bridge or a trap?* Brookfield, USA: Aldershot.

Whyte, A. (2002) 'The real world of work, ' in R. McDonald, J. Figgis and L. Doyle (eds.) *Fresh Thinking about learning and learners: a blue skies project.* Brisbane: Australian National Training Authority, pp. 38-41.

CHAPTER 11

DAVID BOUD AND NICKY SOLOMON

WORK-BASED LEARNING, GRADUATE ATTRIBUTES AND LIFELONG LEARNING

Much has been written in earlier chapters about the value of generic attributes, their generation and their application in varying circumstances. In many of these, the decision to adopt the framework of graduate attributes was discretionary. That is, everyday practices of teaching and learning would be able to proceed without the need for such a framework. They may have added value to what would have been done, but they were not a necessary solution to any immediate problem. In this chapter we relate a two-part story about graduate attributes and how the idea is taken up in practice quite differently in differing circumstances, even within the one institution.

In the first part we examine a new teaching and learning practice in higher education — work-based learning partnerships — to show that a concern for graduate attributes, or something similar, is required for the practice to be enacted. In other words in this kind of program adoption of a graduate attributes framework is not discretionary, but is a necessary feature of its everyday activities. In the telling of this part of the story we describe the introduction of work-based learning into our own university — the University of Technology, Sydney (UTS) — and the institutional and pedagogical response that it demanded, including a particular emphasis on graduate attributes.

The second part of the story describes a related but quite different initiative involving a policy-led introduction of graduate attributes as a framework for the design and accreditation of *all* UTS courses. We track these two initiatives and consider the ways in which graduate attributes were taken up within the institution. We focus in particular on the ways in which teaching staff responded to them in the two sets of circumstances. We wish to argue that, no matter how desirable features of graduate attributes might be, they will not necessarily be

207

P. Hager and S. Holland (eds.), Graduate Attributes, Learning and Employability, 207–220.
© 2006 *Springer.*

actively taken up at the local level, and may indeed be resisted, unless there is a strong and immediate pedagogical imperative for doing so.

1. WORK-BASED LEARNING

Perhaps the most radical challenge to conventional assumptions in recent years has been the introduction of new forms of work-based learning (Boud and Solomon 2001). While many innovations in work-related learning have been introduced, the one that has done most to disturb what we take for granted is that of work-based learning partnerships. Students in such programs are typically involved in full-time work and undertake study in which their own work is the key part of the curriculum they pursue. Courses built around the idea of work-based learning partnerships focus on the knowledge and learning requirements of their work and this becomes the curriculum. Courses are negotiated between three parties — the learner, and representatives of their organisation and of the educational institution which supports and accredits the program.

Work-based learning challenges many everyday assumptions about courses and about teaching, learning and assessment. It raises questions about the nature and content of courses and about what we can take for granted in a university education. Questions it requires us to consider include: What is it legitimate to study for a qualification? What can be regarded as a course of study? Who decides what should be included in a program and how it should be assessed? Our own involvement in work-based learning confronted us with the need to consider the issue of what constitutes the successful completion of a higher education qualification. Abstract answers were not enough. They needed to be translated into practice so that judgements could be made about the performance of particular students at a given level of qualification.

In accord with its practice-based orientation to higher education, innovations in work-based learning that were occurring in the UK raised interest in establishing similar kinds of courses at UTS. Presentations by advocates from the UK focused attention on new kinds of program that could meet the needs of those already employed to engage in learner-managed programs of benefit to themselves and to their employer. Ideas about work-based learning were taken up in three Faculties and links forged initially with two employers.

The magnitude of the innovation and the educational challenges identified were such that the University decided to create a new mechanism for the accreditation and monitoring of work-based awards alongside its longstanding committees for undergraduate and postgraduate courses. A Board of Studies for

Work-Based Learning reported to the University Academic Board, was chaired by the first author, and had representatives from those Faculties with an interest in work-based learning. One of these representatives was the second author. She was invited to participate as her experience in non-traditional forms of knowledge and learning were considered to be relevant to the interests of the development of work-based learning frameworks and pedagogical practices.

Development of programs progressed rapidly from 1997. Rather than each Faculty inventing its own form of work-based learning and the documentation to have that accredited, the Board of Studies acted as a forum to consider proposals from Faculties. It later developed a standard framework that could be used as a template for work-based learning programs from any part of the University.

A particular challenge of work-based learning is the need to encompass a very wide range of learning outcomes. In particular, to recognise that work-based knowledge may be disciplinary or interdisciplinary, but is often transdisciplinary. That is, work itself, in its different manifestations, generates and sustains knowledge that cannot be reduced to the disciplinary or professional knowledge commonplace in the university, but is a type of knowledge which needs to be recognised in its own right. Conventional university frameworks of assessment, governed as they are by disciplinary or professional cultures are not sufficient to embrace the scope of more diverse knowledges found in organisations. At some later date these may be codified and represented in ways that academics find comfortable, but until that time they are intrinsically provocative within the academy, as they are essentially alien forms.

A central problem for all Faculties was to determine how a negotiated program of study could meet the requirements for a given level of award. The first set of courses were at postgraduate level and the question arose of what constituted appropriate performance to warrant the award of a Graduate Certificate, Graduate Diploma or Masters degree. The obvious source for this was the earlier experience in the United Kingdom. Derek Portwood from Middlesex University was employed as a consultant and processes from that university (Portwood 2001) as well as the framework from the South East England Consortium developed initially by Frank Lyons of Portsmouth University (Lyons & Bement 2001) provided a useful starting point.

What did this framework consist of? At its most basic level, there were statements of outcome at given levels of achievement (Graduate Certificate or Masters, say) in a number of categories. These categories represented learning and research processes such as planning, identifying and sourcing information, analysing and synthesising information, applying and demonstrating new learning and communicating this learning. Together these constituted what might be regarded as the set of attributes required of a graduate at the defined level. The distinctions in levels related to the degree of complexity and diversity of these processes as well as the degree of uncertainty and ambiguity of the context. An example of the different levels can be seen in the following criteria. At the Graduate Diploma level one of the criteria is 'choice and execution of appropriate communication mediums in a number of contexts', while at the Masters level it is 'choice and execution of appropriate communication mediums extending to unanticipated situations' (UTS 1997).

This framework of graduate attributes acts as a guide to students and to those who advise them on what is required to meet the requirements at any given level of academic performance. Typically, any given workplace learning project has, in order to meet the demands of the workplace, a strong emphasis on a limited number of areas covered by the framework. The work produced without any additional involvement might be at the desired level. However, further study, investigation, reflection and documentation is needed to show that the work involved has *de facto* met the full range of requirements for the particular academic level for which recognition is sought.

It can be seen therefore that work-based learning necessarily demands a focus on generic attributes; there is no disciplinary or professional framework to draw on when learning is constructed from the demands of actual work rather than framed within the particular cultural traditions of an existing codified body of knowledge. Generic attributes are not an add-on to existing assessment frameworks; rather they create a new framework from which decisions about academic worth are derived.

2. GRADUATE ATTRIBUTES ACROSS THE UNIVERSITY

While the challenges for both students and teachers in the work-based learning program were in some ways peculiar to the radical nature of that program, the university was at the same time confronting other challenges and repositioning itself in a number of complementary ways. This repositioning was a response to broader agendas and drivers that were influencing higher education conditions in Australia and elsewhere (Boud & Symes 2000). While some of the conditions were shaped by changing government funding arrangements, others were related to changes in understandings about knowledge and the increasing relationship of the academy with the world external to the university, in particular the world of work.

While not all academics were closely connected to the larger challenges around the role and function of universities, and indeed many continued to work in familiar ways, university-wide there were a number of curriculum and policy initiatives responding to the new context. Part of this related to a new concern with transdisciplinary or cross-disciplinary knowledge as well as different ideas about learning, ideas that marked a shift away from traditional understandings about disciplinary knowledge and their learning outcomes.

The *Statement of UTS Graduate Attributes* is located within this context. A story about its development though is a fragmented one—fragmented because it did not unfold in a linear or continuous way, but it came to be through a combination of responses to intersecting agendas and initiatives. What follows is an attempt to provide a brief account of the various institutional initiatives that contributed to the development process. While it reveals some of the messiness of the process, the many 'corridor' conversations that were involved to make the process 'work' are invisible.

From as early as 1994 there had been university level initiatives driven by educational and quality assurance agendas. One of these focused on the development of a document that could be used to guide curriculum development across the university as well as be used for promotion and marketing purposes. In a context where transdisciplinarity and generic capabilities were considered to be characteristic features of contemporary work (and thus educational) practices, the purpose of this document was to provide a common reference point for university courses. It was anticipated that this reference point would inform course developments within and across faculties as well as communicate to public audiences, such as the community, employers and potential students.

The complexities around the development of such a document cannot be underestimated. At a policy level it may have been understood as relatively apolitical and non-controversial but such a view ignores the strength of academic disciplinary communities and the resistance by academics to what could be understood as a top-down intervention. As an attempt to counter this kind of resistance the process began with the establishment of a working group. Its aim was to prepare a discussion paper that addressed a number of questions: How does/should the university ensure that its graduates' skills meet reasonable employer expectations? Should there be a core component for all undergraduate curricula? What assumptions can be made about the abilities of school-leavers?

Once the paper had been distributed each faculty was requested to prepare a graduate profile. These profiles were then submitted to Academic Board in 1996 and a second working group was established, this time with the aim of developing a generic graduate profile that took account of the faculty variations. The implementation of this draft profile though became tied into another project and this one emerged from the university's membership of the Australian Technology Network (ATN). The ATN is a network of universities in Australia who have grouped themselves as the major technological higher educational institutions. An ATN Teaching and Learning Committee within the university was established to develop strategies to foster the generic capabilities of ATN graduates. Its draft report discussed the concept of generic capabilities and illustrated how these contribute to graduate quality and highlights key issues in their development. The report includes principles covering the development of curricula for, and assessment of, generic capabilities. Graduate attributes were defined as 'the qualities, skills and understandings a university community agrees its students should develop during their time with the institution. These attributes include, but go beyond, the disciplinary expertise or technical knowledge that has traditionally formed the core of most university courses. They are the qualities that also prepare graduate as agents for social good in an unknown future.'

Importantly though the draft report was greeted with a mixed response by staff. By and large the main response was one of silence. Interestingly, while there were positive comments, some groups, such as the union representing academic staff, were concerned about the implications for work practices and a loss of freedom for academics in the curriculum development process. (UTS 2000a).

Meanwhile, in 1999 in parallel with the ATN project the university established yet again another working group on graduate capabilities. The connections with the work-based learning initiative in developing a capability framework indicated the need to include in the group staff connected with work-based learning. Furthermore, two other university level projects had connections with the ongoing development of the *Statement of UTS Graduate Attributes*. One was the BELL (Being an Effective Lifelong Learner) Project that was also initiated in 1999. Its aim was to establish a University-wide program for the development of lifelong learning skills and it involved investigating existing cross-disciplinary programs (such as those conducted by the Library, English language support units and information technology development unit) and also examined similar initiatives in other institutions.

In May 2000 the Academic Board approved the *Statement of UTS Graduate Attributes* (UTS 2000b). As indicated in the report that explained the development process, this statement built on work completed, or being undertaken, by a number of other university level projects, all of which referred to, or assumed desired characteristics of UTS graduates. In the consultative stage, there had been enthusiasm from those who had been active in making substantial changes to their undergraduate courses and there was little apparent resistance to the adoption of the Statement.

The stated goals of the statement were to:

- provide a common reference point for all courses
- develop a consistent terminology for describing learning outcomes
- develop a language for assessing the academic standards of undergraduate and postgraduate courses
- act as a quality assurance tool.

As described in the approved document the intention of the *Statement of UTS Graduate Attributes* was not to delete or deny existing processes or descriptions but rather to build on and develop previous UTS graduate profiles in order to 'facilitate current course development and review processes'. The Statement provided both general and specific descriptions of the attributes of a UTS graduate. At the most general level the Statement described three attributes, suggesting that these constitute 'graduate capability':

1. Learning to Learn Attribute — a UTS graduate is equipped for ongoing learning in the pursuit of personal development and excellence in professional practice
2. Professional Attribute — a UTS graduate operates effectively with the body of knowledge that underpins professional practice
3. Personal Attribute — a UTS graduate is committed to the actions and responsibilities required of a professional and a citizen.

A breakdown of the detail of these attributes is then provided in order to draw attention to their interrelationships and to offer some explanation of the various domains or categories which constitute and define the characteristics of each. For example the Learning to Learn attribute is described as comprising two domains:

1. *Knowledge literacies domain* – Academic literacies that encompass the learning of disciplinary, cross-disciplinary and transdisciplinary knowledge, and the ability to gain access to, utilise and critically assess knowledge from a number of sources. This domain links primarily, though not exclusively, with the Professional Attribute.
2. *Autonomy domain* – The ability to learn independently and analytically. It includes identifying things to learn, planning how to learn, and monitoring, reflecting on and thinking critically about that learning. This domain links primarily, though not exclusively, with the Personal Attribute.

There was little regulation around the way the Statement should be interpreted or written up by various courses and programs. What follows is one illustration of the way the Statement shaped a description of a graduate profile of the Work-based Learning programs (UTS 2000c):

Learning to Learn
A graduate of the work-based learning awards:

- understands the relationship between academic post-graduate learning and workplace learning
- is able to translate work experiences and activities into areas of learning and learning outcomes that are organised within an educational framework
- develops independent learning strategies, such as critical thinking and strategies for planning, monitoring and reflecting on one's learning.

Professional
A graduate of the work-based learning awards:

- understands and applies a body (or bodies) of professional or disciplinary knowledge
- engages with social and communicative relationships at work
- relates learning to the organisational context and directions.

Personal
A graduate of the work-based learning awards:

- engages in personal professional development that balances short term learning needs with career directions
- responds effectively, ethically and responsibly to work and learning requirements.

3. ISSUES AND OBSERVATIONS

As illustrated above, statements of graduate attributes were seen to be an appropriate way of addressing a number of different issues. Many of these initiatives have been directly driven by responses of the institution to the complexities universities face today. UTS, in common with most other universities, is positioning itself in a competitive marketplace and as such has been attempting to define and project itself as a unique and distinctive institution. At the same time it is also positioning itself to draw strength from a network of universities with common interests (the ATN) and facing the increasing accountabilities of government.

3.1 Pedagogical Imperatives

Along with the system-wide move to develop statements of graduate attributes or profiles, as discussed above, another set of initiatives also contributed to the development of the UTS Statements. These initiatives, which are to do with the university's work-based learning program, were also driven by university imperatives, but they were not played out only in university committees and working parties. Rather, the interest in developing generic statements of learning outcomes for work-based learning was directly related to the pedagogical practices of teachers working in the program. In this case the developments were pedagogically rather than institutionally driven. In other words there was an imperative to develop statements of graduate attributes within the work-based learning program in order for the program to operate. As described in earlier sections, work-based learning programs are by definition concerned with multi or transdisciplinary knowledges. Unlike other programs in the university the learning outcomes in work-based learning programs do not sit within familiar single disciplinary or professional areas. Teachers cannot rely on disciplinary communities to describe or recognise learning or to make judgements about a program. Teachers therefore needed a different kind of learning outcome framework to support the development of a cohesive and coherent program. Without such a frame they can neither advise students on their learning plans, nor judge when their work is sufficient for submission.

Furthermore, work-based learning programs were under a particular kind of scrutiny by the university community. Certainly, on the one hand academics have been encouraged to be innovative and develop programs that take advantage of the university's relationships with industries and workplaces and that help to produce new markets. However on the other hand there has been increased debate and questioning around the need to maintain academic standards. Without these standards, it is often argued, universities would struggle to sustain their particular role and status within the ever-increasing competitive educational marketplace.

3.2 Lack of Uptake

Academics involved in work-based learning therefore could not avoid the pedagogical imperative to develop a generic framework. They needed some kind of transparent transdisciplinary frame in order to support the development and assessment of each individualised work-based learning program. And this accounts for the relative ease in the way they have taken on generic statements. However this has not been mirrored in the uptake of the Statements outside of the work-based learning program. In 2002 a review of the *Statement of UTS Graduate Attributes* revealed a rather uneven engagement with the statements to say the least. Feedback suggested that there was a lack of commitment. A number of reasons were given, ranging from questions about the 'language' of the statements to a perceived concern with the limited scope of the statements. Of particular interest was a point made by one of the respondents who gave a 'cultural' explanation. This academic saw the necessity of a team approach to using the statement in curriculum development but such an approach was 'not necessarily a part of the work culture of most faculties or courses'. The various groups involved in the review have, at the time of writing, been engaged in a redrafting process of the Statement. This is attempting to respond to these concerns by reframing the statements and 'simplifying' the language as well as taking on board the outcomes of more recent university-level initiatives such as projects on the tracking of graduates following graduation.

We wish to draw attention to a number of issues that are likely to be contributing to academic resistance to taking up statements of graduate attribute in mainstream programs. In part the issues we identify and discuss here, have come to our attention by comparing and contrasting the two initiatives: the Graduate Attribute Statements and the use of graduate outcome statements in work-based learning programs. As discussed earlier the coexistence of these initiatives is not coincidental. They are both located within the same institution but importantly both are particular kinds of responses to the challenges confronted by universities and academics within a particular set of contemporary political and cultural conditions.

3.3 Resistance to Policy Initiatives

While theorisations about these conditions vary in their focus, there is a shared understanding that globalisation and the emergence of a knowledge economy have resulted in a new way of conceptualising knowledge and knowledge production and understanding universities as involved in the 'new business of learning' (Symes & McIntyre 2000; Boud & Solomon 2001). At the local level these practices may be manifest in differing ways. However, it is likely that stories told about contemporary academic practices resonate across many locations as academics and their institutions reposition themselves in relation to the different accountabilities increasingly required by government, industry and workplaces, as well as those of students.

As knowledge itself becomes a contested and diversified concept, the cultural practices of both universities and academics also become contested and diversified. The previous cultural meanings around being an academic working within a particular disciplinary community no longer have the same currency. As academic work becomes increasingly managed, commodified, quantified and sold, academics find themselves identifying as workers and understanding themselves as working in a workplace — rather than a university in a more conventional sense.

The policy directions of the university as it positions itself to the government and the marketplace have resulted in academic practices that suggest a loss of autonomy and a change in their identity (Chappell et al. 2000). Academics respond to these changes in different ways but frequently though can be seen to resist policy impositions that bureaucratise their everyday practices. The *Statement of UTS Graduate Attributes* can be understood as one of these policy imperatives that are experienced as motivated by institutional accountability and this is experienced as incompatible with 'normal' academic work. It is understood as a bureaucratic task that has little meaning to the everyday world as they experience it and as such can (or should) be avoided. The Statement is a document that is seen to service the accountability pressures experienced by the institution. It is not a document that provides for or even relates to academics' everyday pedagogical practices.

It is not as if the concept of a graduate profile or graduate attributes is intrinsically problematic for academics. Rather the problem lies in its bureaucratic and centralised location and this means that it can be experienced as a managerial tool for regulating academic work rather than facilitating it. It can be understood as a technology of power in a Foucauldian sense, and as such can become a site of resistance (Scheeres & Solomon 2000). It is likely that it is not the 'words on the page' that are puzzling or obscure, but it is rather what the document symbolises. Nor is it that the language of the document is inconsistent with understandings about knowledge, skills or learning, nor that it has no educational value. But rather it is to do with the source of that text and the way its meaning signifies accountabilities and cultural practices that are institutional ones rather than those that have meaning within disciplinary communities or relevance to individual teacher practices.

3.4 Central-local Tensions

However the reasons for a lack of uptake go beyond the manager–employee power relations. It may also be explained in curriculum design terms. Conventionally academic course design practices are bounded by knowledge and learning areas that lie within a particular disciplinary territory, which may or may not be explicitly articulated. This curriculum design work does not involve local translations of university level global statements. Yet in order to operationalise the statements, they have to go through a translation process in order to have meaning within the context of a discipline. This process is not one that is usually part of academic practice, nor is it one that responds to what might be experienced as a pedagogic problem. It is not understood as a tool for resolving a perceived problem and is therefore not considered to be helpful or useful.

By contrast, in work-based learning programs, generic statements of graduate attribute do relate to the curriculum practices of the academics. In a program that sits outside conventional academic or disciplinary boundaries academics are in need of tools and texts that can assist them in their efforts to design and judge areas of knowledge and learning. They cannot do their work without it. They need something to mark out the curriculum territory. Furthermore, they can use their application of it to respond to the critical eye of sceptical colleagues and use the document for quality assurance and equivalence arguments.

4. CONCLUSIONS

Policy initiatives in educational institutions always need to be justified in terms of the benefit to students, but members of the institution may not accept all of these justifications, and, even if they are, they may not be taken up with enthusiasm. The extent and pace of such initiatives, driven by the need for universities to position themselves in the external environment, are creating an overload on staff who themselves are under considerable pressure to perform more with less resources. This means that some of these policy initiatives are going to command more attention than others and the degree to which they are acted upon will vary greatly.

In the case of graduate attributes we have seen contrasting responses within a single institution. When graduate attributes were needed, as illustrated in the work-based learning story, in order for staff to engage in a desired new practice and to justify it to others, then they were accepted and used with almost no resistance. However when they were seen to be part of a culture of compliance with respect to a new course approvals process, there was significant resistance. That this took the form of using them as required, rather than rejecting them out of hand, was no less a form of resistance. The pedagogical imperative may have been persuasive, but the positioning imperative was not.

In many ways this does not reflect on the value of graduate attributes at all. It says nothing about whether the use of graduate attributes in course design and accreditation is desirable or not. What it does do is to draw attention to what the idea is taken to be and how it is enacted in practice, by whom and for what purpose. New educational ideas are used for many purposes. For some, it is to solve a previously insoluble problem, for others it is to ease others into compliance with a position which while not rejected, is not one they would have adopted if left to their own devices. Such ideas need to be judged not only on their intrinsic merits, but also on the ways in which they are promoted and taken up in practice. No matter how apparently seductive they may be, they only work if those to whom they are exposed are willing players in the process and are in a position to appreciate the qualities displayed.

5. REFERENCES

Boud, D. & Solomon, N. (eds.) (2001) *Work-Based Learning: A New Higher Education?* Buckingham: SRHE & Open University Press.

Boud, D. & Symes, C. (2000) Learning for real: work-based education in universities, in C. Symes & J. McIntyre (eds.) *Working Knowledge: The New Vocationalism and Higher Education.* Buckingham: SRHE & Open University Press, pp. 14-29.

Chappell, C., Farrell, L., Scheeres, H. & Solomon, N. (2000) 'The Organization of Identity: Four Cases', in C. Symes & J. McIntyre, (eds.) *Working Knowledge: The New Vocationalism and Higher Education.* Buckingham: SRHE & Open University Press, pp. 135-52.

Lyons, F. & Bement, M. (2001) 'Setting the standards: judging levels of achievement,' in D. Boud & N. Solomon (eds.) *Work-Based Learning: A New Higher Education?* Buckingham: SRHE & Open University Press, pp. 167-183.

Portwood, D. (2001) 'Making it work institutionally', in D. Boud & N. Solomon (eds.) *Work-Based Learning: A New Higher Education?* Buckingham: SRHE & Open University Press, pp. 74-85.

Scheeres, H. & Solomon, N. (2000) 'Research partnerships at work: new identities for new times', in J. Garrick & C. Rhodes (eds.) *Research and Knowledge at Work: Perspectives, case-studies and innovative strategies.* London: Routledge, pp. 178-99.

Symes, C. & McIntyre, J. (eds.) (2000). *Working Knowledge: The New Vocationalism and Higher Education.* Buckingham: SRHE & Open University Press.

UTS (1997) *Manual for Work-Based Learning Programs,* Sydney: University of Technology, Sydney.

UTS (2000a) Memo from Secretary of the UTS Branch of the National Tertiary Education Union to Director of Centre for Learning and Teaching, UTS, 15 March 2000.

UTS (2000b) *Statement of UTS Graduate Attributes,* Sydney: University of Technology, Sydney.

UTS (2000c) Accreditation Document of Work-based Learning Programs 2000, Sydney: University of Technology, Sydney.

CHAPTER 12

INA TE WIATA

GENERIC ATTRIBUTES AND THE FIRST JOB:
GRADUATES' PERCEPTIONS AND EXPERIENCES

1. INTRODUCTION

So far the chapters of this book have focussed mainly on the role of higher education institutions in the fostering of generic graduate attributes. This chapter shifts the focus to the realities of the generic attributes as experienced by a group of new graduates in their first one to two years of work. The study from which the information is drawn began with eleven graduates. They were from a medium sized Australian university and had completed their first undergraduate degrees (sometimes double degrees), in Commerce, Law, Arts, Information Technology, Computer Science, and Engineering. The eleven graduates were initially interviewed after four to six months in full time work. Those seven who remained in the study were interviewed again after approximately twelve to eighteen months. Four remained in contact for approximately twenty four months. For the seven who were available for re-interview more in-depth information was gathered, including perceptions about the usefulness and importance generic attributes have in determining job satisfaction. This was done using the critical incident technique (Flanagan 1954; Tripp 1993; Christie & Young 1994). This technique is ideal for gathering qualitative data as it is grounded in common sense procedures. It essentially involves the identification of and reflection on an incident that has had 'real' significance for the individual concerned, it is personal, and memorable. The reflection then ought to lead to some sort of action, for example, a change in attitude, thinking or behaviour.

A critical incident in this study was defined and emphasised as 'an incident or situation that occurred that has affected the way you think, feel or act in relation to your work or workplace'. It was highlighted that the actual incident did not necessarily have to occur at work, so long as it impacted on work in the way(s)

221

P. Hager and S. Holland (eds.), Graduate Attributes, Learning and Employability, 221–242.
© 2006 *Springer.*

indicated. More specific information on what might constitute a critical incident was provided, e.g. an experience (either positive or negative) that did not go according to plan. Guidance was also given as to 'where' critical incidents might be found, e.g. something that happens to you in your current job or activities that has an effect on your work. This might be something as straightforward as your team being called into your manager's office to discuss a problem that a customer is having with one of your team members. Or it might be something more unusual such as a past experience influencing the way in which you practise. For example, the manner in which you provide feedback to work colleagues may be a result of the way in which you received feedback as a member of a sports team.

The specified clusters of generic graduate attributes identified in this study comprise critical thinking, problem solving, communication, and interpersonal understandings. These clusters were chosen firstly because all Australian universities advocate, and indeed expect, that their graduates develop these during their university experience, and, secondly because they were the basis of the initial Graduate Skills Assessment (GSA) instrument(s), which was being trialed at the university from which the research participants were drawn. The GSA, developed by the Australian Council for Educational Research (ACER) is based on pen and paper tests, that is, it assesses, for example, written communication as opposed to other forms of communication.

Definitions/descriptions of what is meant by each of the specified clusters of graduate generic attributes are based on the information provided by the ACER documentation and Nightingale et al. (1996) They are as follows:

Critical thinking – reasonable, reflective thinking that is focused on deciding what to do or believe. It might include the ability to develop arguments, reflect, evaluate, assess and/or judge.

Problem solving – a mental activity leading from an unsatisfactory state to a more desired 'goal' state. It will include activities where you might have to:

- identify, comprehend, diagnose, restate a problem, pose problems;
- analyse information/data relevant to a problem;
- review information/data, represent features of a problem;
- identify, synthesise and apply information relevant to a problem;
- explore, speculate, identify, generate solutions and; evaluate solution strategies and their outcomes.

Communication - includes communicating in writing, orally, and visually. This involves activities where people need to get their ideas across to others and vice versa. This category may include skills such as arguing, describing, advocating, interviewing, negotiating, presenting, and listening.

Interpersonal understandings - understanding the features of interpersonal relationships that enable people to work and live together. This is likely to include skills such as

- working co-operatively/collaboratively,
- identifying individual differences and cultural diversity,
- identifying the features of effective team workers and factors that could affect team performance, and,
- interpreting team dynamics, making inferences about feelings, attitudes, motives, values, personality.

Graduates in this study were provided with a working description of each of the clustered attributes prior to their first interview, and these descriptions were referred to throughout the study.

The two case studies below illustrate the use and development of some of the generic attributes necessary in the workplace today. All cases revealed that no one cluster of generic attributes is used in isolation but rather they are interwoven into the tapestry of the workplace.

These case studies provide stories – i.e. narratives grounded in context – that illustrate the experiences of Richard and Raewyn in their respective workplaces. They demonstrate the ways in which graduates acquired their generic attributes, how they use them in their day to day activities, and the importance and meaning they have for them both in their current roles in the workplace and for their role in lifelong learning.

The framework for describing each story (based on Bennett, Dunne & Carre 2000) comprises 5 categories – the context, the main generic attributes used, origin of attributes, development of attributes, attributes and lifelong learning. These categories have been derived through analysis of the whole sample (11 graduates), and represent the main issues and concerns from graduates.

Case study 1 focuses on interpersonal understandings (team dynamics, team-work) and communication.

Case study 2 concentrates on communication in the workplace.

2. CASE STUDIES

2.1 Richard

Richard graduated with an honours degree in electrical engineering. He studied for four years to gain his qualification. Richard gained a position in a large national engineering firm just prior to his graduation. Richard considers himself to be a good communicator and team worker. He felt he could "handle" himself in the workplace.

2.1.1 The context

Richard, although not designated as a supervisor, performs a supervisory role at his current workplace. This is in contrast to the initial role, in which he was employed, where as a junior staff member the nature of his work primarily involved the drawing of technical specifications as the company was in the design phase of a major project. Although employed with the same company, Richard's geographic location has moved from the company's office to on-site and the nature of his work has changed significantly as the company moved into the installation phase of a major project. He regards his job ".... as a completely different job now."

2.1.2 Main attributes used

In Richards's first position within the company he emphasised three categories of generic attributes as being important:

Problem solving, for example, various aspects of drawings and designs required problem identification, and application of relevant information in order to generate a suitable solution, which was needed in order that the project team could continue to progress. Richard was able to develop this attribute in a supportive environment.

> ...like every day I sort of got a few more questions for them (line managers) so they can see what I'm up to. My designs are checked by the drawing office, checked by my supervisor before being sent off..... they're not leaving the whole thing up to me...

This reinforces the idea that a community of practice (Lave 1990) is important in developing and consolidating generic attributes and achieving successful outcomes.

Interpersonal understandings, for example, working as part of a team, which included other specialists also engaged on the same project.

> That's the real "trick" isn't it?..... at work sometimes it is quick to get it sorted out...other times... ...the electrical guys want to know how to get the cables....... whether they should stay there..... so you got to go backwards and forwards...yeah doing that takes some time...

In this example the team could be viewed as using polycontextual skills (Engestrom, Engestrom, & Karkkainen 1995). They crossed the boundaries of their own work area in order to collaborate with other communities of practice (Lave 1990)

Communication, for example, written reports and drawings on all phases of work had to be communicated to supervisors and verbal communication to team members (not necessarily electrical engineers) had to be clear.

> Trying to describe a concept over the phone is nowhere near as easy as drawing it on a drawing. If someone doesn't have a drawing in front of them and you are trying to explain it you've got to be very clear and not waffle on and get off the point because it makes it quite difficult for that person to receive your point.

Effective communication requires among other things, "an appreciation for the context or culture in which the communicative act occurs" (Hyslop-Margison 2000: 62). In Richard's case, communication as presented in his university course simply did not encompass this appreciation.

2.1.3 Origin of generic attributes

During his time at university Richard claims that he was never told or given any explicit instruction regarding the generic attributes he would need in the workplace. For example, he had the all too common misunderstanding of the experience of what is learnt through 'group work' (part of the 'interpersonal understandings' category of this study). Although Richard was part of a group on two occasions, he did not have any knowledge of the attributes that the lecturer may have been attempting to develop in students, did not therefore value the experience, nor find it useful in enhancing his own skills in this area. Richard certainly knew that group work, or teamwork was an attribute that was valued in the workplace, but viewed it as one learned outside of the university. In fact, when asked at his employment interview how he worked in a team environment, he spoke of his experience at playing sports, and managing a soccer team in order to illustrate this.

> I went to the interview and it was .... they basically just asked how I worked in a
> team environment.....
>
> I said I'd played on team sports before and I was also managing a soccer team at the
> time.....yeah I just said umm...I get on well with people and...

Richard's shared purpose as part of his soccer teams, as both a player for one, and coach for another, illustrate Beach's (Beach 1999) contention that it is the meaningful and dialogic engagement in a 'community of practice' inspired by a shared motives that helps in the development of capabilities such as team work.

Richard attributes his communication skills to his family environment.

> ....living in a family environment. You learn to communicate with your parents
> and brothers and sisters. You learn to share and to value each other's time and be able
> to make time for each other and be able to stick to that commitment. And they are
> very important skills as well at work.

This perception is noted in the literature (Virgona *et al.* 2003a; Virgona *et al.* 2003b), who found that over half of the participants in their study regarded home and community as one significant source of their skill development.

Where Richard did mention further development of generic attributes at university it was not the curriculum *per se*, but the university experience that made the contribution. For example, he commented that he was able to practice his time management skills in, "not running out of time in an exam".

2.1.4 Development of generic attributes

The initial role that Richard had was challenging and stimulating for him. He enjoyed learning the new skills offered by the workplace, for example, learning how to handle himself as a team member when aspects of the project don't go according to plan. Incidents such as seeing a senior colleague re-negotiate time lines with a small group of team members who hadn't met a deadline, and watching that same senior colleague sort out an awkward interpersonal interaction between another two different team members has benefited Richard enormously. He found the learning he took from these situations advantageous in his next role within the company.

A year or so after Richard had started work with his company, it moved into the second phase of the major project. Both his geographical location and the nature of his work changed. Richard found himself acting much more as the supervisor, instead of the "junior" being supervised. For Richard, this was the critical incident that he identified. The change of role had a huge impact on not only the emphasis given to particular generic attributes, but on both the level to which he needed to develop and use them, and the frequency with which he employed them.

Generic attributes according to (Hager *et al.* 1996) are overlapping, and Richard highlighted all four categories as essential in his second role in the company, although problem solving and critical thinking were not the prime attributes he emphasised.

With regard to these two categories though, Richard made the following comments:

> I think I am using the skills (problem solving) differently now, yeah. I assist others now in translating our design work into the actual installation you see on site (as opposed to doing the translation alone).

And, in terms of critical thinking, for example, assessing different aspects of a situation, making decisions about what to do, he said,

> .... you've got to make good decisions quickly and you've got to be practical and you've got to be able to pass your knowledge on to the guys who are doing the actual work.

These attributes can be viewed both as outcomes as well as processes (Hager *et al.* 1996) and illustrate the more complex learning that Richard has undergone in developing these skills compared with his initial use of these attributes.

Interpersonal understandings, in particular, teamwork (i.e. working collaboratively, interpreting team dynamics and so on) on the other hand was an attribute that Richard emphasised as essential for the role he now had in the company. For example, to relieve some of his own stress and to enable his team to function more effectively Richard has found it necessary to spend more time than he initially thought with co-workers.

> Installation work is a very time-consuming job. Sort of feeling like my job is a little more stressful now than it was. I'm starting earlier and finishing later, spending more time with people.

Through acknowledging the common pressures, he and his co-workers are experiencing he is developing camaraderie, and a shared understanding of issues. Although initially thinking that the other aspects of his job took priority, Richard genuinely values this extra time he has spent with team members. He is finding that his stress levels have dropped and the team is responding well to the challenges that they face in working together on a substantial project.

> I enjoy contributing (to the team). I don't feel that I am any different to anyone else and I enjoy the friendship and being able to discuss things with other people.

Once again it is the 'community of practice' (Lave 1990) that defines the norms and behaviours for a work group. Richard's camaraderie in the group, like Gidden's survey workers (Giddens & Stasz 1999) are both part of an 'intimate' situation – one where members rely on one another in an atmosphere of mutual respect.

Richard values communication, in particular negotiating, listening, describing:

> ..... especially when it's stressful it always helps if you're courteous to each other and just think about them for a minute rather than always focusing on your own problems. I think it makes it a lot easier for other people to do their work. More work gets done and everyone's happy about it.

Communication skills need to be sophisticated in stressful situations which may be potentially adversarial (Giddens & Stasz 1999). Richard is an effective communicator – he has learned and continues to learn how to communicate in a variety of contexts. Falk, Millar & Owen (2002) contend it is this constant re-learning and not the application of skills from one context to another than enables a person to be effective in using generic attributes. Combined with the increasing development in his confidence, Richard is able to demonstrate his communication skills in a variety of 'communities of practice' (Lave 1990) in a purposeful way.

Along with the above attribute categories that Richard emphasised, he spoke about his need to "self-manage". He has had to adjust to, and manage his feelings and expectations about "keeping on top" of his work. While this had been easy for him in his previous role, he finds now he ".... sometimes spends the whole day putting out fires... before even getting to your own work".

He has also had to "get used" no direct supervision. Initially this was unsettling for him but he now believes he is capable of, and trusted enough to complete a task independently. As (Sandberg 2000) suggests, the key to moving forward in the development of more sophisticated and complex use of generic attributes is in understanding how the learner conceives a task. Richard has had to re-think his conceptions about his role and his tasks and although finding his new role somewhat stressful it is very enjoyable. "I'm definitely liking the challenge – I'm enjoying what I'm doing".

2.1.5 Generic attributes and lifelong learning

Richard's learning from his critical incident describes some of the attributes that he takes with him as he continues his journey in the workforce:

- adjusting to and manage feelings and expectations about "keeping on top" of his work. Whilst this was easily done in his previous job, in this current job he "sometimes just spends the whole day putting out fires", and feels like he has done none of his actual work;
- dealing with "real" time and the pressures to work to time based deadlines have required him to develop strategies to help manage his stress levels and his job;
- finding that the common pressures he and his co-workers are experiencing produce a camaraderie that helps him enjoy his job and relieves some of his own personal stress;
- feeling a bit uneasy about not knowing whether or not his supervisor (who is not on site with him) actually knows what he is doing, and/or what he is capable of is "OK". Richard's confidence to work independently and self evaluate is increasing. He is learning if and when he needs to "check in";
- discovering that he likes and needs a workplace that can provide him with change and challenges (this discovery came about as a result of his change in his role and job – it wasn't something he had "really recognised"); and,
- how the completion of a significant work assignment (i.e. one phase of a project), can bring him satisfaction plus excitement – the latter coming with the progress to another new phase of the project.

In response to being asked what a "good" job was, he offered the following:

> working in an organisation that offers challenges and stimulation to remain employed with them.

This involved the workplace valuing and utilising appropriately the skills, expertise and interests Richard had at any given point in time. Enabling him to use particular generic attributes *per se* was not enough; the opportunity to use them to a level that Richard himself perceived that he was capable of, was essential.

Richard values his independence, and his self-discovery, for example, that he was due for a change of role and job even though he hadn't initially recognised this. He has learnt that satisfaction, anticipation and excitement are three key ingredients in making his "life" in any workplace enjoyable and satisfying. The generic attributes Richard has developed and uses could not be reproduced in the university "classroom". Feeling the pressure of "real" time to work as part of a team to complete a large national project is quite different to that of needing to have a university assignment finished on time (whether it be group or individual). The consequences for the former are far-reaching and significant. They have relevance and a meaning that cannot be reproduced in the university setting. The teamwork and other skills needed to deal with situations such as this are learnt 'in action' and by 'reflection on action' (Schon 1983; Schon 1987) in the workplace. Richard's learning is enabling him to both function more effectively in his current "supervisory" role and to reach out for increasingly demanding roles in his chosen profession.

2.2 Raewyn

Raewyn graduated with a double degree in arts and commerce. She studied for three years to gain her qualification and commenced her current job upon graduation. Raewyn describes herself as enthusiastic and organised. She enjoys having a fair degree of responsibility and thinks she works "better under pressure".

2.2.1 The context
Raewyn is a marketing manager in her current job with the company, the same one that she commenced with after graduation. This role is different to the two roles she has had with the company – the first as an assistant to a marketing manager, and in the second she was engaged in sales analysis. Although employed with the same company, Raewyn's geographic location has moved and while she enjoyed her first two roles, the nature of her current work is what she believes she is qualified to do best and what she really likes doing.

2.2.2 Main attributes used
Raewyn's initial role with the company was of assisting the marketing team in a moderately large urban shopping centre. She commenced this job with a minimum amount of induction (half a day), and believes the attributes she required to "survive" in this environment are best described in the following categories:

- Communication, where she found herself constantly asking her manager for the guidance she needed to perform her tasks.
- Interpersonal understandings, in particular having to work collaboratively with other members of the shopping centre team.

The above attributes coupled with qualities such as initiative, self confidence, and self efficacy meant that although she was, "….thrown headlong into it (job)", she not only survived but went on to take up a different position at the Head Office of the company after three months of work.

2.2.3 Origin of generic attributes

During her time at university, Raewyn cannot remember any explicit instruction regarding the generic attributes she would later find useful in the workplace. Having said this, she does remember on a few occasions being aware of the lecturer(s) asking her and her classmates to do particular exercises in order to learn certain skills. For example:

> …. In some group assignments they'd (lecturers) say you've got to do it in groups so you can build up your teamwork skills…....

Although on the face of it teamwork is one of the 'workplace useful' generic attributes (a subset of 'interpersonal understandings'), the nature of teamwork 'taught and learnt' in the classroom is quite different to that which Raewyn experienced in the workplace. (Berge 1998; Candy & Crebert 1991; Giddens & Stasz 1999). To highlight her point, Raewyn said this:

> It (the classroom) is such an artificial situation. ….when we're in a job we are all working in the same office together and we have scheduled times when we can get together and we'll all committed. When we were at uni, I was working with someone who lives…. (in another town) and someone who lives …(a long way from uni). It was just dumb. We found other ways around it that were completely different to how you would do it in a work environment.

So, for Raewyn the learning of generic attributes had to be both relevant to her work and in an authentic environment. This did not happen for her in the university classroom. Instead the majority of her generic attributes were initially learnt in environments outside of the university classroom, for example, in the university college where she was an office holder, and in workplaces (both as a part time and full time employee).

I was heavily involved in running my college back at uni, ...so I've built up all the
problem solving, teamwork, communication, that all came from there. I also worked
all the way through uni, and built up a lot of skills in communication there, and also
just what I've learnt on the job.

Raewyn does however believe that she got at least one "practical thing" from
university – the marketing jargon. Her statement that "I can now sound like a
marketing person", might appear superficial, but on closer examination actually
means that she has increased confidence in performing in her role. She stated "this
jargon has given me the ability to express my marketing ideas in the way a
marketer would". She believes she "already had the ideas, but being able to
express them in jargon buys me credibility." This notion of "identitiy," of being
able to "look and act like a worker in a particular context" (Falk, Millar & Owen
2002: 53) is important in enabling effective communication to take place.

2.2.4 Development of generic attributes

In her second position in the company, the nature of Raewyn's work was vastly
different to that she had been doing. Having survived one "sink or swim" situation,
Raewyn coped well with only three days of on-the-job-training to prepare her for
her role as Reporting Analyst. In this role, Raewyn found herself analysing sales
figures for staff from several divisions of the company. She emphasised the
following two categories of generic attributes as being particularly important in
this role.

- Communication, for example, presenting information in diagrammatic
  form, negotiating time lines with other workers.

  Often, I make sure that everyone gives me a timeframe of how soon they need it.
  Sometimes I'll have the General Manager saying "I need this" but he doesn't need it
  for a week, and I've got a Centre manager saying "I need this in two hours" so
  obviously I know that I can push the GM back a bit and worry about that later. ....
  it's one of the big skills that I have learnt while I've been at work, having to say "I can
  do that for you, but I'm not going to be able to do it until next week." So it's been
  something that I've had to sort of master.

- Problem solving, for example, analysing information, synthesising and
  applying information relevant to a problem.

  It's generally, it's a lot of problem solving, a lot of things I get asked to...I do a lot of
  work on spreadsheets, it's all numbers based .... I get asked to plot a trend over the

last three years of how a particular company's gone to compare say, sales of white
goods to sales of books, all that kind of thing.

Because she was now engaged in a more global role, i.e., working across
several different divisions of the company, she had to learn how to juggle the
competing needs of senior staff members while maintaining a reasonable
workload for herself. Raewyn was "warned" that this was one of the pressures she
would face. This warning came from both her direct manager and another staff
member. Being told by her manager that an inability to prioritise had been a
problem for the staff member previously in Raewyn's role, and knowing that she
could check priorities at any time with the General Manager if necessary, helped
Raewyn to develop the skill of prioritising. She has learnt how to manage the time
frames that the various staff members give her through asking for time frames
from people and then negotiating those if necessary.

This skill of prioritising is one of the "big" skills Raewyn believes she has
learnt in the workplace. Having the ability to say, "I can do that for you, but I'm
not going to be able to do it until next week", to senior managers requires a degree
of self-assuredness that Raewyn believes was/is unable to be taught or
experienced in the university "classroom". Bandura's (1977) work in social
learning theory shows us how important the experiential base is particularly for
the development of self efficacy, i.e. believing that you can perform certain
actions. For Raewyn, her workplace was the necessary base.

Raewyn's third position commenced in the second year of her employment
with the company. She was appointed to a position as Marketing Manager at a
facility in another city (2 hours away from Head Office where her last job had
been). It was in this position that Raewyn experienced her critical incident.

The generic attribute that is the focus of Raewyns' critical incident is the role
of communication in the workplace. As mentioned at the beginning of this
chapter, no one generic attribute is used in isolation, and indeed this was also the
case here where Raewyn had to also draw on other attributes and specific skills.
Hager (1999) notes that generic attributes are not 'free floating' but are used in
unison in actual work situations along with other more specific competencies.

Unlike the previous case study where Richard's critical incident could be
labelled as "positive", i.e. his move into a "new" role and job with the company,
Raewyn's incident, was a less pleasant occurrence. It occurred about one month
into her new role and is best described within the generic attribute category of
communication.

The incident involved. a significant misunderstanding on Raewyn's part in negotiating work that another agency would be doing for her (and her company). She inadvertently agreed to give the "other" agency extra work, which resulted in a significant "blow-out" of her budget.

> I was working with the (other) agency... they would say something like "we can do this here", and at the time it sounded like a really minor thing and I would say "yeah that's a great idea" not realising that what they were saying to me was "we could do this here and it would cost you $5,000". So it was one trivial bit in the whole landscape ....but having suddenly blown my budget, I went "oh no what have I done!

Although the incident left Raewyn somewhat shell-shocked, she knew that she needed to address the situation promptly. She did so by first apprising her manager of the situation, informing (via email) the other agency that all agreements would need to be in written form in the future, and by altering her own practice (ensuring that all future communication with this agency is followed up in writing – to ensure a shared understanding is reached.)

Admitting to her manager that she had made a mistake was not particularly difficult for Raewyn, as she believed her manager and indeed her work environment was supportive, and as such would welcome its employees learning through their mistakes. She appeared to be correct in this belief

> I have a really good relationship with my Centre Manager...he was understanding knowing that I was thrown in the deep end (into her current job).

> "I said ....so look you know, I've made a mistake,...... I'm going to be careful about it in the future.". He obviously went a bit ooo gee, ok – we've lost a bit of money... and then just said, "we really need to work and make sure that we do get everything in writing".

Once again, this illustrates that communication skills needed to be sophisticated in order to achieve a satisfactory outcome. For Raewyn, who was working in a potentially adversarial position to the "other" agency, her ability to negotiate with other parties, to give them a fair hearing, and to maintain this under pressure, were paramount. Giddens & Stasz (1999) found in their study that 'An amicable and professional demeanour is highly valued in all spoken communications'. Such a demeanour is perceived to improve the ability and willingness of the listener to engage in communication. This was certainly the case for Raewyn.

This experience was simply not reproducible in the "classroom" or indeed in a work experience situation as part of a formal curriculum. It required the context of a "real" role in a "real" workplace for Raewyn to both experience and deal with the misunderstanding and its consequences. That is to say, participation in 'communities of practice' (Lave 1990) and consequently shaping by the actual context of work (Boreham 2002).

In further conversation about the attributes she is currently using and the contexts in which they have been developed, Raewyn is now using all of those attributes described at the beginning of the chapter, but in particular the 'interpersonal understandings' and 'communications' groups. She restated (initial statement was in her first interview) that she believes she developed the generic attributes outside of the university curriculum (including her University College experience as Captain, and "on the job" experiences) and stated that she didn't believe that any exposure to generic attributes in the university curriculum enabled her to "take something" into the workplace.

2.2.5 Generic attributes and lifelong learning

Raewyn has engaged in critical reflection (self) and dialogue (with the researcher) in response to her incident. She believes the factors that contributed to this incident occurring included her inexperience in the job (which was at a level she did not expect to attain for at least another year), and her inexperience and unfamiliarity with the other agency, meaning that she did not recognise or realise precisely what she was agreeing to in the meetings. Put another way, she was being required to use skills that she hadn't previously developed.

Raewyn's learning from this incident relates directly to her work practice. She believes that she:

- needs to follow-up every verbal business interaction (particularly with the agency above) in writing.

This change in practice has challenged Raewyn's beliefs about herself. She had always heard that her company was "into ... covering exercises" but didn't want to think of herself as one who would engage in this practice. Raewyn commented here that she "doesn't necessarily like this about herself because she used to think those that engaged in it were stupid." And she now feels that she spends "more time on 'useless' things, but simply must cover myself."

As well she:

- is now using many more interpersonal skills with different people than
  she has in the past, and that this requires constant attention to detail.

  I work in a very close team now - there are only six of us that run the whole Centre. I
  have to be good at working in a team.

Also she:

- had/has to work very hard to stand firm in asserting what she needs/wants
  and to maintain good working relationships with other parties at the same
  time.

  I have to ... use a lot more negotiating skills .... and that's actually been very hard
  for me to be firm about what I want and maintain a relationship. I thought ...I'm a
  really firm person.I can say 'no I want this', but I'm realising I also have to maintain
  a relationship with these people so I can't just say I want this, give it to me and be
  done with it. I have to make sure that I don't put them off, and know that in two
  weeks I have to deal with them again.

In response to being asked what a "good job" was, Raewyn identified the
following characteristics:

- being given a fair amount of responsibility;
- having independence;
- being able to make her own decisions and being responsible for them;
- having some pressure to perform; and,
- identifying and utilising her expertise appropriately.

Expertise for Raewyn included using the generic attributes she perceived she
possessed and, like Richard, they needed to be used at and to a level at which *she*
believed she was capable of operating.

Raewyn is faced with some uncertainty regarding her next performance review
and what she wants to do, as she did not expect to be in her current role for a few
years yet. Having said that, she is not "fazed" by this though, as she believes that
she is a self-starter, and when the "right" opportunity presents itself she will take
advantage of it. She is developing her generic attributes to a much more
sophisticated level than previously, and while this development continues she
remains happy in her job. Unlike the university "classroom" which provided for
Raewyn, "such an artificial situation", for developing her generic attributes, she is
thriving in the learning environment of the workplace. Raewyn's learnings are

enabling her to function well in an environment of ambiguity and uncertainty. She will undoubtedly continue to succeed in her chosen profession.

3. DISCUSSION

The two graduates whose stories have been illustrated are representative of the seven who were interviewed at twelve to eighteen months, in that they either are, or feel as though they are, in quite different jobs to when they first began their employment. Of the seven, four have moved from their initial employer, with the other three having had substantial role changes (this includes Richard and Raewyn).

So, what influenced these changes in role and or job? It was primarily the need to be in a "good" job. A job that was challenging, and stimulating, one that both supported and enabled learning to occur, one where graduates' believed they were able to use and further develop their generic attributes in an increasingly complex and sophisticated manner, and one where company values, and workplace practices were congruent with individual graduates' beliefs and values. Apart from Richard whose move was initiated by the company, all other graduates were proactive in seeking new jobs, roles and responsibilities. (It is also likely that Richard would have been proactive in seeking further challenges within 3–6 months of his second interview.)

The importance of generic attributes to work performance is described by Virgona et al. (2003a; 2003b). Similar results were found in this study. All graduates believed before they entered the workforce, that generic attributes were important in the workplace. By the end of eighteen months in the workplace this statement had "real" meaning for them, and was restated as generic attributes are vital for survival in the workplace. Being placed in what they described as "sink or swim" situations brought graduates face to face with honing their generic attributes such as communication, critical thinking and interpersonal understandings. After survival came the satisfaction and challenge of using generic attributes to develop lifelong learning skills as their job responsibilities changed and grew. Even when a job was described as "bad", generic attributes were perceived as vital for enabling an improvement, either in the existing environment, or for finding and taking opportunities to move to another employer.

All graduates felt that the major dilemmas (critical incidents) they faced were not replicable in a university context (that is, in a course of study), yet having the generic attributes to work through these dilemmas was and is crucial to survival and success in the workplace. This has been illustrated by the two case studies.

All but one participant restated they had learnt the majority of the 'workplace useful' generic attributes in contexts outside of the university 'classroom' environment. The university course they had undertaken at best served to reinforce this learning; at worst, it played little or no part helping them acquire these skills. For example, four, including Richard and Raewyn, believed that teamwork/groupwork, whilst, covered in their university courses was different to that experienced in the workplace. Differences included, the relatively short duration that 'classroom' groups are in existence in comparison to those in the workplace, and the lack of individual and collective motivational factors in the 'classroom' groups as compared with those they had worked (or were working) with in the workplace.

Having said this all graduates did believe that their university courses of study were helpful in some way in enabling them to practise effectively in the workplace. Some participants described developing generic graduate attributes that were specific to a particular discipline. These were perceived as useful if and when practising in a given occupation. For example, one participant described how she "learnt to argue like a lawyer", appropriate for the courtroom, but not useful she believed, for everyday interactions in the workplace. Another spoke about problem solving in a commercial information technology environment being quite different to "life" situations where you had to "figure out" what to do when managing people with a problem in another workplace.

Other participants gained different skills. Raewyn, in her story above, mentioned that her course provided her with the language of her chosen profession, and thus afforded her some credibility. Richard believed that his discipline content knowledge gained through his course increased his confidence in being able to operate in the workplace, for example he felt he could give an oral presentation in the workplace more effectively and confidently as a result of his declarative knowledge.

4. CONCLUSION

The study at the centre of this chapter suggests that the role that universities play in the development of generic attributes is complex and problematic. For one thing, the generic attributes appear to be significantly contextual, and for another, their development is ongoing as job responsibilities change and grow.

In contrast to a lot of the existing research that supports the acquisition and development of generic attributes through the curricula, this study has highlighted some of the contentious issues that must be considered. Although Crebert (Crebert *et al.* 2004) proposes that attributes such as communication, teamwork skills, problem solving and analysis lend themselves to development at university provided the 'right' environment, conditions and processes are in place, this study has suggested that even this may not be enough to ensure that the attributes that are needed for the workplace are developed.

It may be that university courses play an important role in the development of some of the "specific discipline generic attributes", but can only lay the ground-work that will facilitate the development of the broader generic attributes in the workplace and elsewhere.

The study at the centre of this chapter has highlighted the following:

- Generic attributes that are useful in the workplace are not the same as those attributes labelled "generic" in the classroom. This has important implications for universities curricula and workplace learning environments;
- Generic attributes that are most useful in the workplace are most effectively and most often learnt outside of the university classroom. These attributes are most successfully acquired and developed through some form of experiential learning, which may or may not include the university experience as a whole. On the other hand, generic attributes specific to a particular discipline may be able to be developed through university curricula;
- Despite the apparent acquisition of 'workplace useful' generic attributes, graduates may not feel prepared for entering the (full time) workplace environment;
- The development of 'workplace useful' generic attributes, especially interpersonal understandings, is essential for surviving and operating effectively in the workplace;
- Some 'workplace useful' generic attributes may only be able to be learnt in the workplaces themselves. Self-confidence or self-efficacy is an important factor for graduates in believing they can successfully demonstrate their skills in the workplace. Increases in self-efficacy can occur in a variety of ways, with performance accomplishments arguably the most dependable; and,

- The appropriate deployment and level of application of generic attributes is essential for job satisfaction. These two factors can play a major role in determining whether a job is perceived as stimulating and challenging (that is a good job).

Graduates need to be capable workers in their chosen professions. If we agree with Stephenson's argument (1994), that to be capable people need 'justified confidence' which is based on real experience of their:

- Specialist knowledge and skills;
- Ability to manage their own learning and to learn from experience;
- Power to perform under pressure;
- Ability to communicate and collaborate effectively; and
- Capacity for dealing with issues – their own and other peoples,

then it becomes obvious that the workplace environment will become increasingly important in the development of generic attributes.

5. REFERENCES

ACER, http://www.acer.edu.au/ (accessed July 2002).

Bandura, A. (1977) *Social Learning Theory*. Englewood Cliffs, New Jersey: Prentice-Hall Inc.

Beach, K. (1999) 'Consequential Transitions: a socio-cultural expedition beyond transfer in education', *Review of Research in Education*. Vol. 24, pp. 101-139

Bennett, N., Dunne, E. & Carre, C. (2000) *Skills development in higher education and employment*. London, UK: Society for Research into Higher Education Ltd.

Berge, Z. L. (1998) 'Differences in teamwork between post-secondary classrooms and the workplace', *Education and Training*, Vol. 40. No. 5, pp. 194-201.

Boreham, N. (2002) 'Work Process Knowledge in Technological and Organisational Development' in N. Boreham, M. Fischer & R. Samurcay (eds). *Work Process Knowledge*. London: Routledge.

Candy, P. C., & Crebert, R. G. (1991) 'Ivory tower to concrete jungle: The difficult transitions from the academy to the workplace as learning environments', *Journal of Higher Education,* Vol. 62, No. 5, pp. 57-592.???

Christie, M., & Young, R. (1994) *Critical incidents in vocational teaching.* Darwin: NTU Print.

Crebert, G., Bates, M., Bell, B., Patrick, C., & Cragnolini, V (2004) 'Developing generic skills at university, during work placement and in employment: graduates perceptions,' *Higher Education Research and Development,* Vol. 23, No. 2, pp. 147-165.

Engestrom, Y., Engestrom, R., & Karkkainen, M. (1995) 'Polycontextuality and boundary crossing in expert cognition: learning and problem solving in complex work activities', *Learning and Instruction,* Vol. 5, No. 1, pp. 319-366.

Falk, I., Millar, P., & Owen, C. (2002) *Non/Working lives: Implications of "non-standard work practices" for literacy and numeracy.* Tasmania, Australia: Adult Literacy and Numeracy Australian Research Consortium.

Flanagan, J. (1954) 'The critical incident technique', *Psychological Bulletin*, pp. 327-355.

Ghaye, T., & Lillyman, S. (1997) *Learning journals and critical incidents: Reflective practice for health care professionals.* Wiltshire: Mark Allen Publishing Ltd.

Giddens, B., & Stasz, C. (1999) *Context matters: Teaching and Learning Skills for Work.* Berkeley, CA: National Centre for Vocational Education Research.

Hager, P. (1999) *Developing judgement: A proposal for facilitating the implementation of the key competencies* (A report prepared for the New South Wales Department of Education Co-ordination). Sydney: School of Adult Education, University of Technology.

Hager, P., McIntyre, J., Moy, H., Comyn, P., Stone, J., Schwenke, C., & Gonczi, A. (1996) *Workplace keys: Piloting the key competencies in workplace training.(A* Report prepared for the NSW Department of Training and Education Co-ordination, Sydney: Research Centre for Vocational Education and Training, University of Technology, Sydney

Hyslop-Margison, E. J. (2000) 'The employability skills discourse: A conceptual analysis of the career and personal planning curriculum', *Journal of Educational Thought/Revue de la Pensee Educative,* Vol. 34, No. 1, pp. 59-72.

Lave, J. (1990). 'The culture of acquisition and the practice of understanding', in J. Stigler, R. Schweder, & G. Herdt (eds.) *Cultural psychology* .Cambridge: Cambridge University Press, pp. 365-399.

Nightingale, P., Te Wiata, I., Toohey, S., Ryan, G., Hughes, C., & Magin, D. (1996).*Assessing Learning in Universities*. University of NSW, Sydney: UNSW Press.

Sandberg, J. (2000) 'Understanding human competence at work: An interpretive approach', *Academy of Management Journal*, Vol. 43, No. 1, pp. 9-25.

Schon, D. (1983) *The Reflective Practitioner*. San Francisco: Harper Collins.

Schon, D. (1987) *Educating the Reflective Practitioner*. San Francisco: Jossey Bass.

Stephenson, J. (1994) 'Capability and competence: Are they the same and does it matter?' *Capability*, Vol. 1, No. 1, pp. 3-4.

Tripp, D. (1993) *Critical incidents in teaching, developing professional judgement*. London: Routledge.

Virgona, C., Waterhouse, P., Sefton, R., & Sanguinetti, J. (2003a). *Making experience work: Generic skills through the eyes of displaced workers*. Vol. 1, Leabrook, Australia: National Centre for Vocational Education Research.

Virgona, C., Waterhouse, P., Sefton, R., & Sansuinetti, J. (2003b). *Making experience work: Generic skills through the eyes of displaced workers* . Vol. 2, Leabrook, Australia: National Centre for Vocational Education Research.

CHAPTER 13

DAVID BECKETT AND DIANNE MULCAHY

CONSTRUCTING PROFESSIONALS' EMPLOYABILITIES: CONDITIONS FOR ACCOMPLISHMENT

1. INTRODUCTION

Doubts have been cast on the current trend to develop definitive lists of graduate attributes of employability. At least two problems present in this development work. Firstly, knowledge and skills reside in *shared practices* as much as in individuals. In recent years, the focus has shifted from treating knowledge and skills as something that people possess to something that they do as part of practice (Cook & Brown 1999; Lave & Wenger 1991; Wenger 1998). It is commonly understood that knowledge and skills are inevitably embedded in a wide set of considerations, such as work organisation, organisational routines, employment relations, industrial relations and community relations.

Secondly, generic skills profiles do not explain why (and more importantly perhaps how) a particular graduate emerged and whether this graduate can perform the required skills in a specific work situation. Graduates get better (at some particular course of action) as they gain confidence and competence in some socially important categories of practice. Recent research on generic skills suggests that the primary context for the development of generic skills is work, and that the main mode of development is experiential learning (Virgona et al. 2003: 6).

It can be argued that currently established discourses of employability – most particularly the competence movement's appropriation of employability in which employability skills are narrowly defined as functional skills – are better at describing the *outcomes* of change(s) in graduate attributes than at analysing the

P. Hager and S. Holland (eds.), Graduate Attributes, Learning and Employability, 243–265.
© 2006 *Springer.*

processes behind them. Experiential learning is one such process. The deliberate design of learning and teaching strategies is another.

Employability is a complex concept that has both formal and non-formal dimensions. Employability skills are commonly put together as skills frameworks or skills schemes for national industry or professional bodies and, as such, they are formal descriptions of skill.

Consider this example from an Australian federal government-sponsored Report:

> Enterprises participating in the research placed a strong emphasis on the need for both entry level and ongoing employees to exhibit a broad range of personal attributes. Employers suggested that entry level and ongoing employees needed to reflect attributes that were acceptable to the rest of their peer working group and the customer and in line with the company's approach ... [They] stressed the need to ensure future employees developed these personal attributes, as they are an integral feature of an employable person, and a key component of the Employability Skills Framework *(DEST 2002: 6)*.

What are these personal attributes?

> ... loyalty, commitment, honesty and integrity, enthusiasm, reliability, personal presentation, commonsense, positive self-esteem, sense of humour, balanced attitude to work and home life, ability to deal with pressure, motivation, adaptability *(DEST 2002: 7)* .

The Report notes that '[t]here is no doubt that enterprises saw the inclusion of these attributes as a new and essential component of employability skills', which are as follows: communication, team-work, problem-solving, initiative and enterprise, planning and organising, self-management, learning, technology (2002: 7).

Because such lists of desired attributes omit the details of actual practice, they may be less important to an industry or profession's capacity to prosper than descriptions that do include these details. Formal representations of skill, such as these lists, cannot easily capture elements of knowledge which remain specific and tacit. In developing profiles of skill, one can easily fall into the trap of 'believing that all knowledge is verbalisable, so that important knowledge is left out' (Stevenson 2001: 658). Typically, this important knowledge is embodied and embedded. As Eraut (2000) has it, 'the limitations to making tacit knowledge explicit are formidable...'. The probability is that "thick" tacit versions will coexist alongside "thin" explicit versions: the thick version will be used in professional practice, the thin version for justification' (2000: 134–5).

This chapter focuses on 'thick' descriptions and ascriptions of abilities to professionals, that is to say, in their work practices – in the very doing of their work. The particularities of the immediate workplace context are, we argue, the signifiers of identities, which are at once both social and embodied. Our argument proceeds in two ways.

Firstly, in the next section, a new conceptual account of how somebody comes to 'understand' something is given. This locates a worker's agency in making judgements about how to proceed, in the conduct of the work, in the sociality of particular workplaces. These judgements are articulated in peer contexts which partially construct not only what counts as workplace practice, but also the identities of the practitioners.

Secondly, in the following section, two case studies of identity formation, through practice, are presented.

The intention throughout is to show that close attention to the particularities of work practices generates the attributes or capacities required for employment – that one learns *for* work by *doing* work – and that, by extrapolation, lifelong learning occurs across the lifespan in diverse settings, with particularistic 'accomplishments', beyond which what could be claimed as 'generic' is vaporous.

2. ACCOMPLISHING 'UNDERSTANDING' THROUGH PRACTICAL INFERENCES

Some of our current work shows how embodied actions at work re-present not just the work practices, but also the identities of the workers (Mulcahy 2000; Beckett & Morris 2001; Morris & Beckett 2004). The *doing* drives the emergence of practices, and of the workers, whose identities are co-constructed through those practices. These ontological considerations are raised afresh in the next section, but this section (drawing substantially upon Beckett 2001, 2004) deals with a fundamental epistemological aspect: how can 'understanding' be accomplished through practice? The short answer is: through the social articulation of inferences. But what is an inferentialist approach?

Almost fifty years ago, the American philosopher Wilfred Sellars (1912–1989), in his most influential work, *Empiricism and the Philosophy of Mind (EPM)*, consistently attacked what is known as foundationalism, or the 'Myth of the Given'. DeVries & Triplett (2000) characterise it in this way:

... very roughly, the idea is that direct knowledge does not have to be achieved or arrived at by inferring, pondering, sorting of evidence, calling forth memories, comparing data, or using other constructive cognitive processes. All it has to do is simply be there. It requires only the person's attention, if even that, in order to be knowledge for that person. As such, it is given. And the rest of one's knowledge, the indirectly known, has to be built up from what is given by the sorts of cognitive processes just noted. It follows that direct knowledge must be noninferential *(2000: xix)*.

The Given is presumably an endangered species, if not already extinct. Blackburn's *Oxford Dictionary of Philosophy* (1994) describes it as a 'name adopted by Sellars for the now widely-rejected view that sense experience gives us particular points of certainty, suitable to serve as foundations for the whole of empirical knowledge and science'. We are not about to resurrect the Given, which is the non-inferential, directly available basis of knowledge. Instead we take seriously a broadly Sellarsian resurrection of the *contrasting* view: inferentialism. Inferentialism is a conceptualisation of claims which:

- account for what is 'epistemically efficacious' about experience, (that is, how we come to know what to do next) and
- are at several points 'ostensively tied' to reality (that is, are about this world now), and
- *emerge with new properties, amidst public justifications (articulated inferences).*

'Inferential understanding', as advanced herein, requires all three of these criteria, since all are required for the achievement of understanding, but our interest is only in the third criterion: the emergent articulation, as 'understandings', of particular practices, in one's public context, that is, amongst one's professional peers.

Instead of grounding knowledge in the refinement of a state of the mind (which fits with the Cartesian origins of the Given), inferentialists like Brandom (2000) argue for 'a form of linguistic pragmatism that might take as its slogan Sellars's principle that grasping a concept is mastering the use of a word' (Brandom 2000: 6; he acknowledges a Deweyian, Jamesian and Wittgensteinian heritage). Brandom's expressivism – this 'usage' – sees the mind not as a mirror (representing what is inner and is outer), but, similar to a lamp,

> ... making explicit what is implicit. This can be understood in a pragmatist sense of turning something we can initially only do into something we can say: codifying some sort of knowing how in the form of a knowing that. *(2000: 8)*

Educators have gone some way further with this already: workplace learning and especially the Schonian 'reflective practitioner' at work are redolent of this conversion of what is done (acted) into what is said (articulated). This directs attention to the emergence of understanding, with its propositional form (knowing *that*) regarded as an accomplishment – the outcome of a *process* – rather than (as traditionally) a product. The contrast with Cartesian epistemology could hardly be more dramatic.

The Givenist claim on 'experience', as such, matches, and perhaps grew out of, the broader Cartesian epistemology that first-person reports of how one thinks or feels (avowals) provided ineffable knowledge of the world and one's place in it ('what I know best is what I know first'). We now acknowledge that this Enlightenment epistemology was underpinned by, and in turn supported, an ontology: that there were two kinds of stuff in the world (mental and material), with all the implications this has had for educational provision, for pedagogy and for labour markets. Cartesian dualism required that the material world make a mentalistic 'impression' or footprint, which became a representation or image of experience, to be corrected and refined by formal education, which had as its first priority the inculcation of an 'idea'. The mind as a *tabula rasa* (blank slate) on which education was inscribed was popular.

In contrast to this Cartesian epistemology, Brandom's expressive 'linguistic pragmatism' sits well with certain educational and pedagogical innovation, in adults' workplaces, as we shall see shortly. And the Sellarsian backdrop is congenial. Instead of a Givenist foundationalism, Sellars provides the resources for a countertradition in both epistemology and in ontology, one that does not require Cartesianism. As DeVries & Triplett (2000) summarise:

> According to Sellars, we know first the public world of physical objects. We can extend that framework to include persons and their language. What we know best, however, are those beliefs that are the most well-supported pieces of the most coherent, well-substantiated explanatory framework available to us ... our best knowledge will be provided to us by the efforts of science. *The picture of knowledge created is that of a communal, self-correcting enterprise that grows from unsophisticated beginnings toward an increasingly detailed and adequate understanding of ourselves and the world* *(2000: xlvi) [emphasis added]*.

We believe the way forward is to unpack that notion of the articulation of inferences as a 'communal, self-correcting enterprise'. Expressive, pragmatic understandings of experience are really *how adults' workplaces are shaped*. Beckett & Hager (2002) show what this centring of 'knowing *how*' does to and for traditional education. In a nutshell, 'knowing how' to proceed at work, for most adults, requires a series of decisional actions, some of them articulated, which issue in change. To give these experiences the epistemological significance they deserve, we need to add the 'knowing why'. The argument here, and in our other current work, is that inferentialism – the 'communal, self-correcting' justifications given by an individual at work of why she or he acted thus-and-so – looks promising.

It follows that if we are serious about how understanding at and through work is accomplished, then the reflective action of making a 'judgement' is central. Workers do this all day, every day, and we claim these adult learning experiences are central to a new epistemology of practice, and therefore to exploring generic skill formation.

Briefly, our claim is that how a person goes on to do something (what 'know how' consists in) is not about something other than itself (like a propositional state, or a product, such as is Given), but rather about what that person finds herself or himself undergoing, in what it is to be human. Frequently, what humans find themselves doing is making decisions (judgements) about what to do next. Workplace learning is increasingly shaped by this sort of fluid experience ('knowing how' to go on), but it needs to be *made explicit* (as in Brandom's 'expressive approach', above). The 'making explicit' is what the best adult teachers and trainers can do, in facilitating, even revealing, adults' experiences for educational purposes. Mentoring schemes are an example.

Judgements under this latter, inferentialist, model of agency are *practical* in that they are expected to be efficacious: they deal in what is thought to be good (that is to say, appropriate) *in specific contexts in which they are embedded*. This contextuality is crucial and is further developed in the two case studies in the next section.

There has to be this pragmatic point to it all, especially for coming to understand practice through generic skill formation. 'Problem-solving' for lawyers will carry inferences for and from practice differently than for masons. Earlier, we noted that Brandom (2000) locates inferentialism in the *pragmatic expression* of knowledge claims. He means, as a Sellarsian, to move the achievement of understanding beyond static representationalism into a more dynamic, process-focussed mode (what may be called the 'counter-tradition' in epistemology). He unpacks this when he states:

> According to the inferentialist account of concept use, in making [an explicit truth] claim one is implicitly endorsing a set of inferences, which articulate its conceptual content. Implicitly endorsing those inferences is a sort of doing. Understanding [sic] the conceptual content to which one has committed oneself is a kind of practical mastery: a bit of know-how that consists in being able to discriminate what does and does not follow from the claim, what would be evidence for or against it and so on. *(2000: 19)*

In expressing this personal mastery at and through work, adults find themselves committed to and bound up in socio-cultural expectations, specific to their practices, that thus-and-so (whatever the course of action is) will be justifiable – and can be justified.

These practical understandings *emerge*. What can this mean? Acts of judgments are 'doings', and they possess new properties, not reducible to their origins in workplace experiences. DeVries and Triplett (2000), in their useful Glossary, define 'emergent properties' as:

> The often murky but persistent idea that, in at least some complexes (such as organisms) some of the properties of the complex as a whole are (1) genuinely novel; or (2a) unpredictable ... or (2b) not reducible to ... the properties of the parts; or (2c) not explainable by the occurrence of the properties of the parts. The notion of an emergent property is not that of a property, the initial temporal instantiation of which succeeds the temporal instantiation of other properties, but of *a property that is in some way ontologically distinctive from the kinds of properties true of the parts of the whole (2000: 183) [emphasis added]*.

Now workplaces that are serious about the productive exercise of generic skills are keen to support them in favour of novel, unexpected outcomes, albeit those that contribute to strategic as well as individual purposes. Inferential understanding thus provides a theoretical underpinning for this support for 'ontologically distinctive' properties that are not merely more general properties with antecedent components: they are a new entity, or phenomenon, or process. In brief: the making of a judgment ('knowing how' to go on) is the exercise within adults' workplace experiences of an 'emergent property'. Such an exercise is a form of doing, where there are distinctive reasons articulable in that process of doing (the 'knowing why'). Thus the inference of understanding is available to others, as well as to the individual: "I/She did x, because I/we/they can justify it like this ... ".

An example of this is the model of holistic, or integrated competence, which has been developed in Australia, in the 1990s (Gonczi, Hager & Oliver 1990; Hager & Beckett 1995). This is explicitly based on the *inference* of competence from an array of performative evidence, and is sensitive to the 'contextual' nature of generic skill formation and development. It fits with the judgement-driven nature of workplace learning, and it invites a diversity of assessment evidence in support of judgements – inferences – of competence. Furthermore, this 'Australian model' (labelled by Hyland 1997) generates an ontologically distinctive outcome: the competent practitioner, whose practice is defensibly competent, by reference to the public standards of a work-based peer group (such as profession, or occupational association or industry). It is an example of what Brandom (2000) called the 'communal self-correction' of individuals' actions – and even of identities. It also appears that generic skill formation, if it were to have any purchase on particular workplace experiences (that is, in the case of graduates, enhancing their 'employability') would need to make available opportunities for this 'communal self-correction'. Group-based project work would be a workplace-specific example of this communal self-correction, where a new graduate (or someone on field placement whilst still in tertiary studies) could endeavour to display her or his generic skills in real life with real peers. Without such a context for the claim to possess or to have acquired generic skills, they float off the planet.

We have in this section shown how a Sellarsian approach to 'understanding' gives due significance to the dynamics and realities of adults' workplaces, and to the processes now acknowledged in many workplaces which advance this 'communal self-correcting'. This self-correction is the public articulation of reasons for acting, and in this way, professionals' practices shape the accomplishment of 'understanding'.

But there is an ontological dimension to this accomplishment, as we stated earlier. The co-construction of the Self through workplace practices establishes identities as 'competent' or 'skilled' workers. Central to these constructions and reconstructions are communal self-corrections: we are both subject to and objects of our Selfhood. Understanding, and identities, emerge in these agentive processes. We turn now to identities.

3. PROFESSIONALS' FORMATION:
IDENTITY, HETEROGENEITY AND EMPLOY-ABILITY

In this section, we draw on the understanding of the learning experiences of a student teacher and practising teachers, as case studies, to examine further the relationship between professional identity formation and employability, showing in particular how employability is primarily to be seen not in terms of personal attributes or sets of skills (so called employability skills) but rather performances of practice in 'ecologies of practice' (Stronach et al. 2002). The term 'ecology of practice' refers to "the sorts of individual and collective experiences, beliefs and practices that professionals accumulate in learning and performing their roles. They relate mainly to 'craft knowledge', and may be intuitive, tacit or explicit" (2002: 132). The notion of 'community of practice' (Lave & Wenger 1991; Wenger 1998) does much the same work.

The primary performance concerns identity formation and change – 'the hidden dimensions that make "generic skills" appear as they are' (Falk 2002: 8). Formal representations such as the knowledge representations encoded in generic skills profiles hide all manner of heterogeneity within (Mulcahy 1999). In what follows, we attempt to render these hidden heterogeneities (Law 2002) more visible. In so doing, we shift the grounds on which questions pertaining to the reality of employability may be addressed. We shift the question from what it is to *have* employability skills, or *be* employable, to what it is to *do* employability: employability is constructed as a component of a practice, or rather of a variety of different practices, hence employabilities.

3.1 Asha's Story: Student Teacher Formation Through Problem-Based Learning

Teacher education has come under increasing scrutiny by governments in Australia over the last decade. Faculties of Education are under pressure to improve the quality of teacher graduates and to align the underpinning knowledge and skills produced through teacher education programs to the needs of schools, the profession and the community. Accordingly, a group of teacher educators began, in 2001, to talk and think about a new design for a program in initial teacher education:

> Beginning teachers face a future that will be very different, in unimagined ways, from the present. They will need to be flexible and cope easily with diversity and ambiguity. They may be asked to function in both local and global communities, arriving at curricular, pedagogical and policy decisions after due consideration of evidence and possibilities. They will be expected to work in innovative ways as members of professional learning teams, actively researching their practice and contributing to the growth of these teams. They will engage in the development of the curriculum, the formation of policy, the improvement of the schools within which they are located, and the enhancement of the teaching profession. ... The problems

that they will encounter in schools, and in other learning contexts, will require cross-disciplinary thinking and complex problem-defining and resolving skills. These skills are at the heart of teachers' work *(Hildebrand, Mulcahy & Wilks 2001: 1).*

Student teachers elect to join the Problem-Based Learning (PBL) program which attempts to ensure that graduates develop broad-based generic skills such as critical thinking, problem-defining and problem-resolving. The three domains of professional knowledge, professional practice and school concerns provide a platform for this development.

Asha, one of these student teachers, tells of tensions between these domains, in this instance, between 'trying to get the best possible marks' and maintaining a reasonable relationship with the school supervisor:

> If … you're in a situation where you're not always comfortable with the supervisor that you've got … that's a big issue. And a lot of people that I spoke to (who) weren't contemplating doing PBL said to me 'Why would you do it? You're going to be in the same school twice. What happens if you don't like your supervisor?' I mean it's not a question of liking or disliking the supervisor. At the end of the day you are trying to get the best possible marks. You're trying to make the most out of your situation. And so if there are any uneasy kind of feelings you're going to be at that school for quite a long time. I suppose that teaches you how to deal with different types of situations but I can see how that might really affect someone who isn't quite ready for it *(Interview: 20/10/2001).*

As it happened, Asha managed this (and other) tensions particularly successfully. She did indeed make the most out of her situation, moving on, after her studies, to a full-time teaching position in a prestigious private school. How was this movement accomplished? For Asha, as for various other students, the formal well-bounded requirements of her course – for example, the espoused attributes of flexibility and coping with ambiguity – are met in and through nests of practices within the networks of practice that grow up both on campus and at school:

> I think working with (other) PBL students is great. They challenge you. They make you rethink your opinions. You can challenge them. Everyone is quite free and, you know, quite ready to speak up for themselves, which is great. And because it's a smaller group you get to bond together and you get to know one another in a way that you probably wouldn't … if you were just doing the straight course.
>
> Teachers are very busy. … You don't really have a lot of meeting(s) with teachers just on PBL issues. But you soak it all up. You soak it up especially during your

rounds. You try and establish relationships. ... I found it was my initiative that brought out anything that happened. My school contact person was a very, very, very busy person. He does everything by schedule and he's a fantastic dynamo of a person. But, at the end of the day, again, he had a lot of commitments. He did try to share his time with me but I almost had to soak it up through just his presence.

Taking initiative, Asha establishes relationships with peers and experienced teachers. Professional identity formation involves being challenged by peers and keeping company with experienced teachers – soaking up professional knowledge through 'just their presence'. Contemporary conditions of teachers' work do not lend themselves to formal meetings with student teachers; rather, these teachers build knowledge and skill in a tacit, concrete, bodily way. In the context of PBL, Asha's identity is an enactment that comes in many forms: bonding with peers, 'shadowing' skilled practitioners, observing their practice, participating in the observed practice, reflecting on the outcomes of this participation, both individually and in a group, researching the underpinnings of the practice, and so on. It is also emergent.

In practice, if not in principle, employability skills are the outcome or product of *collective work*, some of which, at least, appears more felt than said:

(The facilitator) picked up the mood of the group quite well. And she would often get us to work with that and, finally, with those, sometimes, mood issues which you sort of don't have words for. You knew; you just felt things.

Here, generic skills take the form of learnt capacities embedded in a shifting set of considerations or conditions – staff facilitation; student personal and collective understanding.

A successful enactment of the identities of employable graduate and prospective teacher would appear to involve mobilising a complex set of identifications – with peers, school supervisors, teacher educators – in response to shifting contexts. This mobilisation or 'self work' is largely hidden from view. Among other things, it involves working the space between sites of learning: ' ... making a link between the learning on campus and learning in schools. I was constantly reflecting on that'.

Bhabha (2001: 136), writing in the context of debates around post-coloniality and the postmodern, draws attention to 'those moments or processes that are produced in the articulation of cultural differences'. The contesting claims of peers, campus and school can be negotiated in 'in-between' spaces. Bhabha describes these thus: '"In-between" spaces provide the terrain for elaborating strategies of selfhood – singular or communal – that initiate new signs of identity, and innovative sites of collaboration, and contestation, in the act of defining the idea of society itself' (2001: 136-137).

Asha initiates new signs of identity in a relational, cross-locational way:

> Making a student feel important is very important because as a student you're walking around and you have to ask all these tough questions to people that are so much more experienced than you. You do need a bit of resilience, you do need to feel supported. For instance at (x school) with (x supervisor), even though I didn't always have him around, when I did, after the meeting, I always felt important. I always felt good. So that was something very useful. And that's why I valued his contribution so much.

> If you see a person from (x university) walking around with a student teacher, that immediately adds a bit more status, I guess, to that person because, ultimately, especially if that person is walking around by himself or herself, it does help to have a bit of back up.

Her resilience as a prospective teacher is a product of staff support and institutional standing. It is built out of the materials to hand and in relation to local practice and conditions: 'even though I didn't always have him around, when I did, after the meeting, I always felt important'.

For one of Asha's peers, identity appears to be a matter of linking 'knowings' of various kinds:

> ... really worthwhile learning is when it almost becomes a part of you. You know, the whole experience becomes a part of you and stuff. And I think that is what the PBL is like. Because you've got all these ideas and you've linked them to memories, and things that happened to you, and things that you had to work out the hard way, and things that you saw and things that you felt. It's real context based and multiple intelligence learning *(Interview: 25/10/2001).*

Practical understandings formed in the sociality of particular learning spaces emerge as important:

> We were always talking all the time. That communication. But that's where you do get a lot of your ideas from. And those ideas were the ones that actually helped me when I did go to lectures and listen to the more theoretical stuff and when I did look at the literature. And I often found that most of us ... we'd almost thought of all the ideas in the literature before we read them. And when we read them it was a bit more like there was a recognition ... that, yes, they're useful ideas because we thought of

them ourselves pretty much. We've seen that they occur, rather than reading the literature and thinking: 'Oh this is something that I've got to make myself learn and understand'.

These understandings are emergent; importantly, they are achieved in conjunction with others: 'We'd almost thought of all the ideas in the literature before we read them'. This case material suggests that employability is not a private, personal substance, but socially constructed and distributed: spread out over students, staff and sites. Located in the whole array. As Asha comments:

The learning experience I had was fantastic. I learnt things which I wasn't always aware I was learning. Again I just soaked up so much from other PBL students, from staff at schools, from actually doing my assignments, from my facilitator. Drawing all the information together for tasks, for looking at problems, for coming up with solutions. So there was a lot of hands on learning. There was a lot of practical learning.

Like the picture of knowledge painted by Sellars, the picture of employability that emerges is that of a 'communal, self-correcting enterprise that grows from unsophisticated beginnings toward an increasingly detailed and adequate understanding' (DeVries & Triplett 2000: xlvi).

3.2 Stella's Story: English Language and Literacy Teachers' Formation Through Standards

The project, Standards for Teachers of English Language and Literacy in Australia (STELLA), began in 1999 as a three-year research project funded by the Australian Research Council. The purpose of the project was to develop subject specific standards for primary and secondary teachers of English that acknowledge the complexity of teaching. With the assistance of two national subject associations (the Australian Association for the Teaching of English and the Australian Literacy Educators' Association) teacher panels were set up in different states to develop the STELLA standards. The standards were derived from panel discussions about criteria for good teaching and narratives about good teaching (Gill 1999: 74).

The STELLA Standards Framework (http://www.stella.org.au/) consists of statements of what accomplished teachers of English and Literacy believe, know and are able to do. Standards statements are grouped under three broad headings:

Professional knowledge;
Professional practice;
Professional engagement.

Each statement contains a *core description* (of what accomplished teachers of English and Literacy believe, know and are able to do) and *key words* and *focus questions* for reflection and discussion. The key words identify *attributes* that can be used to describe accomplished teaching as shown in Table 1:

Table 1. Extract from STELLA: Standards statement 3.2 – teachers continue to learn

3. Professional Engagement	
3.2 Teachers continue to learn	
Standards statement (core descriptions of what accomplished teachers of English and Literacy believe, know and are able to do	Key words & Focus questions (For reflection and discussion)
3.2 Teachers continue to learn	**Reflection**
Accomplished English / Literacy teachers recognise that the context of their teaching is continually evolving. They reflect on, analyse and are able to articulate all aspects of their professional practice, constantly reviewing and refining their teaching to improve students' learning opportunities, and searching for answers to challenging pedagogical questions. They seek opportunities to discuss the effectiveness of their teaching with colleagues, students, parents and care givers. With their own learning goals in mind, accomplished English / literacy teachers pursue new knowledge through professional renewal activities such as …	How does the teacher maintain and further develop his / her personal and professional growth? **Critique** To what extent does the teacher contribute to and learn from current debates about teaching and learning? How open is the teacher in questioning and evaluating classroom, school and wider literacy practices? **Development** What professional learning goals does the teacher have? What opportunities are taken up to learn from courses, colleagues and the workplace?

For English/Literacy teachers, continuing to learn and get better at teaching is determined by processes of 'reflection', 'critique' and 'development'. For the purposes of the present discussion, these processes are not only attributes used to describe accomplished teaching but also employability skills. As Field comments, employability skills 'should be taken as skills required not only to gain employment, but also to progress within a company so as (a) to achieve one's potential and (b) contribute successfully to company strategic directions' (2001: 11).

As the STELLA Standards Framework has it, should teachers of English and Literacy want to progress in the teaching profession, they require the capacity to reflect, critique and develop professionally. *Doing* employability here is a matter of practising in particular ways (reflectively, critically ...). This practising is always condition and context dependent, partial, inconclusive and indeterminate. One of the interesting features of the STELLA Standards Framework is that conditions and contexts are kept in view. The developers of these standards have practised a style of developing in which teaching standards (and, by extension, employability standards) are not produced as entities in and of themselves but rather as indissolubly linked to teaching practice. The focus throughout is on what the professional practitioner finds herself or himself undergoing in practising well (or failing to practise well).

Each of the attributes used to describe accomplished teachers of English and Literacy is embedded in a teacher narrative in which questions pertaining to the reality of accomplishment (employability) are addressed. For example, in the narrative, 'We are teaching kids, not subjects', a teacher of a year 8 English class, tells of tensions surrounding teaching a set text. He questions an established discourse and practice of English teaching and, in so doing, enacts curriculum *critique*:

> We all know good teaching is good acting, at least in part; but maybe I hammed my lines. Perhaps they picked up on my insincere enthusiasm for the book. But how could they have when my initial enthusiasm was genuine, at least in part? What a thing to get hung up on. I should have turfed the book and found something else. Yet, if I did that, it would set a precedent, and there would be ignited a raging subversive fire of refusing to read set texts: or so I was told. Where would it all end? If we weren't careful we might be in a position where we would not be able to teach Of Mice and Men at Year 10 (http://www.stella.org.au/narrative_content.jsp?id=41)

Forming part of the standards statement 'Teachers continue to learn', critique is not extracted from practice but rather linked to various and different practices – personal ('What a thing to get hung up on'), professional ('I should have turfed the book') and political ('Where would it all end?'). These practices in turn are nested within, or networked with, other practices. Curriculum, pedagogy, policy and teacher identity are under examination here. As are classroom, school and wider literacy practices. Teacher identities are co-constructed through these.

Thinking back to the last section, we are witness to a teacher making decisions (judgements) about what to do next. Self-correction takes a communal form. If this teacher 'turfs the book', 'it would set a precedent, and there would be ignited a raging subversive fire of refusing to read set texts', or, so he *was told*. The correction of teacher action is at the same time the correction of teacher identity. The decision not to turf the book carries along with it the decision not to initiate a different teacher identity (teacher-who-sets-a-precedent; ignites-a-raging-subversive-fire). Contextuality, or better perhaps, specificity, is also crucial: had the teacher turfed that particular book and 'found something else' the issue of student disengagement may not have arisen.

Enacted variously in various situations, critique comes in the plural. While in some schemas critique might be thought a single, separate skill, in the STELLA Standards Framework it takes multiple and diverse forms. There are as many critiques as there are practices in which critique is performed. In this further teacher narrative, critique carries inferences from practice somewhat differently than the narrative above:

> My class programs consisted of a series of discrete units of work with the systematic coverage of a range of genres being the main organizing factor. Upon reflection, my major dissatisfaction with this practice was that it allowed little real choice for students and, as a consequence, students were frequently not really fully 'engaged' in the writing and speaking tasks that the class program generated. In comparison, the essence of the writing workshop approach … is that students basically learn to write by writing and therefore need to spend a significant proportion of available class time in actual writing. In an effort to achieve the real engagement with tasks previously perceived to be missing, I now have students work on writing tasks of their own choice rather than ones set by the teacher. The principle at work here is a version of the old adage that one volunteer is worth ten pressed men (http://www.stella.org.au/narrative_content.jsp?id=9).

The object of this teacher's critique might be called theory-in-practice: which approach to teaching writing assists writers to be 'really fully "engaged"'? Tensions exist between two epistemologies of practice, 'the systematic coverage of a range of genres' and 'the writing workshop approach'. Enacting critique, this teacher works the tension between these two: 'My classroom practice is currently based on an endeavour to marry a form of process writing … with a genre / functional grammar approach'.

In attempting to understand practice through generic skill formation, we are compelled to consider *practices*. Understandings shape the conduct of practice and practices shape the accomplishment of understanding. Thus, in the vignette above, we see a teacher striving to improve existing practice through articulating understandings of alternative practices that might make this improvement. The close attention given to the particularities of work routine and practice generates a capacity for critique: 'My class programs consisted of a series of discrete units of work with the systematic coverage of a range of genres being the main organizing factor'.

Similarly, identity shapes the conduct of practice and practices shape the accomplishment of identity. This teacher grows dissatisfied with a class program where 'a range of genres' is covered; he performs a self that is less teacher-centred and creates conditions for students to learn (and form identities) as volunteers rather than as 'pressed men'. The practice of self work and teaching work go hand in hand: each is caught up in the other. Importantly, this work is of a public kind – undertaken as part of the project of developing subject specific standards for the English teaching profession. It is inherently social (communal) in character. The categories of self work, teaching work and project work tend to merge. Altogether, the STELLA project would appear to have created the right conditions for the accomplishment of teacher professional standards ('understanding') and of a particular kind of teacher practitioner, the *accomplished practitioner*, whose practice is defensibly accomplished by reference to these standards.

4. CONDITIONS FOR ACCOMPLISHMENT: THE SHARED, THE LOCAL AND THE PARTICULAR

Once one starts to ask how employability is *practised*, there are a number of different answers to the question 'what is employability' or, our preferred term employ-abilities. These 'answers' are given with respect to two *genres* of employability: (i) a 'representationalist' genre in which employability is talked about as if it were in isolation – able to be described more or less accurately by a text, such as a 'list' – and (ii) an 'enacting' genre in which it is talked about as a component of practice. Our concern in this chapter has been to make the latter genre more visible. Employability skills are statements – formalisations or abstract representations – of knowledge and skill which are put together by a particular group of people (employers, practising professionals) in a particular way (as skill sets or skill profiles). These skills only exist however, if they are practically performed. In other words, we need to acknowledge their intimate relationship with – their co-dependency on – practice. The conditions of this performance, the salient aspects of practice, are what interest us here.

In STELLA's story, teacher narratives are the bridge between *what is done* (practice) and *what is said* (understandings, standards, employability skills). Grounded in practical judgments, they draw attention to the inter-section and co-implication of these two. The STELLA standards are built around sets of case studies, in essence, 'thick' descriptions of teaching performance. The special contribution of case material is to locate generic skills in the 'recognisable and indeterminate realm of professional judgment' (Louden 1993: 18). Our attention is directed to this indeterminate realm as well as the processes by which this realm is rendered more determinate (more explicit, more immutable). In STELLA's story, this rendering work is made very visible. As noted above, the standards were derived from panel discussions about criteria for good teaching and narratives about good teaching. They are the product of *shared* work – the emergent articulation, as standards, of particular practices, by members of specific subject associations.

The making of knowledge (and representations of knowledge) is a highly *local* affair. As Smith and Comyn have it:

> employability skills are context-bound, in that different industries and employers value and weight the skills and attributes quite differently. The worth of employability skills can only be fully appreciated in the workplace where the consequences of such skills can be seen *(2003: 10–11).*

The STELLA skills are not causes but consequences of teacher-researcher and teacher-professional work. The position that a skill may be seen as a consequence, and not as an antecedent, is axiomatic to the pragmatist approach. Unable to be developed in isolation, conditions for accomplishment apply and these conditions are quite *particular*. A skill is a property of some actions rather than others. For example, certain workplaces provide rich opportunities for participation in learning and development. The skills that Asha builds in pursuing the problems presented in Problem-Based Learning are conditional upon the opportunity afforded by her practice school to 'walk around and ... ask all these tough questions'. Certain projects, such as action learning and (some) standards development projects, provide rich opportunities for participation in communal self-correction: 'Upon reflection, my major dissatisfaction with this practice was that it allowed little real choice for students and, as a consequence, students were frequently not really fully "engaged"'.

In respect of workplace learning, Evans & Kersh (2003) identify two types of workplace environment: *restrictive* (or non-stimulating) and *expansive* (or stimulating). 'The expansive or stimulating workplace environment is closely related to recognition and development of *tacit skills* and opportunities to engage in non-formal learning' (2003: 68, emphasis in original). Given the argument made throughout this chapter, inferentialism – the 'communal self-correcting' justifications given by an individual at work of why she or he acted thus-and-so – also needs to be taken into account. A workplace that creates a range of opportunities, both formal and informal, for (re)constructing workers' employabilities might be considered an expansive workplace.

5. IMPLICATIONS FOR LIFELONG LEARNING

In the Australian context, discussions around lifelong learning have tended to emphasise skill training and employability issues (Robinson 2000; Stanwick 2003). The technical-rational basis of much of this discussion has meant that attention has been directed to the outcomes of lifelong learning and away from the processes that secure these outcomes. Accordingly, we have sought in this chapter to redirect attention to questions of process and practice. Like employability, lifelong learning is primarily to be seen not in terms of intrinsic capabilities or potentialities but rather performances of practice in ecologies of practice. It is inevitably implicated in the *everyday of concrete practices* which promote the formation and reformation of skills and identities.

Identifying the conditions for the accomplishment of employ-abilities is an important issue in the facilitation of lifelong learning. The picture of learning created is that of a shared, self-correcting enterprise (such as the Problem-Based Learning program, the STELLA project) in which understanding is accomplished collectively. We have set out a new understanding of 'understanding' itself. If intelligent action contributes to this new approach, it is because it starts with a serious focus on agency and then approaches it in a new way. Rather than asking how learning, through acquisition of generic skills from some national list, for example, is *represented* to the learner ('Has there been a change in the state of the learner?'), a more profound question is 'What *inferences* can now be articulated by the learner?' (Lifelong) learning takes on a more agentive look and feel.

Emergent properties of inferential understanding at work will take any number of forms depending on the variables in particular workplaces. And it is this that should guide the way generic skills are theorised: are there public ways workers (or learners, still in formal studies) can articulate their judgments which are, by definition, located in local and particular workplace experiences? This supplies the 'knowing why'. Teamwork, and other forms of socially-reflective practice (for example, 360 degree appraisals, 'retreats', role plays, simulations, project- and problem-based groups) are some ways these articulations are made public, and similar activities should be pedagogically central in formal studies, especially in tertiary education. And these can be manifest in multiple and diverse settings across the lifespan. As Smith & Comyn comment, 'Employability skills are developed throughout a person's working life and hence employers need to view the process of employability skills development as a whole-of-workforce issue' (2003: 10).

This is, then, to say in summary, that the accomplishment of employ-abilities depends on two things, and neither of them are lists of generic attributes. First, a prior commitment to undergoing diverse and socially located experiences from which one can learn, and, second, a continuing commitment to the public articulation of reasons for one's judgments at work – one's daily business. Lists of generic skills make no sense unless they show they are grounded in practical judgements and that the reasons practitioners can give for their judgements are publicly articulated amongst their peers.

6. REFERENCES

Beckett, D. (2001) 'Hot Action at Work: A Different Understanding of 'Understanding', in: T. Fenwick (ed.) *Sociocultural Perspectives on Learning Through Work*. New Directions for Adult and Continuing Education Series, San Francisco: Jossey-Bass, pp. 73-84.

Beckett, D. (2004) 'Embodied Competence and Generic Skill: The Emergence of Inferential Understanding', *Educational Philosophy and Theory*, Vol. 36, No. 5, pp. 497-509.

Beckett, D. & Hager, P. (2000) 'Making Judgements as the Basis for Workplace Learning: Towards an Epistemology of Practice', *International Journal of Lifelong Education,* Vol. 19, No. 4, pp. 300-311.

Beckett, D. & Hager, P. (2002), *Life, Work and Learning: Practice in Postmodernity*. Routledge International Studies in the Philosophy of Education 14. London & New York: Routledge,

Beckett, D. & Morris, G. (2001) 'Ontological Performance: Bodies, Identities and Learning', *Studies in the Education of Adults*, Vol.33 No.1, pp. 35-48.

Bhabha, H. (2001) 'Locations of culture: the post-colonial and the postmodern', in: S. Malpas (ed.) *Postmodern Debates*. New York: Palgrave, pp. 136-144.

Billett, S. (2001) *Learning In the Workplace: Strategies for Effective Practice*. Sydney: Allen
& Unwin.

Blackburn, S. (1994) *The Oxford Dictionary of Philosophy*. Oxford & New York: Oxford University Press.

Brandom, R. (2000) *Articulating Reasons: An Introduction to Inferentialism*. Cambridge, Massachusetts: Harvard University Press.

Cook, S. & Brown J. (1999) 'Bridging epistemologies: The generative dance between organisational knowledge and organisational knowing', *Organization Science*, Vol. 10, No. 4, pp. 381-400.

Department of Education, Science and Training (DEST) (2002) *Employability Skills for the Future*. Canberra: Commonwealth Department of Education, Science and Training.

DeVries, W. & Triplett, T. (2000) *Knowledge, Mind, and the Given: Reading Wilfred Sellars's 'Empiricism and the Philosophy of Mind'*. Indianapolis, USA: Hackett Publishing Company Inc., (contains the full text of EPM)

Eraut, M. (2000) 'Non-formal learning and tacit knowledge in professional work', *The British Journal of Educational Psychology*, Vol. 70, pp. 113-136.

Evans, K. & Kersh, N. (2003) 'Recognition of Tacit Skills and Knowledge: Sustaining learning outcomes in workplace environments', *Proceedings: Book VI*, of 3rd International Conference of Researching Work and Learning, *Work and Lifelong Learning in Different Contexts*, July 25th-27th 2003, Tampere, Finland.

Falk, I. (2002) 'The New World of Work: Implications for literacy and numeracy'. Discussion paper prepared by Adult Literacy & Numeracy, *Australian Research Consortium (Tasmania) for the ALNARC National Research Program 2001-2002*, Launceston: University of Tasmania, pp.1-12.

Field, L (2001) *Industry Speaks: Skill requirements of leading Australian workplaces*. Canberra: Commonwealth Department of Education, Science and Training.

Gill, M. (1999) 'If we don't do it, someone else will … ', *English in Australia*, Vol. 124, April, pp.70-75.

Gonczi, A., Hager, P. & Oliver, L. (1990) *Establishing Competency Standards in the Professions: NOOSR Research Paper No. 1*. Canberra: Australian Government Publishing Service.

Hager, P. & Beckett, D. (1995) 'Philosophical Underpinnings of the Integrated Conception of Competence', *Educational Philosophy and Theory*, Vol. 27, No. 1, pp. 1-24.

Hildebrand, G., Mulcahy, D. & Wilks, S. (2001) 'Learning to Teach Through PBL: Process and progress', Paper presented at the Australian Teacher Education Association Conference, *Teacher Education: Change of heart, mind and action*. 24-26 September, 2001, Melbourne.

Hyland, T. (1997) 'Reconsidering Competence', *Journal of Philosophy of Education*, Vol. 31 No. 3, pp. 491-501.

Lave, J. & Wenger, E. (1991) *Situated Learning: Legitimate peripheral participation* Cambridge & New York: Cambridge University Press.

Law, J. (2002) 'On Hidden Heterogeneities: Complexity, Formalism and Aircraft Design', in
J. Law & A. Mol (eds.) *Complexities: Social Studies of Knowledge Practices*. Durham, North Carolina: Duke University Press, pp. 116-141.

Louden, W. (1993) 'Researching Teacher Competencies – Portraying competent teaching: Can competency based standards help?' Research Project 1, *Unicorn*, Vol. 19, No. 3, pp. 13-23.

Morris, G. & Beckett, D. (2004) 'Performing Identities: The New Focus on Embodied Adults' Learning', in P. Kell, S. Shore & M. Singh (eds.) *Adult Education @21st Century: Studies in the Postmodern Theory of Education*, New York: Peter Lang Publishing, pp. 246-254,

Mulcahy, D. (1999) (actor-net) 'Working Bodies and Representations: Tales from a Training Field', *Science, Technology, & Human Values*, Vol. 24, No. 1, pp. 80-104.

Mulcahy, D. (2000) 'Body Matters in Vocational Education: The case of the competently-trained', *International Journal of Lifelong Education*, Vol. 19, No. 6, pp. 506-524.

Robinson, C. (2000) *New Directions in Australia's Skill Formation: Lifelong learning is the key*. Adelaide: National Centre for Vocational Education Research.

Smith, E. & Comyn, P. (2003) *The Development of Employability Skills in Novice Workers*. Adelaide: National Centre for Vocational Education Research.

Stanwick, J. (2003) *Skills for Life: Lifelong learning systems in Australia*, Adelaide: National Centre for Vocational Education Research.

Stevenson, J. (2001) 'Vocational knowledge and its specification', *Journal of Vocational Education and Training*, Vol. 53, No. 4, pp. 657-662.

Stronach, I., Corbin, B., McNamara, O., Stark, S. & Warne, T. (2002), 'Towards an Uncertain Politics of Professionalism: Teacher and nurse identities in flux', *Journal of Education Policy*, Vol. 17, No. 1, pp. 109-138.

Virgona, C., Waterhouse, P., Sefton, R. & Sanguinetti, J. (2003), *Making Experience Work: Generic skills through the eyes of dispaced workers*, Vol. 1, Adelaide: National Centre for Vocational Education Research.

Wenger, E. (1998) *Communities of Practice: Learning, meaning, and identity.* Cambridge: Cambridge University Press.

CHAPTER 14

SUSAN HOLLAND

SYNTHESIS: A LIFELONG LEARNING FRAMEWORK FOR GRADUATE ATTRIBUTES

1. INTRODUCTION

The purpose of this chapter is to examine graduate attributes in relation to learning processes, employability and leadership as the basis for developing a framework for 'lifelong learning'. By this is meant learning taken up at different times for different purposes throughout life, including learning at work. As it is the ultimate chapter the opportunity has been taken to draw on the preceding theoretical discussion of graduate attributes which is outlined in the first part of the book. This chapter also takes into account the implications of the case study material reported in the second and third parts of the book. Some of this case material goes beyond the usual educational settings of the lecture room or laboratory to include work settings and examples of professionals in practice. Accordingly these cases provide a number of insights concerning the dynamic interplay between learning processes and the factors influencing employability as well as leadership in the workplace.

At this point it is necessary to clarify terminology. Given the diversity of qualities encapsulated by the phrase 'generic skills', and the ambiguities inherent in any definition, the use of this terminology will be restricted. Instead, in line with the convention adopted throughout the book, 'generic attributes' will be used to refer to the collection of skills, capacities, dispositions and values that together represent the more general outcomes of learning. In the context of tertiary study, 'graduate attributes' will be used to distinguish general as opposed to more disciplinary-based attributes.

Initially, for novice professionals, as the reflections captured by Te Wiata (chapter 12) exemplify, the interplay between learning and employability is typically manifest in the way that recent graduates develop, apply and often come

P. Hager and S. Holland (eds.), Graduate Attributes, Learning and Employability, 267–307.
© 2006 *Springer*

to rely on generic attributes, in comparison to disciplinary knowledge and skills. Indeed it seems that this reliance on generic capacities is part of a coping strategy in the early years in the workplace. It will be argued, following Beckett & Mulcahy (chapter 13) in particular, that as graduates become more capable practitioners with deeper forms of engagement within their respective professions, including feedback and assessment by peers, the interplay between learning and employability contributes to the refinement of 'professional capabilities'. The term 'capability' is used as it implies clustering of various elements or attributes, of which only some are cognitive in character, as well as a sense of agency. The emergence of this form of generic capability after significant experience in professional practice is a further development and so represents a later and mature phase in terms of lifelong learning.

Notwithstanding the valuable connections that are highlighted in the various case studies, none of the other chapters in this book explicitly addresses issues concerning learning and leadership, or indeed employability and leadership. The nature and importance of these kinds of relationships is explored in the present chapter in the context of considering aspects of continuing professional education and the potential for what will be called 'leadership capabilities'. While not all professionals necessarily aspire to, or may be capable of, leadership in their professional practice, none the less it can be identified as the ultimate phase of lifelong learning. In describing the possible conditions whereby this phase may occur in practice, 'leadership' is taken to mean a state of being. As such leadership capabilities may not be attributed to someone merely as a result of their appointment to a senior management position.

Traditionally much of the organisational development and human resource literature as well as structured programs, such as the increasingly ubiquitous Masters in Business Administration (MBA), focussed solely on management skills, that is management of resources, strategy and people. In recent decades the changing nature of workplaces and the impact of technology has meant that there is now more recognition that knowing how to harness and expand 'learning' capability is important for sustainable development and success, both for individuals and for organisations as a whole. Binney & Williams, for example, have concluded that, 'successful leaders in charge combine leading and learning: they lead in such a way that learning is encouraged; they learn in a way that informs and guides those that seek to lead' (1995: 7). Based on their years of practical experience concerning leadership and change management they have combined the notions of 'leading' and 'learning' in coining the phrase, 'leaning into the future' in order to make the point that in contemporary workplaces successful senior managers need to be *both* leaders and learners.

So, instead of the typical scenario of the leader only driving change from the 'top down' as if the organisation or enterprise is some kind of machine, a more effective and sustainable approach is to also invest in people by facilitating learning processes as part of the work situation. In this more complex and integrated scenario employees are more likely to become self-aware and so be able to achieve their potential, including finding better ways to improve their work practices. Such outcomes are of benefit to themselves as well as to the enterprise. However, as will be elaborated in later sections, while there is obvious merit in recognising organisations as places for learning as well as for working, the development of learning capability, at an individual or collective level, is not necessarily easily or quickly acquired in the workplace. The work settings need to be configured in such a way that learning is not only encouraged but also valued as an ongoing and important part of the work situation.

While the crucial lesson to be taken from this book overall is that there are difficulties in uncritically describing, embedding or assessing generic aspects of learning, there are still sound educational and work-based arguments for pursuing a graduate attributes agenda. It will be contended that the development of generic capabilities is necessarily a continuous, though not contiguous, lifelong process involving several phases. The present chapter is a contribution towards understanding how such an agenda may play out and be developed in practice.

Three learning phases are identified each with the possibility of a set of generic outcomes at increasingly higher levels of capability: Tertiary Study, Professional Practice and Leadership Development. This is not to deny the value of social and collective aspects of learning, nor to imply that there is a need to follow a particular developmental sequence in order to become proficient. The phases, together with the prior development of the necessary foundational and basic forms of learning, are proposed as a Lifelong Learning Framework for Graduate Attributes. While the framework is couched in terms of professional qualifications and practices, the phases could apply equally, with some modification, to other occupational forms.

Tertiary study is the first phase in the development of graduate attributes. During this phase learners build on the basic skills and foundational attributes ordinarily learnt in the years of schooling to become more independent and 'authentic' as learners in the sense that Barnett (Chapter 3) uses the term. Engaging in a profession, initially as a novice and ultimately as a 'capable practitioner', is the second phase of lifelong learning whereby 'professional capabilities' emerge. Leadership development is a further phase, which is not necessarily pursued by all professionals. In this phase, leadership is about gaining peer recognition in a profession by demonstrating 'leadership capabilities' as a 'learning leader', that is, a leader who is engaged in learning and is capable of leading others in their learning. While learning processes are fundamental to all phases, employability and leadership, respectively, are of particular importance in the second and third phases.

The following table is a summary of the phases in the proposed Lifelong Learning Framework, which indicates the respective roles of the learners, the prime context for the learning, and the outcomes in generic terms. Further details of each phase are elaborated in the final sections of the chapter.

Table 1. Lifelong Learning Framework for Graduate Attributes

Phases	1:Tertiary Study	2: Professional Practice	3: Leadership Development
Roles	Tertiary Student	Novice Practitioner	Learning Leader
Learning Context	Becoming authentic as a learner	Engaging in practice and professional registration	Gaining peer recognition as a leader in learning
Outcomes	Graduate Attributes	Professional Capabilities	Leadership Capabilities

2. EMPLOYABILITY, GENERIC ATTRIBUTES AND LIFELONG LEARNING

The contemporary focus on the value of generic attributes and lifelong learning has three prime sources. There is, firstly, employer dissatisfaction with the apparent poor suitability of graduates for productive work. Secondly, government concern regarding educational outcomes has lead to national and international education policy reforms focussing on the relationships between schooling, tertiary education and work. Thirdly, new understandings about the nature of learning have generated different approaches by educational providers to pedagogy and curriculum design. Although the same set of global, economic and technological factors is at play each of these stakeholders has a different agenda that reflects their respective core purposes. Employers want 'job ready' graduates for the workplaces of today. Their prime concern is with what has come to be described as 'employability'. Governments want productive economic and social outcomes in return for their significant public expenditure on different forms of educational provision. Educational providers, which are catering increasingly for more diverse groups of students, want better learning outcomes in relation to inputs and available resources.

Despite inevitable policy shifts due to the prevailing political milieu, there is a persistent perception by employers and industry associations that graduates, whether from the secondary, vocational or university sectors, frequently lack the attributes deemed necessary for effective performance at entry level, and also for future success in the workplace. This perception of deficiency is being voiced strongly throughout the Western world, by business and employer groups, and encompasses both technical and professional work. There have been a number of surveys and similar projects that have attempted to quantify the nature of the deficit in practical terms.

In Australia, for example, there have been two such projects in recent times. The first of these projects was the publicly funded report, *Employer Satisfaction with Graduate Skills* (DETYA) which identified a list of desirable skills deemed to be lacking by some graduates. 'While the overall performance of new graduates employed appears to be reasonable, neither particularly low or high...a large proportion of applicants for positions are considered unsuitable, even for other positions within the organisation' (2000: vii). This report attempted to take into account the relative importance of the skills required by employers and concluded that the greatest skill deficiencies among new graduates were perceived to be in the areas of 'creativity and flair', 'oral business communications' and 'problem-solving'. Interestingly, unsuccessful applicants were also seen to 'lack' these skills, and, in addition, the 'capacity for independent and critical thinking'. The report notes that it is 'this skill ...(which) most sets apart successful from unsuccessful applicants: in other words, employers *value* this skill, and *can* find it but it is *rare*' (2000: viii).

The public debate following the release of this report led in turn to another. The second report, *Employability Skills for the Future* (ACCI & BCA 2002), was industry sponsored but also publicly funded. This latter report was designed to identify a comprehensive set of so-called 'employability' skills. The shift in language from 'generic' to 'employability' was deliberate. The employer stakeholders that sponsored the report have an ongoing agenda to exert influence over the nature of the curriculum, particularly in the vocational sector, in the belief that highlighting employability skills will necessarily ensure that more graduates become 'job ready'.

Based on a case study approach with small, medium and large–sized enterprises during 2001 the attributes identified were a mix of the familiar, largely experientially based, job-specific skills such as 'self-management, team work, communication skills, planning and organising skills, using technology, and problem solving skills'. Also identified were more nebulous attributes reflecting dispositions which businesses wish to encourage like 'initiative and enterprise skills' as well as a large number of value laden, personal attributes seen as ideal for success in contemporary workplaces. These latter attributes ranged from 'loyalty' to a 'balanced attitude to work and home life', and even a 'sense of humour'. While this more industry focussed project arose primarily from dissatisfaction with graduate outcomes from the vocational sector it also has relevance for the higher education sector.

While employer perceptions may be flawed, the shift to a knowledge-based economy certainly requires new forms of knowledge, practical capacities and more flexible responses from employees, which in turn requires the ability to share knowledge and understanding with others. Hager, Holland & Beckett (2002) highlight that it is the emphasis on 'intangible inputs' that most clearly characterises the new workplace. These inputs require different kinds of knowledge and practical skills, such as 'creativity, design proficiency, customer relations and goodwill, and innovative marketing' that are generic rather than discipline specific. Such 'intangible inputs' are elusive and so, increasingly, is the kind of employment in which they are manifest. Many employees are now more vulnerable in the workplace due to what Murtough & Waite (2000) term the 'precarious' nature of work. This is most evident at the middle level, where many jobs have disappeared due to fundamental structural changes affecting both production processes and organisational arrangements.

As a result of these types of changes today all job entrants, even those entering the workforce directly from school, need to be able to demonstrate broad rather than narrow skills, including the softer skills like 'communication' and 'team work'. As observed by Hinchliffe (chapter 5) success in this kind of work scenario requires 'insider' experience, and the heightened capacity to 'read' and interpret that culture. Hager (chapter 2) makes a similar point in highlighting the emergence of the notion of 'cultural fit'. Down (chapter 10), based on interviews with employees and their supervisors in various industry sectors, argues that in contemporary workplaces these new skills and forms of knowledge are best learnt by employees as part of their work practice. Following Lave & Wenger (1991) she suggests, using case studies drawn from the vocational sector, that it is the very 'situatedness' of the learning, and the learner, that shapes the what and how of this kind of workplace learning.

If these more elusive generic attributes are important for employment and so, there is a need to develop them, what is meant by 'employability'? Beckett and Mulcahy argue that the key question is not what it is to *have* employability skills but what it is to *do* employability. In their view employability is the construction of different practices, which involves social forms of learning, so they prefer the term 'employabilities'. Indeed, as illustrated by Te Wiata's vignettes of graduates in their initial years of professional practice, the generic attributes perceived as being important and contributing to effective performance are actually a mix of social and cognitive capabilities requiring some maturity and feedback from colleagues as well as supervisors.

Another interesting observation of workplace practice she documents, is, that despite all the talk of 'knowledge workers' these professionals, albeit at a novice stage in their respective careers, are rarely given the opportunity to create any new forms of knowledge. Instead they are engaged primarily in locating, then applying or disseminating knowledge. As her graduates themselves recognise it is generic rather than discipline specific attributes that underpin and are therefore the core contributors to these kinds of work activities.

Even though, as Hager indicates, there are difficulties with the credibility of employer 'skilltalk', and often unrealistic expectations, as argued by Hinchliffe, there is still an apparent gap in employers' perceptions of what they need and what they get in recruiting employees. An important task then, to return to the question posed earlier about 'employability', is to unpack what they are really saying and put this into an educational framework. In other words, "What do universities or other tertiary providers need to do so that employers will be more satisfied with their graduates?" A more sophisticated account of graduate capabilities is needed in which generic attributes are conceived as being central to lifelong learning.

3. GRADUATE ATTRIBUTES AND NEW FORMS OF LEARNING

Workplace changes are so fundamental that proficiency in a broad range of generic attributes is essential for the new worker to obtain and retain meaningful work. Rapid changes in the nature of work mean that workers not only require the capacity to be 'flexible' and 'adaptable' in their present work situation, but also require the knowledge, confidence, and skills to self-manage their careers by continuing to develop their capabilities and matching these to available opportunities. In other words, to view their response to the job market and progression in a trade or profession as the concept of accumulating an appropriate mix of knowledge, skills and experiences, and to take responsibility for retaining evidence of their continuing learning and development via some kind of portfolio.

As will be argued below such notions lead naturally to an interest in, and an increasing commitment to, lifelong learning on the part of workers who often now see themselves as both 'earners and learners'. Since so many jobs are now requiring the kinds of capacities that previously were not so important for most workers, it is not surprising that participation in all forms of post-compulsory education has increased. At university level longer degree structures which combine different disciplines are more in vogue, a significant number of graduates subsequently undertake some form of vocational training, and there is an increasing tendency for graduates to obtain jobs which are outside of their initial field of study. These shifts in emphasis and the blurring of previously rigid distinctions between 'learning' and 'working' have profound implications for educational providers as much as for employers.

Even for graduates in professional occupations there is now more emphasis on continuing professional education beyond the initial requirements for registration, certification and the right to practice. Indeed many professions such as medicine, accounting and psychology now require compliance with a formal system for regulating continuing professional education. Participation in activities deemed to be relevant to further learning and development as a professional practitioner is typically the basis for maintaining registration and recognition. To count as legitimate professional development these activities generally include but go beyond the traditional annual conference to encompass engagement, for example, in the trial of new processes, products or services and a commitment to be exposed to peer review as well as other forms of reflective practice.

From the perspective of educational providers these workplace changes and new types of professional requirements have created demand for different types of vocational, undergraduate and postgraduate programs. Increasingly there is dissatisfaction with the typical course structure for professions, for example, which has been documented by Hager (1996). There is more interest in combinations of vocational and university level study, double degrees, and integrated or sandwich type undergraduate programs, which incorporate practical as well as theoretical elements. In some cases too, in the Australian scene most notably in Medicine, the entry program to the profession has been shifting over recent years from undergraduate to postgraduate level. In summary, irrespective of whether the exit credential from tertiary study is a vocational diploma, or an undergraduate or postgraduate degree, it is no more than a necessary basis for the commencement of practice. Further development and continuing practice is required over the life of a practitioner.

This is the genesis for the deepening interest in lifelong learning and the trend to credential learning in the workplace, even for tertiary forms of study. Boud & Solomon (chapter 11) detail the way in which one university has successfully embarked on an alternative approach to curriculum design, learning and assessment by using the workplace as a legitimate site for academic learning. Other authors such as Candy, Crebert & O'Leary (1994) argue, on the basis of practical case studies, that the attributes that are commonly taken to characterise lifelong learning are heavily reliant on a range of generic capabilities.

Linked to this, as noted earlier, is the emerging notion of the 'learning organisation', where the nature of the generic attributes of staff, particularly their learning capacities, is regarded as the most important factor in ensuring sustained business success. Senge (1990) first articulated this concept and since then it has been refined and applied by many others to a range of contexts, including vocational development (for example, Billet 2001). Indeed it is now fairly commonplace for human resource professionals to think in these terms when designing staff development programs (see, for example, Marsick &Watkins 1999; Teare & Dealtry 1998).

Governments whether national, regional or state are seeking a return for their various public investments in education at secondary, vocational or tertiary levels. So they are being more concrete and prescriptive about the kinds of outcomes they are expecting in each case. Leaving aside cultural differences, the general expectation is for more highly skilled and educated citizens who will increase economic productivity in the short term, and help to build social cohesion over the longer term. Here the focus is more to do with 'accountability'.

Discussion of this agenda is dealt with, at least in part, by Gonczi (chapter 6) elsewhere in this book. He outlines the rationale for, and implications flowing from a large scale, international project, *DeSeCo,* which arose in response to the question of whether citizens of developed countries are learning the skills appropriate for the new age. The *DeSeCo* project, auspiced by the Organisation for Economic Cooperation and Development (OECD), attempted to identify and classify generic attributes as part of a cross-cultural agenda to improve educational and social outcomes for all citizens across their life spans. Not surprisingly, the notion of learning throughout life is implicit in this kind of policy research.

Thus the OECD agenda provides some guidance for the task of determining the criteria for a credible lifelong learning framework. In other words, a framework, which explicitly incorporates generic attributes in such a way that developmental and reflective learning processes are recognised, and which at the same time can encapsulate the related, and equally developmental, processes of employability and leadership. All these processes are seen as contributing, potentially at least, to sustaining and interpreting a meaningful lifelong journey, a lifetime of development and reflective engagement, which can be achieved via a number of pathways.

From various perspectives, the validity of a lifelong approach for graduate attributes is emphasised by Scanlon (Chapter 7), Barrie (Chapter 8), and Atlay (Chapter 9). This set of chapters collectively records the main difficulties as well as some notable successes in embedding, describing and teaching generic attributes in bridging and tertiary settings. Accordingly, these analyses provide some basis for considering the phased development of generic outcomes resulting from different kinds of learning processes, and as such they provide a useful backdrop against which to assess the 'practicality' of developing graduate attributes in different educational settings.

In detailing the phased development from graduate attributes through professional capabilities to leadership capabilities, the concluding section of the chapter draws, in part, on research cited in the final part of the book concerned with graduate attributes and employability. The different but related accounts by Down, Boud & Solomon, Te Wiata, and Beckett & Mulcahy consider a number of germane issues. These include, respectively, the role of personal agency and 'affordances' in learning from and at work, the credentialling of work-based learning, the initial career experiences of professionals, and the development of professional capabilities – coined 'employ-abilities'.

The book chapters taken together highlight two kinds of constructs. Firstly, there are conventional, individualistic, approaches to the acquisition of knowledge and practical understanding, including engaging in academic endeavour for the advancement of self-knowledge, or at more mature levels, following Barnett (chapter 3), the development of 'authenticity' as an integral aspect of being. Secondly, there is an alternative construct, which places more emphasis on socially-derived, collective forms of learning, whether in the academy or in the workplace, where 'situational' aspects of learning influence the nature of the processes involved as well as the learning outcomes. The differences in these ways of describing learning processes and outcomes require some kind of resolution for any coherent, developmental conception of lifelong learning

Accordingly, note is taken of the theoretical and practical implications of the cases in outlining a lifelong learning framework for graduate attributes. The framework will set out three interconnected phases:

- Tertiary study when students learn to become independent and start to be 'authentic' as learners;
- Professional practice when novices through engagement in their profession meet the requirements for registration and gradually become more capable as practitioners ; and ultimately,
- Leadership development when more accomplished even expert performance, as adjudged by peers, is achieved as a precursor to the development of the capacity to lead others in their learning as a 'learning leader'.

The purpose of the framework is to highlight the need for further personal, and even collective development, if what will be termed, respectively, 'professional capabilities' and 'leadership capabilities' are to emerge. Whether or not such further development occurs in practice for individual graduates depends on a range of personal and contextual factors, including the kind of learning pathway pursued, the range of professional experiences encountered, and the nature and extent of engagement in continuing professional education.

As already cautioned, this will not be an argument for an immutable or overly prescriptive developmental hierarchy. Rather the intention is to leave open the possibility of a progressive agenda for generic aspects of lifelong learning. It will be argued that the development of generic capabilities is an ongoing and accumulative process that requires contextually rich learning environments and conditions, including a mix of educational and work-based settings. Examples of the learning strategies and settings that are likely to facilitate these kinds of long term and necessarily reflective processes will be suggested in respect of each of the phases.

4. COMPLEXITY AND WORKPLACE CHANGE: DRIVERS FOR LIFELONG LEARNING

The twenty-first century has been heralded as a golden and prosperous age. The common expectation is for continuing rates of economic growth, including in the developing countries, due to the widespread impact of micro-electronic technology and more open terms of trade with border-less markets. Our world is now seen as a small planet. Communication can be with anyone, anytime, anywhere. We can expect to live longer and in better health. Yet in this era where technology both enables and pervades there are uneven outcomes. At the individual level, for example, there is the issue of access to, and potential misuse of, private and confidential information. More broadly, economic and cultural resources remain unevenly distributed, as is the corresponding technological capacity of nations.

As well the pace of change is accelerating while at the same time the choices or pathways available to even those in relatively modest circumstances are expanding. As a result our world has become more complex and challenging in both a personal and social sense. Even if all of us were to aspire to become truly global citizens, we cannot rely on technological solutions alone to address fundamental and perennial issues such as how to use our collective capacities to live together peacefully for mutually beneficial purposes. Individually, and collectively, we need now, more than ever, for example, the capacity to make sound and ethical judgements balancing private interests with public concerns, and considering national objectives in the light of global impacts. Clearly these kinds of capacities have generic as well as discipline specific elements.

Ordinarily the capacity for individuals to make such judgements is not lightly or quickly gained. This is so, because, to ably deploy in practice a complex capacity of this kind, which is multi-layered and contingent, requires engagement over time in a developmental and contextually rich set of learning processes. This is necessary to gain the range and breadth of practical experience as well as the self-confidence that comes with the opportunity for reflection and mature insight. While competent performance of a value-laden capacity may be difficult to judge since it is subject to many interpretations, it is clear that it is not merely a matter of mastering a particular technology or skill set. One cannot just be trained to act or think ethically, for example, as it is not an easily identified or narrowly defined technical skill. In what Barnett calls the age of 'super-complexity', technology, despite its many potentials, cannot provide clear answers to the question of how to live a happy, peaceful, and productive life. It is only through education that we can learn, grow, and develop as individuals as well as doing so as members of different groups. This is not to suggest that all forms of education are equally useful. Here it is worth noting in passing, for the subsequent discussion about graduate attributes and tertiary study, the useful distinction made by Winch (chapter 4) between 'technical knowledge' and 'technological knowledge'. While the former puts into effect a body of theoretical knowledge in a particular context for a particular purpose, the latter encompasses the capacity to contribute to the theoretical component of that applicable knowledge. Both forms of knowledge are important and he does not privilege one form of knowledge over the other. Rather, he reminds us that the latter category of knowledge formation requires higher order conceptual capacities which are usually only taught in a formal sense in universities.

From an historical perspective, higher education institutions specifically universities, have played an important role in pointing to possible answers to the kinds of big issues just posed. It is after all the form of education with a long and explicit tradition of advancing socially useful as well as technically relevant knowledge based on the twin notions of free inquiry and independent thought. Barnett and Winch each provide brief but complementary accounts that set the historical context for the traditions and purposes that, despite recent changes, still underpin contemporary forms of higher education.

Although, in an increasingly competitive environment with more institutions offering private forms of higher education, several nations have found it necessary to articulate the defining characteristics of universities in order to protect their special character as places of higher learning and research. In broad terms this special character has been taken to be that teaching is underpinned by research, which is undertaken to advance new forms of knowledge as well as to improve pedagogic practice (Guthrie, Johnstone & King 2004). The National Protocols for Higher Education Approvals in Australia, for example, include a Protocol concerning the recognition of institutions as universities. Similarly, in New Zealand, there are five characteristics or tests set out by the New Zealand Qualifications Authority (NZQA) all of which must be met by any local tertiary institution aspiring to be designated as a university.

Alongside these regulatory developments there have been many other factors that have changed forever the shape and operating principles of the higher education sector. Significant global trends include the expansion in the range and rate of participation, adoption of 'user pays' as a necessary element of the funding base, and more explicit expectations for outcomes or performance measures to assure quality and accountability. This latter factor accounts for the renewed emphasis on governance while 'massification' and cost drivers have resulted in significant shifts in the academic profiles of many universities. In Australia, as elsewhere, most universities now offer a spectrum of disciplines together with multi-disciplinary and inter-disciplinary studies. The level and focus of study also varies from the traditional professions to paraprofessional and vocationally oriented programs, as well as more overtly 'populist' courses like 'Surf, Science and Technology' (ECU 2005: 12), that have weaker though not necessarily illegitimate claims to belong to the academy.

While higher education itself has been subject to these kinds of changes, its core teaching and research purposes, at least, remain intact. That being said, new approaches to pedagogy and curriculum design have arisen, such as 'e-learning', due to the convergence of technologies and pressing commercial imperatives. Inevitably these emerging forms of teaching and learning are subject to debate, trial and revision as academic practitioners try out what works and discard what does not. This is generally a peer review process as much as a reflection of individual endeavour. As with similar journals based elsewhere, recent articles in the journal, *Higher Education Research and Development* (HERD 2004 a, b, c) confirm the value of these kinds of activities in the Australian context.

Whatever the pros and cons of new approaches to pedagogy, there is no escaping the imperative for higher education to cater more effectively, in an educational and economic sense, for diverse groups of students. There is concern about how to improve learning outcomes in the immediate term, as well as to assist students to achieve their career and self-development goals in the longer term. The case of Luton University's attempts to cater more effectively for its culturally and educationally diverse student population, documented by Atlay, provides useful insights into the nature of the curriculum and pedagogic challenge involved in being explicit about career development and the acquisition of generic type capabilities. It is in this changing educational landscape that the nature of graduate attributes has become more of a focus for attention in tertiary forms of education.

Overall, these kinds of changes coupled with demands for better governance and quality assurance presents serious challenges to university leaders. Indeed in accountability terms, the new challenge for all educators across the sectors is how to effectively 'value add'. If Barnett's notion of 'super-complexity' is valid, then it is not difficult to imagine how these kinds of challenges in the academic environment now require leaders in the academy to develop 'new dispositions, new qualities, new forms of being' to cope with their changed world. Meade (2003) provides a balanced discussion about how to acquire such new dispositions or qualities and some useful practical suggestions for university leaders. This theme is explored further below in describing the third phase of the lifelong learning framework, the development of 'leadership capabilities'.

Since universities are not insulated from changes in the external environment, they cannot afford to be isolated from the communities and stakeholders they are expected to serve. As a result more serious attention is now being paid to 'community engagement' as well as to pedagogic strategies like 'service learning', which aim to use the 'community' as site for learning and/or research for mutual benefit. Such strategies require new approaches in respect of accrediting and assessing learning. A range of these types of programs incorporating elements of 'service learning' have been in place in the United States of America, in particular, for some time and are a more recent phenomenon in Australia (Metropolitan Universities 2003).

Another consequence of the need for more 'connectivity' has been the emergence of new kinds of partnerships between industry and higher education. This is evident, for example, in the way that it is now commonplace for some categories of research funding to be allocated to projects that specifically encourage 'collaborative' types of research. In Australia, modelling practice elsewhere, the Business/Higher Education Roundtable (B-HERT) is another mechanism in place to encourage interaction between the academy and industry. This commitment is reflected in its charter which is to 'pursue initiatives that will advance the goals and improve the performance of both business and higher education for the benefit of Australian society' (B-HERT 2003).

Other changes are cross-sectoral in character. There are new relationships being forged between the different sectors in education as the previously tight boundaries between learning and working, vocational and professional, secondary and tertiary, public and private are becoming looser. Today there is more opportunity for people, irrespective of their previous formal educational experience, to continue to pursue further study via various pathways that link one education sector with another, frequently on the basis of credit for prior learning. These credentialling processes and provisions for 'staircasing' are now more widely available for school leavers, mature workers re-entering education, and professionals engaging in 'continuing professional education' as well as senior members of the community. While several initiatives designed to promote credit transfer have been developed, in Australia, for example, mostly this approach has not been successful in policy terms. Rather the drivers for individual educational aspiration, and the pursuit of further learning beyond an initial qualification, appear to be economic and social.

Scanlon provides some insights into the factors involved in the aspiration for further learning. She traces in some detail the unfolding learning experiences of one set of mature adults re-entering formal education with the explicit aspiration of seeking university entrance via an alternative pathway. The major conclusion of this case study relates to the perception by all the learners of the importance of the acquisition of generic attributes. While each learner recalled learning events or experiences relating to different kinds of generic attributes, overall, engaging in these processes was seen by these learners to be a crucial and important step in overcoming negative self-concepts arising from earlier educational experiences. This finding suggests that the processes involved even in the embryonic development of generic attributes may contribute to higher levels of confidence and self-esteem. Indeed generic attributes seem to be an important component of self-identity and identity formation.

As Scanlon's case illustrates, the links between the various education sectors are horizontal and vertical as the demand for different combinations of knowledge sets, skills and dispositions changes in line with market demand. In fact in Australia, at least, recent surveys show that there are more university graduates (by a factor of about seven) undertaking some form of vocational education and training – a horizontal link – than vocational graduates articulating to university study – a vertical link (DEST 2002: 7-8). This is especially significant because the phenomenon is not due to any policy agenda, but, is instead a consequence of significant numbers of individuals making pragmatic decisions to further their own educational and vocational interests. Finally, anecdotal evidence suggests that due to economic necessity, most, if not all, undergraduate students in Australian universities, irrespective of whether, in a technical sense, they are designated as part-time or full-time, are both 'learners' and 'earners'.

Against this background there is much policy talk and optimism at national and international forums about the value of lifelong learning and generic skills. In recent years the OECD, as already noted, has pursued this policy agenda systematically. Lifelong learning can take many forms. Even when there is an extended period of education and training for professions such as medicine, psychology or teaching, there is an expectation that the individual will engage in continuing professional education throughout their career. This is one form of lifelong learning. At the other end of the scale it can refer to any type of education or learning process undertaken by adults at different stages in their lives whether for occupational reasons or not.

Increasingly, lifelong learning also has credence in the workplace. In summary, flatter work structures, multi-tasking, and the pervasiveness of micro-electronic technology means that it is increasingly the case that all workers need to update their knowledge and skills. Irrespective of whether they are operating on the shop floor or at senior executive levels people at work need to learn different skills or become more proficient in undertaking their existing tasks, as well as mastering more complex matters such as supervision or decision-making processes. It is in this changing work context that the interplay between learning, employability and leadership is crucial to understanding the potentials for lifelong learning, which encompasses not only the development of graduate attributes, but also higher level professional and leadership capabilities.

5. CHARACTERISTICS OF GENERIC ATTRIBUTES: CONNECTIVITY, CONTEXTUALITY AND CONTINGENCY

In addressing meta–concepts the chapters, respectively, by Hager, Barnett, Winch, and Hinchliffe, collectively distill and distinguish important aspects of generic attributes that help clarify our understanding of these phenomena in the context of recent developments in higher education. Indeed, this set of chapters constitutes a robust and elaborated theoretical discussion regarding the nature of graduate attributes *per se*, specifically the extent to which it makes sense or otherwise to conceive of these in generic terms. A number of fruitful concepts are highlighted in relation to emerging conceptions of 'learning' and 'employability'.

For example, in an uncertain, ever complex and changing world, Barnett proposes that the major challenge for graduates is not so much about knowing and doing as how to become an authentic 'being'. Hinchliffe in emphasising the socio-cultural aspects of contemporary workplaces indicates that the ability to engage in 'situational learning', the capacity to 'read' situations accurately and sensitively, is likely to be as important as cognitive capacities in contributing to the success or otherwise of graduates in seeking and retaining employment.

The present chapter draws broadly on these kinds of theoretical distinctions to identify some important characteristics of generic attributes. In line with the fore-mentioned authors, in particular Hager and Winch, it is argued that in considering the application of generic attributes to different learning situations; whether foundational learning at school, vocational, work-based or higher forms of education, the features of most relevance are 'connectivity', 'contextuality', and 'contingency'. Each of these characteristics is explored below as a precursor to proposing the lifelong learning framework, including the latter phases of professional learning whereby 'professional' and 'leadership capabilities' may be developed.

5.1 Connectivity of generic attributes

The term 'generic attributes' is typically used to refer to a diverse collection of qualities that are seen as important in relation to learning but are nevertheless distinct from discipline-based knowledge and related technical skills. Hager argues convincingly that, in fact, this set of things is quite diverse. Not only does the term embrace higher order thinking and related skills like applying mathematical principles, or logical and analytical reasoning it can also refer to more elusive things that are actually skill components and dispositions. The latter category includes capacities like communication skills, teamwork skills, accessing information or using technology as well as more personal dispositions like creativity or aesthetic appreciation. This category also includes values, one example of which, as already discussed, is 'integrity' and its application in ethical practice.

Indeed, in practice the situation is even more complicated. While some generic capacities are essentially mental or conceptual, in practice others involve both mental and physical elements. Furthermore, only fairly narrow and discrete skills can be improved solely on the basis of routine practice. As already noted more is required for effective acquisition or deployment of dispositions and values drawn from the affective domain. It is the case, too, that life circumstances, including genetic profile, quite apart from socio-cultural influences, can constrain or enhance the way that we, as unique individuals, develop and acquire these different types of generic attributes.

It is useful in developing our understanding of generic attributes to consider them individually. However, in practice, as Hager suggests, based on his own occupationally specific research as well as that undertaken by others, generic attributes 'overlap and interweave' to such an extent that it is more accurate, particularly in workplace situations, to talk about and conceive of these as 'clusters'. So, attempts to identify generic attributes *per se*, or graduate attributes in the university or tertiary context, as separate traits are misguided and reflect seriously flaws in the understanding of the way learning processes actually work in individual and group situations.

Indeed Hager goes to some length to identify five kinds of misunderstandings:

- perceiving attributes too narrowly or atomistically as if these were discrete entities;
- over relying on the notion of acquistion as a metaphor for learning;
- ignoring collective forms of learning;
- over-stating what can be measured as generic attributes; and
- using inappropriate language to describe generic attributes.

Winch in also considering the character of generic attributes in the context of the contemporary graduate attribute agenda applies some tests. In summary these are, whether or not it makes sense to define a particular attribute coherently, the extent to which an attribute of this kind is context dependent and hence whether there is the possibility of transferability, and the practicality or otherwise of learning or developing such an attribute. For example, he considers that 'understanding and applying mathematics' is a generic attribute as it meets the conditions implied by his tests, including conceptual coherence, whereas being able to 'problem solve' does not. Here Winch's notion of coherence is similar to Hager's argument concerning holism, except that in the former case it is a conceptual issue which applies at a lower level of generality.

Many activities in daily life, the workplace or social settings such as applying first aid to someone in an emergency, composing a letter or dealing with interpersonal conflict are mutli-layered. While they can be broken into discrete components in theory, in the actual 'doing' the components are applied concurrently and holistically as a total activity. The discrete components represent a mix of attributes. Some of these are knowledge and skill based, while others, strictly speaking are attitudes and values. Someone might be able to demonstrate each of these discrete attributes yet still be incompetent in terms of the whole task.

The notion of the coherence of generic attributes appears to make sense at the level of individual attributes. And, if the notion of holism is also valid because clusters of attributes have to be combined in particular ways for effective performance, then the important characteristic in both cases seems to be 'connectivity'. In other words for generic attributes to apply in practice there must be some connection both within the elements that define the attribute in the first place and also in the way that individual attributes link together to form a holistic activity.

5.2 Contextuality of generic attributes

There is, too, a relationship between the connectivity of generic attributes and contextuality. Professional practice is characterised by the variability of both context and conditions. Each interaction between a patient and a medical practitioner, for example, is unique. Patients have their own medical and social histories, so, even if the remedy being sought in a large number of cases is the same, say, the alleviation of the symptoms associated with the 'common cold', the appropriate treatment and way of interacting with the patient will vary in each case. Competence performance of this kind of holistic activity depends mainly on a capacity to bring together the various 'discrete' attributes in an appropriate way. So, it is not just any combination that will suffice, but particular combinations tailored to suit the purpose.

Furthermore, the changing conditions and contexts will generally require different combinations or clusters of attributes. Thus, the generic capacities of individuals, including their capacity to deploy appropriate clusters of attributes, whether as learners or workers, tend to reflect their present sense of being, as well as, importantly, their level of confidence about how they can develop in the future. As noted by Scanlon, in the case of mature adults seeking to commence tertiary education, developing and refining generic capacities may well have a positive impact on self-esteem and self-confidence. However, it is while engaged in professional practice that graduates may be more likely to see themselves as competent people, and be perceived as competent by others, including prospective employers. This form of further learning and self-development is evident in the case of the novice professionals documented by Te Wiata.

According to research undertaken by Hager (1997: 13-15), in specific industry and work place settings, the tendency for generic attributes to be connected to each other as clusters is primarily shaped by the *context* in which the 'work' is carried out. This means that it is unhelpful to attempt to identify the generic attributes of an occupation or profession without reference to their workplace contexts. And, as Hager, Holland & Beckett (2002) elaborate the notion of 'context' is itself complex and includes a multiplicity of workplace-related factors. These factors include such matters as the history, values and culture of an organisation, its career development policies and practices, the deployment of technology and business strategy as well as a range of other variables likely to result in short or long term change.

As already highlighted the emergence of concepts such as the 'learning organisation', which have provided new insights into how to understand and describe workplaces, strengthens the case for the inherent contextuality of generic attributes. In contemporary workplaces in a global, competitive and ever-changing world the organisation is no longer concerned solely with the competencies of individual employees. What is at stake is the overall capacity of the organisation to 'learn', that is, the extent to which it can adapt, be innovative and so be able to develop new or modify existing products or services to meet changing circumstances, including market demand. So, in the new workplace it is not the traditional capital resources so much as the combined intellectual, technical and socio-cultural assets of the employees that determines the future success or otherwise of an organisation.

5.3 Contingency of generic attributes

But the very contextuality as well as the intangibility of generic attributes means that there are a number of challenges to address in practice, or contingencies to consider, in both work and educational settings in regard to the acquisition and further development of these types of capacities. In work settings more than ever employers are placing importance on generic capacities that go beyond the technical, such as 'teamwork', 'innovation', 'taking responsibility', and 'communicating effectively'. Moreover, these softer types of generic capacities need to be deployed in different combinations depending on the actual workplace situation.

While Winch's cautions about defining generic attributes and the practicality of teaching these more elusive attributes are valid, it is none the less increasingly the case that workers are required to be adaptable, multi-skilled and flexible if they are to sustain employment in the face of evolving circumstances. As the cases outlined by Down and Te Wiata illustrate, the softer generic capacities certainly require ongoing learning, and even re-learning, to meet the demands of unique and continually changing work contexts.

Notwithstanding this challenge, as Hager concludes, the marked contextuality of generic attributes does provide a powerful argument for the educational value of developing them. Consequently there are contingent implications for educational settings in terms of the design of pre-service programs as well as for continuing professional education. Indeed it is likely that generic attributes may provide the means for learners to gain the types of knowledge and learning not otherwise readily available to them in typical undergraduate programs. This tacit or practice knowledge is as important as disciplinary knowledge and understanding in preparing novices for successful engagement in professional work. Although, as Eraut (1994) documents, while it is relatively straightforward to identify the latter it is more difficult to be precise in curriculum terms in respect of the former.

Nevertheless this notion of advancing practice as a means of developing new forms of knowledge opens up the possibility for different forms of curriculum in higher education to ensure the development of practice knowledge. For many students, such as those at Luton University, this type of knowledge may be as important for job selection and career progression as the actual qualification being undertaken. As documented by Atlay, reflecting on the Luton experience, successful teaching and learning of generic attributes appears to depend on the extent to which these are made explicit for students, particularly whether or not these are assessed and reported on in some way. If the generic attributes are merely implicit in the course design then there is likely to be little to encourage their learning and development.

But any learning process concerned with advancing practice must, by definition, also encapsulate and reflect the kinds of practice presently being undertaken by professionals in the respective discipline field. Accordingly, the teaching activity is intended to achieve two different but related purposes. Primarily the intention is to transform the learner by the acquisition of new forms of knowledge and capacities, including practical as well as conceptual abilities. The secondary purpose is to transform the professional practice of competent practitioners by sharing and applying these new forms of knowledge and capacities. In other words for university graduates the challenge is not so much to develop a suitable range of generic attributes but to be able to *deploy* suitable combinations of these attributes to deal with the particular professional situations in which they find themselves. In this respect the success or otherwise of their future professional careers may well be contingent on the extent to which they have been exposed to different educational and work, or quasi work, settings in the development of their generic capacities.

Different professions and occupations have somewhat different generic profiles, particularly when they are practiced in many different sorts of contexts. So, for academics the challenge in pedagogic terms is to deal appropriately with the contextuality of generic attributes. Obviously, the more the generic attributes are detailed and distinguished, the less likely it is that a proposed general profile will be suited to every university program. Hence an appropriate level of generality is needed. In the case of the University of Sydney a successful strategy, as described by Barrie, has been to adopt only a relatively small number of generic attributes as graduate outcomes. Another useful approach implemented at the University of Technology Sydney in developing a work-based learning degree (Boud & Solomon) has been to contextualise the generic attributes to the particular profession or discipline area.

There appears to be a contingent and continuing relationship between better learning and an agenda to promote generic attributes, which is consistent with the notion of lifelong learning. As highlighted by Moy (1999: 23-4) generic attributes are frequently part of broader strategies designed to improve teaching and learning. In other words the strategies that foster better outcomes, such as open and more reflective forms of learning, including opportunities for practice, also require learners to deploy some combination of generic attributes if they are to be successful. Barrie & Prosser (2004) describe how by explicitly embedding generic attributes in courses and actively seeking to promote their development, teachers can improve learning overall. The teaching priority then becomes how best to encourage learning rather than how to develop generic attributes as such. Furthermore, as Hager argues, for teaching to actually result in learning the educational settings need to be 'contextually rich, interactive and integrative'. Clearly there are limits in respect of the transferability of generic attributes but it may be, as he goes on to suggest, that it is not so much that the generic attributes *per se* transfer as the capacity to apply them successfully in different situations under different conditions.

Currently most tertiary educational institutions are seeking to assist students to maximise these attributes. A first step is to understand how to reflect the influence of context, the benefits of transferability and overall capability in course design. One group of technology related universities in Australia, the Australian Universities of Technology Network (ATN), have chosen to focus on 'knowledge capability' – the ability to deal with each new situation, by relating what is known to the new unknown, determining what to do about it, and then doing it. Typical lists of generic attributes fit in with this 'relational' approach. For example, drawing on Bowden (1999: 16-7), the ATN group lists the following example of 'graduate attributes':

> Graduates will have:
>
> a commitment to learning from every new situation they encounter and the ability to fulfil that commitment;
>
> the capability to make context-sensitive judgements ...and choose appropriate behaviour in varying professional and social contexts; and
>
> a knowledge capability which enables them to deal effectively with each new situation in their professional or social lives.

The deliberate design of learning and teaching strategies to advance these sorts of relational generic attributes is likely to be as important as the substantive discipline or even field-based studies in influencing the employment success or otherwise of graduates. And, if success in professional practice is contingent on the appropriate deployment of such attributes, then the best way to encourage this is to embed generic capacities in substantive courses and reinforce their development through engagement in a range of contextually rich learning experiences, including appropriate practicum type experiences. Such curriculum strategies would likely lead to more emphasis on, and greater practice in the very kinds of generic attributes, which find expression through employment.

Furthermore, given that it seems by all accounts that it is precisely these attributes that are essential for effective professional practice, it is possible that in implementing these sorts of strategies the so called 'employability gap' could at least be narrowed without compromising the integrity of substantive university studies.

6. TOWARDS A LIFELONG LEARNING FRAMEWORK FOR GRADUATE ATTRIBUTES

On the basis of theoretical discussion, research, and case studies cited elsewhere in this book it is reasonable to conclude that the acquisition of generic attributes is a lifelong learning project. It is a project that has connective, contextual and contingent aspects, and needs to involve a mix of both formal and informal dimensions in terms of the learning settings. Indeed, some of the settings need to be work-based if learners are to be able, over time, to know how and when to deploy their generic capacities appropriately in the range of socio-cultural situations and conditions likely to be encountered in professional life. While undergraduate programs contribute to this development, the graduate attributes that are usually acquired via this means are only the first phase of the lifelong agenda. Continuing professional education, involving both structured feedback and less formal experiential learning as well as reflection, is necessary for a further stage of development whereby professional capabilities emerge. Beyond professional registration and recognition, for those who are prepared to commit to a leadership role in which learning is the key element, there may be the development of leadership capabilities, which, ultimately, can be validated only on the basis of peer recognition.

It is not the purpose of the present chapter to describe each phase in detail, or to outline in depth the distinctions between the phases and the characteristics of the respective generic outcomes. To do so would require further substantive and empirical work of the kind undertaken in the *DeSeCo* project, within and across professions to identify, for example, the difference between 'competent', 'accomplished' and 'expert' performance. Here the intention is merely illustrative with graduate education and professional formation being taken as the particular case, although the broad framework could also apply to other occupational forms and learning pathways. While some specific examples are outlined, in general, reference is made to the kinds of learning strategies and settings that are likely to encourage the development of generic attributes. Accordingly, in the brief discussion of the phases, which follows the next section, a table has been included for each that is a summary of possible approaches designed to promote the learning of generic capacities.

The concern with generic attributes by employers may be a recent phenomenon, however, as already noted, from the perspective of providers these have always been inherent to good educational practice. Indeed what makes generic attributes valuable to a student is not only whether they translate to a workplace (often some time in the future), but also whether they relate to the next level of learning they undertake often quite immediately. Generic attributes are relevant throughout life and are frequently used implicitly, if not explicitly, to distinguish between potential students at different stages in their learning.

Despite the increasing specialisation of knowledge that is inevitably discipline-based, generic attributes have not lost their importance in contributing to knowledge creation. Indeed the convergence of technology, amongst other things, has generated new forms of interdisciplinarity. From the perspective of learners in higher education there are two milestones where generic attributes, specifically the lack thereof, impact on their capacity to progress to further study and/or employment. The first milestone is at the commencement of undergraduate study, and the second occurs at the completion of undergraduate study.

There is not necessarily a straight linear relationship in terms of the development of generic attributes. Rather the process of the acquisition of generic attributes would appear to be merely part of the overall learning process. The process may be somewhat like a spiral or a scaffold as each new insight, understanding or skill-based development is built on and connected to earlier ones through stimulus, practice and reflection. In this way, over time the generic capacities of individuals become integrated with other forms of learning. Following Hager, the important point is that people seem to be able to develop an expanding capacity to deploy generic attributes in more and more diverse situations and conditions if they are given sufficient opportunity to practice how to do this in a variety of educational and work settings.

Leaving aside a detailed analysis of learning theory and cognitive development, which is subject to debate as technological developments provide new information regarding brain function, there is most agreement about generic attributes and what is required for success at the first milestone: entrance to tertiary level study. At the second milestone the picture is inevitably more complex because of the range of discipline studies, different forms of professional preparation and the varying length of undergraduate courses.

6.1 Foundational Attributes for Tertiary Study

Traditionally, entrance to university has been a competitive process based on academic achievement tested via public examination after five or six years of secondary schooling. There has been a tacit understanding of the depth of knowledge required for study in particular disciplines (which is the basis for the use of pre-requisites) and the generic attributes which are critical for tertiary level study. This paradigm, of course, is still dominant, however, the increasing diversity of applicants for undergraduate courses has led to a more careful analysis and explication of just what underpinning knowledge and skills are actually required.

Furthermore, primary and secondary schooling contribute significantly to the development of the foundational capacities which are essential for success as a tertiary student. Indeed it can be argued that the younger years are crucial for developing the base for these skills. This is particularly the case for capacities such as 'literacy and numeracy'. If they are not learnt early then it is more difficult to do so later. The *DeSeCo* project, for example, has affirmed the importance of early childhood education for success in the compulsory years of schooling, and also for further academic study.

It is now easier and more common for students, particularly mature aged students to enter university via a variety of alternative pathways such as that described by Scanlon. The response by universities has been to introduce a range of programs. These are variously called 'foundation', 'orientation' or 'preparation' programs and are designed to provide a bridge to university for students who for various reasons – incomplete school education, mature age and/or vocationally-based entry – do not have the full complement of capacities deemed necessary for tertiary study. In addition, English language skills, which are frequently a specific issue in respect to international students, are provided for through specific 'English for Speakers of Other Languages' type programs.

Entrance to these programs is usually by direct means as an alternative to the competitive examinations. Increasingly the nature of these 'foundation' type programs is outcome-based with assessment against clear criteria to ensure students develop an appropriate repertoire of knowledge and skills. At Edith Cowan University (ECU), for example, all earlier versions of alternative entry pathways were discontinued from 2001 in favour of a university preparation program, which is modular and skills-based to allow for flexibility to meet the diverse needs of the students that require this bridge (Hager, Holland & Beckett 2002).

The introduction of 'recognition of prior learning' (RPL) processes is another response to the diversity of undergraduate students. Many students have undertaken other forms of post-school education and training either in the vocational education and training sector or through professional associations, as well as learning 'on the job' at work. While universities generally have systems for granting exemptions and credit transfer, this is not always systematic or inclusive in practice. Rather than attempting to insist on narrow interpretations of the level of specific knowledge, the trend is towards the granting of 'block' credit by making a holistic assessment of a student's academic background, work and professional experience. In this way the emergence of RPL as a legitimate means of judging student potential for success at undergraduate level has resulted in an even greater focus on generic attributes at undergraduate level.

7. PHASE 1: TERTIARY STUDY

Universities have always had a commitment to ensure graduates develop broad based, generic attributes such as 'critical thinking', 'problem solving', 'analytic capacity' and so forth. Indeed the original notion of a university was generic rather than specialist, broad rather than narrow in focus. But being precise about the level and concrete manifestation of these kinds of attributes is more problematic. Consequently the development of undergraduate programs which concurrently and explicitly develop generic attributes as well as discipline-based knowledge and skills is a challenge in design and pedagogic terms. It is a challenge that most universities are now addressing.

Table 2, that follows, lists a sample of the kinds of learning settings and related strategies that are likely to assist students in developing generic capacities during periods of tertiary study. This summary reflects contemporary teaching and learning approaches (see Ramsden 1998; HERD 2004a, 2004b, 2004c), that can be put in place either by individual academics or a group of staff collaborating as a team.

Table 2. Tertiary Study – Settings Conducive to Developing Graduate Attributes

Role	Educational Settings	Workplace Settings
student practitioner critical thinker *independent learner*	team/group work laboratory & practical work authentic & integrated tasks hypotheticals & role plays trouble shooting tasks	practicum placement real work projects internships simulated work experience sandwich programs

It remains primarily the situation in tertiary programs, even in undergraduate degrees designed specifically as preparation for professional occupations, that there is a strong emphasis on content and scholarship *per se*. Yet, at the same time, increasingly, there is recognition by teaching staff of the value of incorporating into degree programs some form of practical, developmental experience related to the workplace. The expectation of staff is that exposing students to different learning contexts, and experiential types of learning via 'internships', 'sandwich programs' or the more traditional end-on 'practicum', enhances 'employability'. Even though this is not necessarily the case, if such experiences are properly structured so as to encourage contextual and more collective forms of learning, then these opportunities can enrich and deepen theoretical understandings, and hence contribute to the development of generic capacities.

As relatively inexperienced participants in workplace oriented programs, undergraduate learners are very much in the role of 'student' rather than 'professional' practitioner. None the less this type of role complements the typical academic role of the undergraduate as 'critical thinker', and in this way can contribute to the personal intellectual journey, that is required in order to become an 'independent learner'. According to Barnett the challenge for higher education, in these ever changing and super-complex times, is to shift focus from a concern with knowledge and skills to consideration of how to encourage dispositions or qualities concerned with character – the inner structure of a person – their sense of 'being'.

He contends that the value of higher education for individual students depends on the potential for such learning to foster the development of the capacity to *be* 'authentic'. By this he means more than mere individuality. Authentic learners possess a sense of legitimacy and are able to justify their ideas, values and actions. As the full development of authenticity as a form of human *being* is an ongoing, lifetime project, undergraduate programs are an important part of the journey but not the final destination. To encourage the kinds of dispositions encapsulated in Barnett's concept of authenticity, he suggests that undergraduates need to be exposed to situations with multiple descriptions, multiple identities and value conflict.

Obviously workplace settings are more likely to offer these kinds of contextually rich situations than classrooms or laboratories. However, unless these practical experiences are integrated with, or at least linked to, the rest of the respective degree program, then such learning is unlikely to be reinforced or retained in any meaningful way. Thus it is also important to include more open and complex tasks, such as 'hypotheticals', 'role plays' or 'trouble shooting' exercises, as well as projects requiring team effort, in the design of the formal parts of the undergraduate curriculum.

Design issues at the local department or program level amongst like minded colleagues may be relatively straightforward. But, as Barrie has pointed out, for the university as a whole, reaching agreement about how to ensure that the curriculum, teaching and assessment across university programs promotes the development of graduate attributes is a much larger, and more problematic, undertaking. An early question to pay attention to is whether to promote the development of generic attributes within or across disciplines.

The experience at the University of Luton, documented by Atlay and Harris (2000), highlights some of the main issues. These include:

- contextualising graduate attributes for diverse subject and discipline areas;
- determining the appropriate level for development of specific attributes;
- specifying the attributes to be assessed within subjects or modules;
- tracking development of graduate attributes across elective choices;
- generating transcripts for reporting on generic attributes; and
- maintaining consistent standards across faculties and departments.

What is the role of employers in the university-wide initiatives? In many cases this work has not been done in isolation from employers. Indeed employer perceptions have been frequently taken into account in framing the particular sets of graduate attributes. Hager, Holland & Beckett (2002) note the following examples in Australia, as elsewhere, of different kinds of response that attempt to address employer concerns. At the university wide level, the Royal Melbourne University of Technology (RMIT) identified a number of key attributes, highlighted the interpretation of each one from the perspective of prospective employers, and specified the teaching and learning experiences that facilitate their respective development.

At faculty level, the Faculty of Education of the Queensland University of Technology (QUT), developed its own faculty-specific graduate attributes called Teacher Practitioner Attributes (TPAs), which were derived both from the QUT generic attributes and teaching industry standards. Processes were developed for identifying and fostering TPAs within course units, together with a series of exemplars to enhance this process. As well a profile of TPA development in sequences of core units was devised. Another significant aspect of this particular initiative was the involvement of students in identifying the TPAs.

Another example of a successful faculty initiative is the approach used by the Faculty of Engineering at the University of Technology, Sydney. They asked the question, "What education do we believe future engineers need?" And, after reflection as well as discussion with both employers and students, staff concluded that three types of attributes are important for engineers – professional, personal and academic. Accordingly, each of these attributes were explicated further and then used as the basis for the design of a new program.

The process of incorporating graduate attributes into faculty courses is, inevitably, an ongoing and dynamic one, for which considerable professional development is often required in order to create ownership by staff and to allow for some fine-tuning as internal and external conditions change. As each of the faculty initiatives outlined above suggest, successful implementation of an explicit agenda for graduate attributes depends, not only on the curriculum design and staff 'buy in', but also on the extent and utility of the links with suitable workplaces.

Indeed, the increasing importance of links between universities and employers, usually channeled via professional, business or industry associations, in preparing graduates for professional careers has led to a range of curriculum initiatives sandwich programs, work placements, co-operative programs, practicum placements, and internships – that can be described as 'work-based learning'. The purpose of the programs, as already noted, is to give undergraduates an opportunity to link their theoretical knowledge to professional practice as well as to gain an appreciation of the contextual issues likely to impact on professional work.

While aspects of these learning opportunities are specific to the particular profession in terms of the requisite theoretical knowledge, there are also more generic dimensions that can begin to be developed, such as 'making value judgements', 'exhibiting ethical behaviour' and 'using technology'. At their best, such programs impact on university staff to inspire novel teaching approaches that stimulate and model experience, and also encourage more authentic assessment practices. As with RPL, the emergence and proliferation of 'work-based learning' initiatives, such as those described by Boud & Solomon, is further evidence of the increasing recognition and commitment of universities to ensuring that their graduates have an appropriate set of attributes, including generic capabilities.

While these initiatives clearly have value, it remains the case that to be successful in contemporary workplaces and meet the challenges arising from the new world order of 'super-complexity' described by Barnett, graduates need to develop their generic capacities over longer time horizons than the typical undergraduate program. Recalling Hager and Winch's cautions too much credence can be placed on graduate capacities as if these were easily and quickly acquired. As already highlighted, the connectivity, contextuality and contingency of generic attributes means that the development of multi-layered capacities, especially the kinds of dispositions suggested by Barnett – 'courage', 'resilience' or 'quietness', is a lifelong journey involving self-reflection and interaction with others. The continuing development of generic attributes, which builds on, but goes beyond the knowledge and skill sets evident upon graduation, is an integral aspect of engagement in professional practice to which we now turn.

8. PHASE 2: PROFESSIONAL PRACTICE

The initial employment experiences of graduates, as described by Te Wiata, inevitably involves the application of practical knowledge to different workplace contexts, quite apart from theoretical understandings relating to the respective field of specialised knowledge. The former, more elusive, tacit type of knowledge – 'knowing how' – cannot all be learnt in advance, no matter the extent or effectiveness of the experiential learning included in undergraduate degree programs.

Furthermore, as Beckett & Mulcahy remind us, such knowledge cannot easily be made explicit. The tendency for employers, in particular, to narrowly describe 'employability' with mere lists of skills, masks the complexity of the generic capacities actually developed through engagement 'in practice' in contemporary workplaces. Beckett & Mulcahy further contend, from a conceptual (adopting an inferential approach) as well as an empirical point of view (based on cases of professionals in practice), that it is the 'particularities' of work practices, which generate the capacities necessary for employment. This is especially so in the daily business of making judgements about how to proceed in a given situation. In their words, 'one learns *for* work by *doing* work'.

Since work is a social activity conducted with peers the judgements made by individual professionals, as they *do* their work, are mediated by feedback from colleagues, and are also shaped by the context of the particular workplace. Given this dynamic interplay between individual and collective activity, any effective program of continuing professional education must necessarily involve opportunities for reflection on practice and peer interaction, as well as more formal course work. The development of professional capabilities is an ongoing and complex process, which involves more than merely completing the academic tasks or practical activities set as the requirements for professional registration and/or accreditation.

Table 3 below indicates some examples of educational and professional settings that are likely to encourage the development of professional capabilities beyond those exhibited by novice practitioners early in their careers. For convenience the table separately lists 'continuing education' and 'professional' settings, however, in practice there may be little distinction between the two, as both types inevitably involve the workplace as the prime site for learning.

Table 3. Professional Practice – Settings for Developing Professional Capabilities

Role	Continuing Education	Professional Settings
mentee team player peer self-critic *lifelong* *learner*	case studies & practical tasks course work for professional registration/accreditation self-reflection via journal (professional) masterate	mentoring programs cross-discipline project work peer assessment & feedback critical incidents/ethical dilemmas clinical supervision

In this phase of lifelong learning there are a number of work-based roles, which ordinarily arise in practice, whereby professionals can enhance their learning. These range from participation in mentoring or clinically supervised programs as a mentee, to involvement in cross or multi-disciplinary projects as a team member. Accepting the judgements of, and feedback from peers, and pursuing reflective activities, such as retaining a journal concerning responses to critical incidents and/or ethical dilemmas, are other forms of work-based learning that provide professionals with opportunities to become more self aware and critical.

During a given day or week a professional practitioner may be required to undertake, in addition to their usual practice, a wide range of tasks with different levels of complexity, for example, servicing customers/clients, preparing business plans or negotiating a resolution to a situation of conflict. Given this scenario the attainment of formal registration or accreditation is a necessary, but no longer sufficient requirement for the development of the range of professional capabilities generally expected for competent performance. Increasingly, professionals are undertaking postgraduate qualifications and often the further study is not in the same discipline as the original qualification. This horizontal movement across disciplines is part of the same trend, noted earlier, in relation to the changing interface between vocational and higher education. Professional masterate programs are also emerging to meet the demand for new types of capacities and forms of learning that are integral to, rather than separate from, professional practice.

Without going into detail about what is involved in competent performance *per se*, which is beyond the scope of the present analysis, it is useful to note the seminal work of Dreyfus (2004) in regard to skill formation and learning. Essentially, using a phenomenological approach, he argues that learning new skills or extending existing capacities is not just about knowing which rules to follow, it also involves deploying insight and intuition, and these kinds of judgements develop gradually with practice. So, while professionals certainly need to know certain facts, and be conversant with their specialised field of knowledge, before this knowledge can be applied properly, they also need to have an understanding of the *context* in which these facts make sense.

Down's analysis of workplace situations together with Beckett & Mulcahy's cases of identify formation illustrate that contextual knowledge is richly layered and tacitly assimilated. Taking this into account, and accepting Dreyfus's line of argument helps explain how professionals are able to gradually improve their practice and achieve higher levels of performance. For him, it is the nature and accumulative extent of practical experience that makes the difference in performance levels. Experienced practitioners replace rules and principles with situational discriminations, and reasoned responses with intuitive reactions. Thus, the expert not only sees what needs to be done, but is also capable of deciding *immediately*, on the basis of an extensive repertoire of situational discriminations, what tactics to employ to *do* the task (Dreyfus 2004: 5–6).

The precise nature of the distinctions he suggests for his hierarchy of five levels of performance from novice to expert may be problematic. However, drawing attention to the difference between novices and experts, the holistic nature of learnt capacities, and the way that people use their accumulative experience to progress from one performance stage to another is pertinent. In these increasingly competitive times with a greater focus on accountability and quality of service delivery, most professional associations, in the light of community expectations, are strengthening their systems for measuring the capabilities of professionals in terms of standards of performance.

Recent developments in New South Wales with respect to the teaching profession reflect this trend. An Institute for Teachers has been established to provide a mechanism to monitor and assess the standard of teaching practice in the State. Following widespread discussion with stakeholders, reviews of research documenting 'good practice' as adjudged by peers, and taking note of analogous developments elsewhere, a schema for Professional Teaching Standards was formulated and disseminated for validation (NSW Institute of Teachers 2003). This schema sets out the capacities, many of which are generic, that practising teachers are expected to exhibit at different levels of performance.

For individual professionals, apart from the gradual assimilation of experience, which happens naturally through engagement with others in different situations and contexts, improved practice, beyond that which is recognised via initial registration/ accreditation, also results from exposure to continuing education and the myriad informal learning opportunities available in the workplace. Generally, this approach to further learning is sufficient to sustain a level of performance that would be regarded by peers as competent. Indeed, the NSW teaching framework refers to the minimum standard for continuing registration as 'professional competence'. There are two other levels identified, 'professional accomplishment' and 'professional leadership', with the latter being the highest level of performance. Unpacking what might be involved in this level of performance directs us to discussion of the third phase of lifelong learning – leadership development.

9. PHASE 3: LEADERSHIP DEVELOPMENT

There are conceptual difficulties in determining any set of professional standards, and especially in developing the requisite assessment tools. Holland & Louden (2002), for example, provide an overview of the problematics and practicalities involved for the teaching profession. They considered the costs/benefits involved, such as the likely contribution to good practice and the value to the profession of engaging stakeholders, and also highlighted the structural/substantive issues that arise in setting standards, including validity, credibility, fairness and transparency. Notwithstanding these issues, it is useful to examine in some detail the NSW schema for professional teaching standards as this provides an insight into the kinds of capabilities expected of a 'professional leader' in comparison to a 'competent' performer.

One of the generic elements of professional practice in the NSW schema for teaching standards is 'teachers (*know how to*) communicate effectively with their students'. In summary, while it is expected that competent teachers can demonstrate proficiency in respect of this element by explaining goals; probing students' prior conceptions; listening and encouraging contributions; building rapport; and engaging students in meaningful activities, professional leaders operate at a higher learning level (NSW Institute of Teachers 2003: 8–9). The capabilities expected for this level of performance include, promoting collaboration via team teaching; demonstrating communication techniques that assist colleagues to improve their practices; and leading staff in the sharing of innovative ideas and resources.

In essence, the differences between the two levels of performance are manifest in terms of *learning* capability. Whereas the competent professional has the capacity to engage in further learning, which, as outlined in the previous section, irrespective of more formal approaches to continuing professional education, occurs incidentally through the conduct of usual activities; a professional leader has the capacity to *lead others in learning*.

Of course, in the continuing process of refining their capabilities, many professionals may reach further stages beyond mere competence. Indeed, the NSW teaching standards, spell out 'professional accomplishment' as the stage between professional competence and professional leadership. The point is not how many stages are appropriate for a particular profession or the best way to define these, rather, it is that the distinctions between the stages of professional development necessarily reflect different capabilities with respect to learning. For clarity the remainder of the present discussion will focus on the two extremes: professional competence and professional leadership.

While the expectations, which are spelt out in the example detailed above, are specific to the NSW teaching profession, it also seems valid, to distinguish more generally, between 'competence' and 'leadership' on the basis of learning capability, with respect to 'professionals in practice'. Unless some practitioners within a profession are capable of leading others in learning, it is difficult to see how the profession renews itself, remains open to the creation of new knowledge or is disposed to adopt new practices. In any case, as already articulated, for individual members of a profession to engage in learning, the nature of professional practice is such that collective processes are necessarily involved in the form of feedback from peers, participation in team projects and so forth. In other words learning in professional settings is both an individual and collective process, which can be enhanced if there are some practitioners in the peer group that are proficient in structuring and encouraging learning activities.

To be able to lead others in learning a professional needs, not only to take responsibility for their own learning, but also to be disposed to being a leader and to promoting learning in others, as well as knowing how to facilitate learning on an ongoing basis. Moreover, facilitating learning for, and with peers, necessitates knowledge of learning processes as well as the capacity to determine on the basis of experience what works and was does not in teaching adults. So, to perform at this meta learning level, professional leaders have to develop appropriate dispositions, possess practical capacities relating to teaching and learning processes and be able to access technical knowledge concerning instructional design and assessment. This requires a cluster of attributes beyond those typical for professional competence. Accordingly, it is appropriate to describe this type of professional as a 'learning leader' and, in this context, to use the term 'leadership' for the cluster of requisite capabilities.

Since not all professionals will necessarily have an interest in pursuing learning leadership, "What kinds of settings might encourage this kind of development"? Table 4, which follows, suggests some settings that are conducive to the development of leadership capabilities. As in Table 3, continuing education settings are listed separately from professional settings, although in practice these will merge. Given the rich nature of the contextual situations that arise in professional practice, and the consequent opportunities to accumulate appropriate experience, most learning of this kind is likely to be in, or directly related to the workplace.

Table 4. Leadership Development – Settings for Developing Leadership Capabilities

Role	Continuing Education	Professional Settings
coach/facilitator teacher mentor moderator/assessor *learning leader*	strategic tasks & change scenarios self-critique to improve practice research projects instructional design work (professional) doctorate	communities of practice quality circles mentoring/shadowing assessment of learning appraisal & expert judgements

Apart from facilitating learning and/or being directly involved in instruction as teachers, professional leaders may also act as coaches, mentors, moderators or assessors. As Rylatt (2003: 7) has argued in outlining strategies to 'win the knowledge game', inspiring higher levels of curiosity and imagination is fundamental to expanding knowledge, both in terms of creating new knowledge (and services and products), and in revisiting and reworking existing knowledge. While the creation of new knowledge is a core function of universities and other research institutions, it is also important that professionals in practice play a part in this renewal process, otherwise the insights derived from their rich collection of practical experience are unlikely to be captured and applied.

Fostering deeper and more open forms of learning requires a culture that sponsors trust, promotes discovery and values collaboration. Establishing communities of practice where peers share resources, use reflective practices and evaluate outcomes, is one way to encourage more systematic learning. Other types of professional networks that focus on improving, and learning from practice, include quality circles, mentoring and shadowing programs. For individual professionals, engagement in strategic tasks and exposure to changing scenarios also provides opportunities to broaden learning and exercise leadership in the process.

In terms of opportunities for continuing education, professional doctorates have emerged in recent years as a new way of providing for high level postgraduate study that is directly connected to workplace practice. As Brennan (1998) has outlined, the new degrees have generated criticism from some quarters in the academy, and debate continues about the similarities and differences between professional doctorates and the traditional doctor of philosophy degree, especially in regard to the rigour and extent of the research component. In turn these issues are enmeshed in changing modes of postgraduate pedagogy and supervision as universities adapt to changing patterns of demand, funding regimes and staffing arrangements. Irrespective of the eventual outcome of these developments, professional doctorates are likely to contribute to more critical inquiry and evidence based practice in professional workplaces. In addition, these programs provide opportunities for practitioners to be given recognition for their research related to practice, as well as creating new leadership roles for suitably qualified professionals as supervisors.

For professionals, becoming a learning leader is not simply a matter of accepting supervisory or management roles. Learning how to manage resources or people are clearly useful attributes for any professional to develop in practice. However, knowing how to create a learning organisation, model lifelong learning practices and promote learning in others, requires different kinds of capabilities, all of which are fundamentally concerned with learning not management. As already exemplified, such leadership capabilities develop gradually, primarily on the basis of experience, and are complex attributes, involving values and dispositions as well as knowledge and understanding. Furthermore, demonstration of leadership capabilities does not sit easily with traditional forms of management appraisal, as these qualities can only be properly validated and judged by peers.

10. CONCLUSION

This chapter has been a synthesis of some of the key ideas outlined elsewhere in the book as well as outlining a lifelong learning framework for graduate attributes. The references to other authors reflect only one interpretation, and have been selected to illustrate aspects of the proposed framework. As such the present discussion does not do justice to all the conceptual or practical issues which are articulated. To appreciate the nuances of the pertinent arguments and the richness of the insights it is necessary to read the respective chapters in full.

While acknowledging the difficulties in describing, developing and assessing graduate attributes, it has been argued that these are none the less so important to learning, and underpin so much of what occurs in professional practice, that attempting to do so is still worthwhile. In terms of the framework, three interconnected phases have been outlined, tertiary study, professional practice and leadership development.

Although there are different ways that developmental processes for professionals could be conceived, elaborating the present framework has provided the opportunity to illustrate that graduate attributes are connective, contextual and contingent in character. Because they are demonstrated in situations rather than being separate entities and are only refined through practice, developing them is a lifelong learning journey. It is a journey of engagement and reflection, involving a gradual accumulation of relevant experiences, which in turns leads to mature insight and the capacity for intuitive judgements; precursors to professional competence, and at a higher learning level, to expertise in leading learning for others.

11. REFERENCES

ACCI & BCA (2002) *Employability Skills for the Future.* Canberra: DEST (Commonwealth Department of Education, Science and Training).

Atlay, M. & Harris, R. (2000) 'An Institutional Approach to Developing Students' "Transferable" Skills', *Innovations in Education and Training International*, Vol. 37, No. 1, pp. 76-84.

Barrie, S. & Prosser, M. (2004) 'Generic Graduate Attributes: Citizens for an Uncertain Future', *Higher Education Research and Development*, Special Issue, Vol. 23, No. 3, pp. 243-394.

B-HERT (2003) 'Developing Generic Skills: Examples of Best Practice', *B-HERT News,* Issue 16, April 2003.

Billett, S. (2001) *Organising and Managing Workplace Learning.* Melbourne: Allen & Unwin

Binney, G. & Williams, C. (1994) *Leaning into the Future: Changing the Way People Change Organisations.* London: Nicholas Brealey.

Bowden, J. (1999) *Foreword in RMIT Graduate Attributes: Information Kit.* Melbourne: RMIT.

Brennan, M. (1998) 'Struggles over the Definition and Practice of the Educational Doctorates in Australia', *Australian Educational Researcher*, Vol. 25, No. 1, pp. 71-89.

Candy, P. C., Crebert, G. & O'Leary, J. (1994) *Developing Lifelong Learners through Undergraduate Education*. Commissioned Report No. 28. Canberra: National Board of Employment, Education and Training.

DEST (2002) *Varieties of Learning: The Interface between Higher Education and Vocational Education*. Issue Paper prepared for the Government Review, 'Higher Education at the Crossroads. Canberra: DEST.

DETYA (2000) *Employer Satisfaction with Graduate Skills: Research Report 99/7*, Feb., 2000, Evaluations and Investigations Program, Higher Education Division. Canberra: DETYA (Commonwealth Department of Education, Training and Youth Affairs).

Dreyfus, H. L. (2004) *A Phenomenology of Skill Acquisition as the basis for a Merleau-Pontian Non-representationalist Cognitive Science*. Berkeley: University of California (available at www.ist-socrates.berkeley.edu/~hdrefyfus/html/papers.html - accessed October 2005).

ECU (2005) *ECUpdate*, Magazine of Edith Cowan University, Vol. 3, No. 2.

Eraut, M. (1994) *Developing Professional Knowledge and Competence*. London: Falmer Press.

Guthrie, G., Johnston, S. & King, R. (2004) *Further Development of the National Protocols for Higher Education Approval Processes*. Canberra: DEST.

Hager, P. (1996) 'Professional Practice in Education: Research and Issues', *Australian Journal of Education*, Vol. 40, No. 3, pp. 235-47.

Hager, P. (1997) *Learning in the Workplace*. Review of Research Monograph Series. Adelaide: National Centre for Vocational Education Research.

Hager, P. Holland, S. & Beckett, D. (2002) *Enhancing the Learning and Employability of Graduates: The Role of Generic Skills*. Business/Higher Education Round Table Position Paper No. 9 Melbourne: B-HERT.

HERD (2004a) *Higher Education Research and Development*, Journal, Vol. 23, No. 1, pp. 1-114.

HERD (2004b) *Higher Education Research and Development*, Journal, Vol. 23, No. 2, pp. 115-242.

HERD (2004c) *Higher Education Research and Development*, Journal, Vol. 23, No. 4, pp. 395-464.

Holland, S. & Louden, W. (2002) *Accrediting Teacher Education Courses in NSW: Perspectives, Problematics and Practicalities*. Commissioned Research Paper for NSW

Institute of Teachers. Perth: Institute for the Service Professions, Edith Cowan University.

Lave, J. & Wenger, E. (1991) *Situated Learning: Legitimate Peripheral Participation.* Cambridge: Cambridge University Press.

Marsick, V. & Watkins, K. (1999) *Envisioning New Organisations for Learning.* London: Routledge.

Meade, P. H. (2003) *Challenges facing Universities: Implications for Leaders.* Dunedin, New Zealand: University of Otago.

Metropolitan Universities (2003) '*Civic Engagement in Australia*', *Metropolitian Universities Journal - International Forum*, Vol. 14, No. 2, pp. 1-108.

Moy, J. (1999) *The Impact of Generic Competencies on Workplace Performance.* Review of Research Monograph Series. Adelaide: National Centre for Vocational Education Research.

Murtough, G. & Waite, M. (2000) *The Growth of Non-traditional Employment: Are Jobs Becoming More Precarious?* Productivity Commission Staff Research Paper. Canberra: Ausinfo.

NSW Institute of Teachers (2003) *NSW Professsional Teacher Standards. Working Draft for Consultation.* mimeographed. Sydney: NSW Department of Education and Training.

Ramsden, P. (1998) *Learning to Lead in Higher Education.* London & New York: Routledge.

Rylatt, A. (2003) *Winning the Knowledge game. A smarter strategy for better business in Australia and New Zealand.* Sydney: McGraw Hill.

Senge, P. (1990) *The Fifth Discipline, The Art and Practice of the Learning Organisation.* London: Century Business.

Teare, R. & Dealtry, R. (1998) 'Building and Sustaining a Learning Organisation', *TheLearning Organisation,* Vol. 5, No. 1, pp. 47-60.

Lifelong Learning Book Series

1. R.G. Bagnall: *Cautionary Tales in the Ethics of Lifelong Learning Policy and Management*. A Book of Fables. 2004 ISBN 1-4020-2214-X
2. K. Evans, B. Niemeyer (eds.): *Reconnection*. Countering Social Exclusion through Situated Learning. 2004 ISBN 1-4020-2520-3
3. S. Jackson: *Differently Academic?*. Developing Lifelong Learning for Women in Higher Education. 2004 ISBN 1-4020-2731-1
4. L. de Botton, L. Puigvert and M. Sánchez-Aroca: *The Inclusion of Other Women*. Breaking the Silence through Dialogic Learning. 2005 ISBN 1-4020-3537-3
5. J. Chapman, P. Cartwright and E.J. McGilp (eds.): *Lifelong Learning, Participation and Equity*. 2006 ISBN 1-4020-5321-5
6. P. Hager and S. Holland (eds.): *Graduate Attributes, Learning and Employability*. 2006 ISBN 1-4020-5341-X

springer.com

Printed in the United Kingdom
by Lightning Source UK Ltd.
130485UK00001B/222/A